UNIFORMS AND INSIGNIA OF THE LUFTWAFFE

VOLUME 2: 1940-1945

UNIFORMS AND INSIGNIA OF THE
LUFTWAFFE
VOLUME 2: 1940-1945

Brian L. Davis

ARMS AND
ARMOUR

Overleaf: Top left, Luftwaffe troops of a motorised flak battery camouflage their light anti-aircraft gun. Top right, Oberleutnant Walter Nowotny, holder of the Knight's Cross and Oakleaves and one of Germany's ace fighter pilots, receiving his Swords from the hands of the Führer, 22 September 1943. Bottom left, a young paratrooper of the German Fallschirmjäger photographed on the occasion of his having been newly decorated with both the Iron Cross Second and First Class. Bottom right, a mixed group of Luftwaffe troops relax in the Norwegian sunlight whilst they listen to instructions given by the unit's Staffelkapitän. Centre, Reichsmarschall Hermann Göring and Generalfeldmarschall Erhardt Milch, accompanied by other senior Luftwaffe officers attending the state funeral of Oberst Werner Mölders, Berlin, 28 November 1941.

This book is respectfully dedicated to Eberhard Hettler, Hauptmann, later Major, in the Reichsluftfahrtministerium and author of the classic work *Uniformen der Deutschen Wehrmacht*, published before the Second World War, with a supplement issued in 1939/40.

Arms and Armour Press
An Imprint of the Cassell Group
Wellington House, 125 Strand, London WC2R 0BB

Distributed in the USA by Sterling Publishing Co. Inc., 387 Park Avenue South, New York, NY 10016-8810.

Distributed in Australia by Capricorn Link (Australia) Pty. Ltd, 2/13 Carrington Road, Castle Hill, NSW 2154.

British Library Cataloguing-in-Publication Data: a catalogue record for this book is available from the British Library

Front of jacket illustration: a painting by Malcolm McGregor showing (left) a Feldwebel of a fighter squadron somewhere on the Western Front in 1944 and (right) a Paratroop Oberleutnant, 1943.

ISBN 1-85409-107-7

Line illustrations by Malcolm McGregor

Designed and edited by DAG Publications Ltd. Designed by David Gibbons; layout by Anthony A. Evans; edited by Michael Boxall and Philip Jarrett; printed and bound in Great Britain by The Bath Press, Avon.

Contents

Introduction

This volume picks up where the first one left off, 1940 being the year chosen as the demarcation point. Each volume contains information relating to organizations that existed only in the relevant period, but much of what was written about the Luftwaffe proper in the 1933–40 volume applies equally to the 1940–1945 period. However, it would be extravagant to repeat text in this book that had appeared in the first; moreover, there is insufficient space in this volume to do so.

These subjects have not been ignored altogether, as can be seen from the contents, but I have in the main attempted to introduce new information where applicable, hopefully without repeating too much. Clothing and garments, objects worn as accoutrements or particular items of insignia introduced before 1939 very often continued in use throughout the war years, although in certain instances their use probably declined as the hardships of the war became increasingly desperate.

I have made a special feature of the many and varied uniforms worn by Reichsmarschall Göring, and this appears in the final section of this volume. With the singular exception of mentioning the two sets of Reichsmarschall's rank insignia contained within the range of Luftwaffe collar patches and shoulder-straps (page 37), everything else appertaining to the uniforms and special insignia worn by Göring is to be found in this final section.

Whenever possible I have attempted to give full references to almost all of the material I have extracted from official or semi-official publications. The majority of these reference notes are to be found at the rear of both volumes. I hope that this will enable those persons who have an interest in this subject to conduct further research themselves.

As before, a considerable number of line drawings have been included. This was a deliberate decision, to avoid a mix of photographs and drawings appearing together on the same page. It also helps to present the subject matter with clarity. Once again I have made a careful selection of photographs to supplement and illustrate both the text and drawings.

With a subject as complex as the German Air Force, covering a 12-year period and rapidly fading into history, there are bound to be errors of omission and faults in both volumes. I have noticed one or two in the first book, but I have done my best to present much of what I know as succinctly as possible. I would be delighted to hear from anyone who can knowledgeably add to what I have written and, where necessary, offer constructive criticism.

Acknowledgements

I wish to thank the following individuals and acknowledge the assistance given to me by the following archives, museums and libraries. All have helped to some degree or other in the research that has formed the basis for these two volumes.

Professor René Smeets of Brussels, Belgium; Fred Walker of Caversham, near Reading; James Lucas of Bromley, Kent, the former Deputy Keeper of the Photographic Library at the Imperial War Museum, London; Roy and Monika Smith of Middleton-on-Sea, West Sussex; and Alex Vangis of London all of whom have assisted me greatly in the time-consuming task of translating official German documents and publications into English.

Jansen Winter of Rotterdam, the Netherlands, and Hans Joachim Nietsch of Ratingen, Germany, both friends who have taken an interest in my efforts and have been unstinting in their generous help in lending me rare but essential handbooks and other contemporary publications. Unfortunately Hans died before the publication of the first volume.

The late Colonel Clifford M. Dodkins, OBE, DSO, who in the past allowed me access to what used to be an impressive collection of German insignia, photographs and research notes, which proved to be a most useful source of reference material. Regrettably this collection is no more, having been dispersed by public auction during 1988.

It has been my privilege to work closely with Malcolm McGregor, a personal friend and a brilliant artist who, in my opinion, ranks as one of this country's leading illustrators. This is the eighth book on which we have collaborated.

Other friends who have contributed in various ways are: James H. Joslyn of Camberwell, London (who unfortunately died before the publication of this volume); Ken Green of Hornchurch, Essex; Pierre H. Turner of Exeter, Devon; David Littlejohn, MA ALA, of Aberdeen, Scotland; Adrian Foreman of London; George A. Petersen, Virginia, USA; Dieter Deuster of Hilden, Germany and Andrew Mollo of Lurcy-Levis, France.

I have received assistance from the following archives and museums: The Imperial War Museum, London; The Bundesarchiv Picture Library of Koblenz, Germany; The Institute of Contemporary History, London (The Weiner Library); Etablissement Cinématographique et Photographique des Armées, Fort d'Ivery, Paris, France.

Photographs appearing in these two volumes are from the author's collection; the Bundesarchiv, Koblenz; the ECPA, Paris, France; and the US National Archives, Washington D.C., USA; and the Imperial War Museum, London.

The National Emblem of Germany and the Reichskokarde

Below: The national emblem (as worn on the Uniform Peaked Cap) and the Reichskokarde, surrounded by a wreath of oakleaves and flanked by stylized wings (worn on the band of the Peaked Cap). These items, worn here by an unidentified Gefreiter, are of pressed silver-aluminium alloy.

Below right: The national emblem and Reichskokarde as worn on the Other Ranks Flight Replacement Cap and the national emblem worn on the Flight Blouse, here worn by an unidentified Obergefreiter.

The Luftwaffe version of the national emblem consisted of an eagle, the traditional national emblem of Germany, with outstretched wings, in an attitude of flight and clutching in its left talon a swastika, the emblem of the National Socialist German Workers' (Nazi) Party. This insignia was required by law to be worn on the right breast of most jackets and tunics (Fig. 1) and, in a smaller version, on almost all cloth head-dress. (Fig. 3)

The National Cockade, which for the Luftwaffe was introduced in May 1935,[1] was made up of concentric rings of the national colours of National Socialist Ger-

many, having a red centre encircled by a band of white or silver with an outer ring of black. The Luftwaffe version differed from the cockades used by other branches of the armed forces in having a narrow band of silver or gold (depending on the wearer's rank) around the outer black band.

On certain forms of head-dress the Cockade was worn as a separate item, on others it was worn in conjunction with a wreath of oakleaves flanked by a pair of stylized 'wings' (Fig. 2).

A point of interest is that two distinct patterns of the Luftwaffe 'Hoheitszeichen', the national emblem, were in existence at various times. The version that had a pronounced downward sweep of the tail feathers is generally agreed to be the early, pre-war version; the type in which the tail feathers were outspread is regarded as being the second pattern, used both before and during the war (see Volume 1933–40, p.10, for details of these two patterns). (For details regarding the colour of these emblems see p.106, head-dress and p. 116, uniforms.)

Right: The national emblem and Reichskokarde, worn on the front of the Other Ranks version of the Flight Cap by an unnamed Flieger.

Far right: The national emblem and Reichskokarde as worn on the front of the Other Ranks version of the Flight Cap by an unnamed Gefreiter.

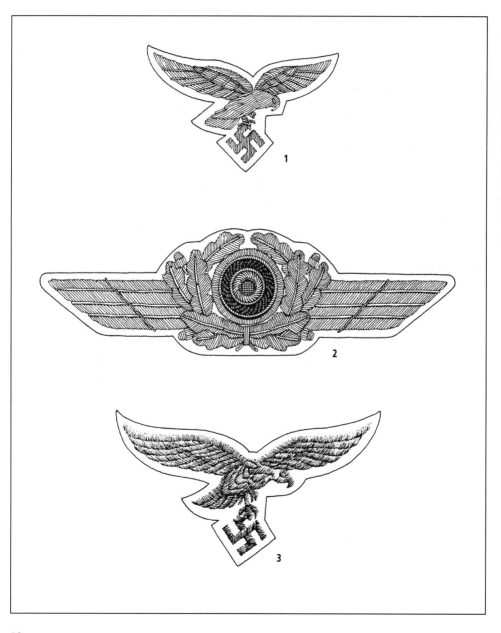

Luftwaffe Version of the German National Emblem and the Reichskokarde.

1 Luftwaffe version of the national emblem.
2 Luftwaffe oakleaf wreath, stylized wings and Reichs-kokarde, hand-embroidered version. Items 1 and 2 were worn together on the Officers' quality Uniform Peaked cap.
3 The machine-woven, second-pattern version of the Luftwaffe national emblem. This size was worn on the right breast.

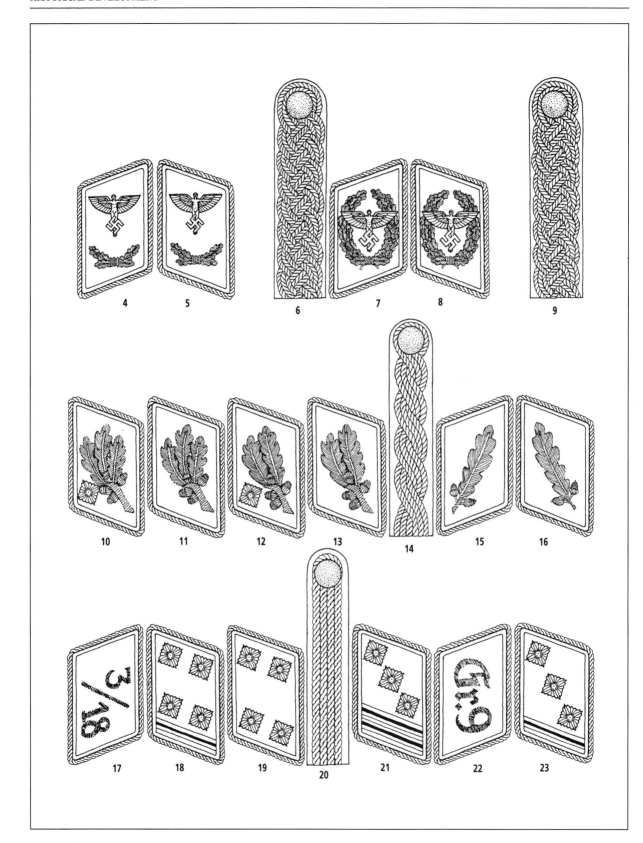

National Socialist Flying Corps (NSFK) Insignia of Rank, Collar Patches and Shoulder-straps, 1935–1945.

All collar patches were produced from blue-grey cloth edged with bright yellow piping. With the singular exception of the collar patches worn by the Korpsführer of the NSFK, all insignia displayed on these patches, embroidered or in pressed, hollow metal, were in white cotton, silver bullion or white metal. Twisted cording worn around collar patches from the appointment of Ehrenführer (Figs. 4 & 5) down to the rank of NSFK-Sturmführer (Fig. 24) was silver bullion.

4 & 5 NSFK-Ehrenführer. Right- and left-hand collar patches. (An Ehrenführer was an individual upon whom the appointment of an honorary commision in the NSFK had been bestowed. This appointment title appeared only in the post-1940 *'Organisationsbuch der NSDAP'*.)

6 Shoulder-strap for NSFK-Korpsführer. All gold plaited braiding on bright yellow underlay. NSFK shoulder-straps were originally worn on the right shoulder only, but were later worn (at least by lower NSFK ranks) in matching pairs. Gilt button.

7 & 8 NSFK-Korpsführer. Right- and left-hand collar patches. The flying man emblem was in silver bullion or pressed white metal on a gold bullion wreath mounted on a blue-grey patch edged bright yellow and with twisted gilt-coloured cording.

9 Shoulder-strap for NSFK ranks from NSFK-Obergruppenführer down to NSFK-Oberführer. The strap had silver and gilt twisted and plaited cording on a bright yellow underlay. Silver button.

10 NSFK-Obergruppenführer. Left-hand collar patch. The right-hand patch was a mirror image of this.

11 NSFK-Gruppenführer. Left-hand collar patch.

National Socialist Flying Corps (Nationalsozialistische Fliegerkorps)

The National Socialist Flying Corps was established on 5 March 1935, eleven days before the reintroduction of national military conscription. Headed by General der Flieger Friedrich Christiensen, it was a State registered corporation subordinate to the Minister for Air and the Commander-in-Chief of the Luftwaffe. Korpsführer Christiensen was an active Luftwaffe General and was directly responsible to Göring.

General Christiensen continued to command the NSFK until, in May 1940, he was appointed 'Wehrmachtbefehshaber (Armed Forces Commander-in-Chief) for the Netherlands in succession to General Alexander von Falkenhausen. Christiensen's position as Chief of the NSFK was taken over by Korpsführer Generaloberst Alfred Keller.

The principal task of the NSFK was to encourage all Germans to be air-minded and to stress the role of air power in modern warfare. By classroom instruction, training and practical experience, it strove to encourage youngsters and teenagers to become the future aircrews of the new German Air Force.

The German Air Sports League (DLV) established two years earlier on 25 March 1933, with a similar purpose, was officially disbanded on 7 April 1937 and all eligible DLV personnel were absorbed into the NSFK.

The pre-war and early war-time organizational structure of the NSFK consisted of seventeen Flying Corps spread across the Reich:

NS-Fliegerkorps 1, 'Ostland' based at Königsberg in East Prussia.
NS-Fliegerkorps 2, 'Nord' at Stettin
NS-Fliegerkorps 3, 'Nordwest' at Hamburg
NS-Fliegerkorps 4, 'Berlin-Mark Brandenburg' in the Reich capital
NS-Fliegerkorps 5, 'Warthegau' in the eastern territory
NS-Fliegerkorps 6, 'Schlesien' at Breslau
NS-Fliegerkorps 7, 'Elbe-Saale' at Dresden
NS-Fliegerkorps 8, 'Mitte' at Eschwege
NS-Fliegerkorps 9, 'Weser-Elbe' at Hanover
NS-Fliegerkorps 10, 'Westfalen' at Dortmund
NS-Fliegerkorps 11, 'Hessen-Westmark' at Frankfürt/Main
NS-Fliegerkorps 12, 'Niederhein' at Essen
NS-Fliegerkorps 13, 'Main-Donau' at Nuremberg
NS-Fliegerkorps 14, 'Bayern-Süd' at Munich
NS-Fliegerskorps 15, 'Schwaben' at Stuttgart
NS-Fliegerkorps 16, 'Südwest' at Karlsruhe

12 NSFK-Brigadeführer. Left-hand collar patch.
13 NSFK-Oberführer. Left-hand collar patch.
14 Shoulder-strap for NSFK ranks from NSFK-Standartenführer down to NSFK-Sturmbannführer. The strap had silver twisted cording mounted on a bright yellow cloth covered underlay. Silver button.
15 & 16 NSFK-Standartenführer. Right- and left-hand collar patches. This was the most junior rank of the officer ranks that wore patches in mirror pairs.
17 & 18 NSFK-Obersturmbannführer of the 3rd Sturm of the 18th Standarte. As for all remaining NSFK ranks, the right-hand collar patch displayed the number of the wearer's unit (or staff appointment, see Fig.31), and the left-hand-patch the wearer's rank.
19 NSFK-Sturmbannführer. Left-hand collar patch. The rank stars (or 'pips') were of white alloy.
20 Shoulder-strap for NSFK-Sturmhauptführer/NSFK-Hauptsturmführer down to the rank of NSFK-Sturmführer. The strap had two strands of silver-aluminium twisted cording laid flat on a yellow underlay to form four lines of cording. White metal button. (The rank of NSFK-Sturmhauptführer was previously, at least before 1940, referred to as NSFK-Hauptsturmführer.)
21 NSFK-Sturmhauptführer left-hand collar patch.
22 & 23 NSFK-Obersturmführer on the Staff of NSFK Group 9. Right- and left-hand collar patches.

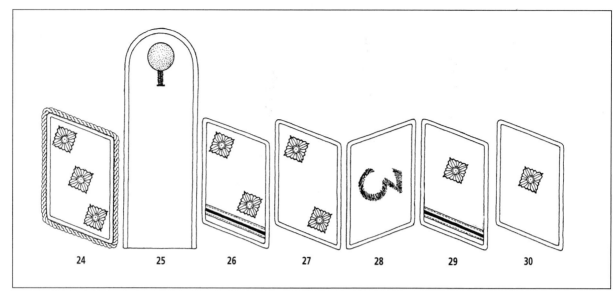

24   25   26   27   28   29   30

NS-Fliegerkorps 17, 'Ostmark' at Vienna

The NS-Fliegerkorps continued to function throughout the remaining pre-war years, and although its personnel and output of fresh recruits for the Luftwaffe declined towards the last year of the war, it nevertheless fulfilled an important function for the German war effort.

The main wartime functions of the NSFK were as follows:

(a) Maintaining schools to train pilots, wireless operators, glider troops and parachutists, as well as other specialized personnel.

(b) Giving instruction to the Flieger-HJ, the Aviation Hitler Youth.

(c) Producing a constant flow of skilled personnel for the Luftwaffe, and thereby functioning as a reserve pool for the air force.

The NSFK 'Flying Man' Emblem

Icarus of Greek mythology was a mortal who attempted to fly. Legend has it that Daedalus, the father of Icarus, had, out of jealousy and spite, murdered his nephew Talos, a gifted sculptor and a brilliant inventor. Daedalus, with Icarus, fled to the island of Crete to escape his crime. Here Daedalus designed the labyrinth for King Minos, but was imprisoned by the king for his efforts. Daedalus and his son escaped from prison by constructing wings fashioned from bird feathers, bound to a framework of saplings and glued into position by beeswax. The flight of Daedalus was successful, but Icarus overreached himself. The higher he flew, the nearer to the sun he went; the wax melted, his wings disintegrated and Icarus fell to his death.

24 NSFK-Sturmführer. Left-hand collar patch. This was the most junior officer rank.

25 Shoulder-strap for NSFK ranks from NSFK-Obertruppführer down to the lowest rank of NSFK-Mann. The strap was of blue-grey cloth piped with bright yellow cording. Buttons were either white metal or painted blue-grey. NSFK unit numbers are found embroidered in yellow threads into the cloth strap.

26 NSFK-Obertruppführer. Left-hand rank patch. The 'rank bars' were produced from silver-aluminium braiding with a central line of black silk. Rank stars were in white metal.

27 NSFK-Truppführer. Left-hand collar patch.

28 & 29 NSFK-Oberscharführer on the staff of Standarte 3. Right- and left-hand collar patches.

30 NSFK-Scharführer. Left-hand collar patch.

31 & 32 NSFK-Rottenführer on the staff of the NSFK-Korpsführer. Right- and left-hand collar patches.

33 NSFK-Sturmmann. Left-hand collar patch.

34 NSFK-Mann. Left-hand collar patch.

31   32   33   34

35 NSFK Breast Emblem. An artistic representation of Icarus was chosen as an appropriate emblem for the membership of the National Socialist Flying Corps. This emblem was used primarily as a badge worn over the right breast pocket of the blue-grey tunic and the tan shirt or blouse. A similar design was used on the flags of the NSFK, the gorgets worn by the NSFK Colour bearers, and as a small device on the collar patches for the Korpsführer and Ehrenführer of the NSFK.

There were two coloured versions of this Icarus emblem. One was produced with a blue-grey backing for wear on the blue-grey NSFK tunics, the other had a light tan backing for wear on the tan-coloured blouse or shirt. A slightly larger version was produced for wear on the front of the all-yellow NSFK Sports Vest.

Photographic evidence shows that the breast emblem was originally worn as an arm badge, on the right upper arm of the blue-grey service dress. On an, as yet, undetermined date the location for the 'Flying Man' badge was moved to the more familiar position over the wearer's right breast pocket.

Doubtless, in 1935, when the figure of Icarus was considered as the emblem for the new air-orientated organization, a man flying by his own efforts, soaring above all adversity and escaping his earthly bonds was felt to be a most appropriate symbol. Ten years later the irony of the choice may have escaped the German authorities.

NSFK Uniforms

In some respects the two basic uniform styles worn by the membership of the NSFK, the Service Dress and the Working Dress, can be considered a combination of, or a compromise between, the dress of the Luftwaffe (the four-pocket, open-neck blue-grey tunic) and the Party uniforms

Right: Under the supervision of an NSFK instructor, boys of the Deutsche Jungvolk are shown the correct way to wear an airman's parachute.

36 & 37 The NSFK Service Tunic and Kepi head-dress, here shown for the junior officer rank of NSFK Sturm-führer on the Staff of the NSFK Korpsführer.
38 & 39 NSFK Working Dress and Beret, here shown for an NSFK Rottenführer.

(the use of a kepi head-dress, the wearing of brown shirts, swastika arm bands and the style of the rank insignia).

The NSFK Service Dress and Kepi
The blue-grey open-neck tunic worn with either matching breeches or long trousers could be utilized for a number of purposes. When worn with breeches, riding boots, brown leather waist belt and cross-strap, brown shirt and black tie, the NSFK dagger and the blue-grey kepi it was considered as the lesser Service Dress (kleinen Dien-stanzug). The same tunic minus waist-belt

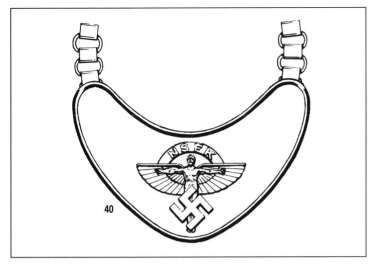

40 NSFK Colour Bearer's Duty Gorget.

Service — or Working — Dress' worn by members of the NSFK consisted of a brown 'political' blouse or shirt and black tie worn with blue-grey breeches, black leather riding boots and a blue-grey beret. The Greater Service Dress also featured a black leather waist-belt and cross-strap worn with the Fliegermesser, literally the 'Flying Knife', the NSFK dagger.

NSFK Colour Bearer's Duty Gorget

Colour bearers of the NS-Fliegerkorps were distinguished by a gorget. This was of a comparatively simple design in that it was half-moon in shape — sometimes referred to as 'kidney' shaped — and was fashioned from polished new German silver. The gilt coloured centrepiece depicted the NSFK flying man emblem with outstretched arms holding a set of wings. Above the man's head was a scroll displaying the initial letters 'N.S.F.K.' A large swastika set on its point strategically covered the man's loins and legs.

The gorget was worn on the front of the flag bearer's chest, being hung around the neck by a matt-silvered nickel chain. The reverse of the gorget was covered in black cloth and, in keeping with other gorgets, it had a single central metal prong that was

and cross-strap but worn with the NSFK dagger, with long blue-grey trousers, black shoes, brown shirt and tie and blue-grey kepi was classed as Walking-Out Dress (Ausgehanzug). Exactly the same combination of dress items, but worn with a white shirt in place of the brown one, was used for Evening Dress (Abendanzug).

The NSFK Working Dress and Beret

The form of uniform dress referred to as the 'grossen Dienstanzug' or the 'Greater

Right: On the occasion of the seventh anniversary of the founding of the NSFK, a special gathering of past and present members took place in the Schulungshaus of the NS-Fliegerkorps (the NSFK House of Instruction) in Berlin. The photographs show, from left to right: NSFK-Obergruppenführer Sauke, representing and deputising for the Korpsführer and Chief of Staff of the NS-Fliegerkorps; Oberleutnant Thierfelder, Knight's Cross holder with Oakleaves and Swords; NSFK-Obergruppenführer Oberst von Bullow, Knight's Cross holder; and Leutnant Fulda, Knight's Cross and Oakleaves. 5 March 1942.

Left: Major Graf, Knight's Cross holder with Oakleaves, Diamonds and Swords, signs the Golden Book of the City of Munich while the Oberbürgermeister of Munich (left) and NSFK-Oberführer Bär (right) look on, December 1942.

inserted into a buttonhole on the front of the blouse to prevent the gorget swinging on the neck chain when the bearer moved.

National Air Raid Protection League (Reichsluftschutzbund)

The early development of air raid precautions was closely connected with the formation of a secret air force and was part of the preparation for the aggressive war which the Nazi leadership had planned at a very early stage.

The German term for 'Air Protection' covered not only air-raid precautions but also the fire protection police, bomb disposal, smoke-screens, decoy sites and camouflage. 'Air Defence' covered the active measures such as fighter aircraft, anti-aircraft artillery, searchlights, sound-location posts and balloon barrages.

On 5 May 1933 the Commissariat for Air Travel, after only three months in existence, was upgraded to the status of Air Ministry. Hermann Göring, the then Prussian Minister of the Interior and Commander-in-Chief of the Prussian Police, was appointed Reichskommissar für die Luftfahrt (Commissioner for Air Travel) and the Ministry of Air Travel took effective control of all air defence measures.

On 29 April 1933 the Reich Air Protection League (RLB) was officially formed and two months later, on 24 June, its existence was made known to the public with the issue of a statement that 'foreign planes had flown over Berlin and dropped leaflets which had insulted the government'. These alleged air raids were used as a convenient excuse to justify developments that could no longer be entirely concealed from the public.

Propaganda was used to depict Germany sitting unprotected amidst neighbours with powerful air forces threatening her from all sides. The hapless citizen was urged to meet the threat by enrolling in the Reich Air Protection League. Volunteers joined in their hundreds of thousands to be taught the skills of domestic air raid precautions.

On 13 March 1935 an announcement was made that Göring had been appointed Minister for Air and Commander-in-Chief of the Air Force, and a few months later the responsibility for air protection was taken over by the Air Ministry.

The Air Protection Law of 26 June 1935 did away with the voluntary status for membership of the National Air Protection League, and future service was made obligatory for almost every German citizen. In 1938 the membership of the RLB was given as 12.6 million, and by April 1943 this number had risen to 22 million.

Before May 1942 the League was divided into two main sub-sections, the Self-Protection Service and the Extended

Above: Von Schröder, Vice-president of the Reichsluft-schutzbund. On 20 April 1939 Hitler appointed him General der Flakartillerie.

woman and who in turn was supervised by a Block Warden (Blockwart). A Block Warden controlled several streets and came under the supervision of a Ward Protection Leader. This system closely followed the organizational structure of the Nazi Party itself. Operationally, the Self-Protection Service units came under the orders of the police chief of the ward. In large towns the Air Protection Police were available to reinforce the Self-Protection Service at any incident beyond its control.

In small towns the Selbstschutz was formed as an 'Air Protection Fellowship', equivalent to street fire parties, which, together with the voluntary fire brigades and, for rescue duties, local technical personnel provided by the Technical Emergency Service (Technishe Nothilfe, TeNo), were the sole forces immediately available. Help could be and was sent from the nearest town when necessary. Members of the Self-Protection Service were expected to supply their own equipment other than respirators and steel helmets.

The Rural Air Protection Fellowship (Landluftschutzgemeinschaft) provided fire-fighting and rescue squads in rural areas too small to be served by any of the other services.

2. The Extended Self-Protection Service was established to cover those institutions, Government offices, hotels and other communal places not large enough or of sufficient importance to the war effort to be provided with a Works Air Raid Protection Service. The Service was administered and operated similarly to the Self-Protection Service, but there were certain additional features such as a leader-in-charge, a control room for the premises and simple rescue and first aid equipment. Shelters had to be provided for employees.

The ordinary German householder was called upon to do far more for him- or herself than was the case in other European countries, even to the extent of providing his/her own equipment and, as a member of the Reich Air Protection League, by subscribing funds out of which, for example, the National Air Protection School was built. (The foundation stone of the new National Air Protection School was laid at Wansee, Berlin on 2 March 1938.)

The main burden for ARP work, however, was borne by the German Police, who

Self-Protection Service. Personnel of these services were recruited, organized and trained by the RLB, and the League was also responsible for propaganda and instruction of the general public in all air protection matters.

1. The Self-Protection Service, known in German as the Selbstschutz, was the organization created for the protection of the ordinary householder, and was based on a warden and fire-guard system. This was the first line of domestic defence against air raids, and its main functions were the equipping of communal cellar shelters and the performance of fire-guard duties under the direction of a House Warden. Each house (generally a block of flats) had a House Warden who was frequently a

National Air Defence League (RLB) shoulder-straps and collar patches.

With the singular exception of the rank of RLB Präsident, all collar patches and the under-lay of the shoulder-straps were made from lilac-coloured cloth. Shoulder-straps were worn singly on the right shoulder and collar patches were worn in matching pairs. Only the right-hand collar patches are illustrated here.

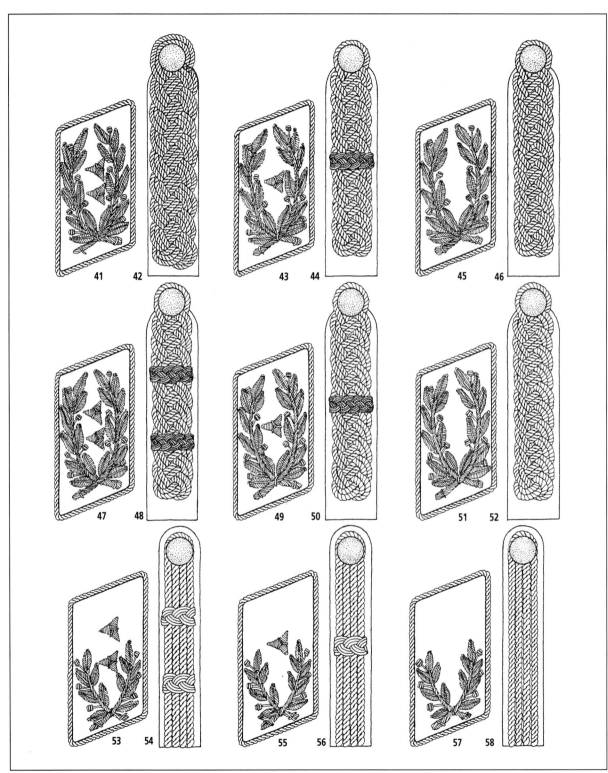

41 & 42 RLB Präsident. Right-hand collar patch and shoulder-strap. The President of the RLB was distinguished from all other ranks by the use of white collar patches and white underlay on the shoulder-strap. The embroidered wreath, three-pointed rank stars and twisted cording were all gilt, as was the plaited cording on the shoulder-strap. The strap button was gilt metal.

43 & 44 General-hauptluftschutzführer (Chef des Stabes). Right-hand collar patch and shoulder-strap. Lilac collar patch with gold wreath, gilt star and twisted corded piping. Shoulder-strap had silver and gold plaited cording with gilt 'rank slide' all on lilac underlay, button in gilt metal.

45 & 46 General-luftschutzführer. Right-hand collar patch and shoulder-strap. As described for Figs 43 & 44, but without gilt star and gilt 'rank slide'.

47 & 48 Oberlutschutzeführer. Right-hand collar patch and shoulder-strap. Lilac collar patch has a silver bullion wreath, stars and twisted cord edging. Shoulder-strap has silver plaited twisted cording on an underlay of lilac cloth. The two 'rank slides' are in gilt, the button in white metal.

49 & 50 Oberstabsluft-schutzführer. Right-hand collar patch and shoulder-strap. Colouring as for Figs 47 & 48.

51 & 52 Stabsluftschutzführer. Right-hand collar patch and shoulder-strap. Colouring as for Figs 47 & 48.

53 & 54 Hauptluftschutzführer. Right-hand collar patch and shoulder-strap. Colouring as for Figs 47 & 48.

55 & 56 Luftschutzoberführer. Right-hand collar patch and shoulder-strap. Colouring as for Figs 47 & 48.

57 & 58 Luftschutzführer. Right-hand collar patch and shoulder-strap. Colouring as for Figs 47 & 48.

59 Shoulder-strap for RLB ranks from LS-Obertruppmeister to LS-Truppmann. Lilac cloth strap with black piping, white metal button.

60 LS-Obertruppmeister. Right-hand collar patch. Lilac cloth patch, flat silver braid, white metal three-pointed rank stars.

61 LS-Truppmeister. Right-hand collar patch. Colouring as for Fig. 60.

62 LS-Obertruppwart. Right-hand collar patch. Colouring as for Fig. 60.

63 LS-Truppwart. Right-hand collar patch. Colouring as for Fig. 60.

64 LS-Obertruppmann. Right-hand collar patch. Lilac cloth patch with single three-pointed white metal rank star.

65 LS-Truppmann. Right-hand plain lilac cloth collar patch.

It is worth noting that at one time a limited run of RLB rank insignia existed, believed to antedate those illustrated here, which were introduced from 1 July 1940. Although their construction and colouring was exactly the same as the later range, the rank insignia shown as Figs. 11 to 25 is believed to be the full extent of these earlier RLB ranks, and they also carried different rank terms to those given above.

51 & 52 LS-Gruppenführer.

53 & 54 LS-Hauptführer.
55 & 56 LS-Oberführer.
57 & 58 LS-Führer.
59 Shoulder-strap used by all RLB ranks from LS-Obertruppführer down to LS-Truppmann.
60 LS-Obertruppführer.
61 LS-Truppmeister.
62 LS-Obertruppwart.
63 LS-Truppwart.
64 LS-Obertruppmann.
65 LS-Truppmann.

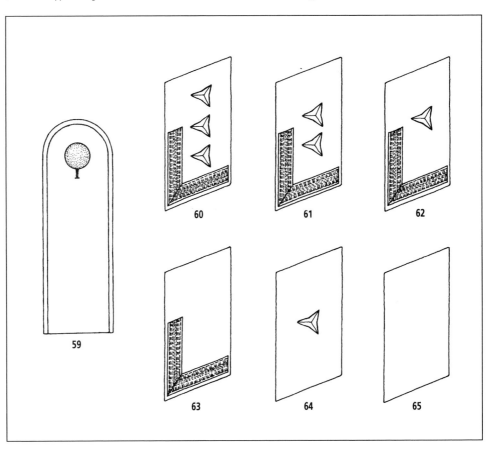

were responsible for all the mobile services in the town, exercised general supervision over the Self-Protection Service and had full operational control within the town limits.

By 1942 the rising scale of the Allied air attacks compelled the German authorities to change the structure of their civil defence organization. These changes did not mean that the existing services were inefficient, but rather that what had been adequate for the scale of raids experienced up to 1942 required drastic overhaul to meet the increasing Allied bombing if they were to have any chance of success.

The Reichsluftschutzbund Emblem

The RLB's Organisational Emblem was used both as a cap badge and an arm eagle. There were two qualities of this one badge, one machine-woven in light grey threads on to a backing cloth of blue-grey, the other hand-embroidered in silver-aluminium threads on to a blue-grey coloured

66

The central design on the front of the first-pattern gorget showed a frosted silver starburst on which were displayed the stylized letters 'RLB' above a small swastika set on its point (Fig. 1). Both the letters and the swastika were in blue enamelling.

The design employed on the second-pattern gorget dropped the letters and at the same time increased the size of the swastika and placed it centrally on the frosted silver starburst emblem. The colour of the enamel used for the swastika was changed to black.

66 RLB Organizational Emblem.

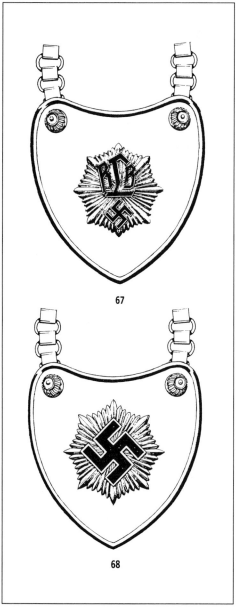

67

68

RLB Gorgets
67 First-pattern Gorget, 1935–1938.
68 Second-pattern Gorget, 1938–1945.

cloth backing. In both cases the swastika was worked in black threads.

When this emblem was used as an arm badge it was worn on the right forearm of the RLB tunic, positioned slightly above the top edge of the cuff. The purpose of the arm emblem worn with either a single or a double silver-aluminium chevron is not clear. The chevrons certainly did not indicate rank. Rank was shown by the use of shoulder-straps and collar patches. It is probable, therefore, that these chevrons had something to do with the wearer holding a particular position of responsibility, or more likely they indicated length of service.

RLB Colour Bearer's Duty Gorgets
The occasion of the first Grand German Congress of Leaders of the RLB, held at the National Air Protection School, Wannsee, Berlin, on 23 March 1939, was also used to dedicate the first of many of the new flags to be carried by the RLB. These new blue flags displayed a large, central, white starburst emblem, in the centre of which was a solid black swastika standing on its point. This same emblem was also used on the second-pattern gorgets (Fig. 2) which began to be introduced after August 1938.

Both the first- and second-pattern gorgets were of identical heart-shape design. Both were of nickel-plated metal, each had a raised, rounded rim, with two prominent silver-plaited bosses on the front of the upper part of the gorget plate, and both had a silver-coloured metal neck chain.

Right: General der Flakartillerie Von Schröder, as President of the RLB, collects Winterhilfswerk donations during the second year of the war, 23 January 1941. Von Schröder is wearing the uniform of RLB Präsident, and has white collar patches with three small gold triangular stars, one more than the number of stars shown in the table on page 21 for the prewar rank of RLB Präsident. It therefore follows that an extra RLB rank was introduced either before or just after the beginning of the war. Exactly what rank this was I have yet to discover.

Below: At a parade drawn up in front of the Reichsluftschutzschule at Berlin-Wannesee on 23 May 1939, Generalfeldmarschall Göring dedicates the new flags of the Reichsluftschutzbund. At least 38 RLB flags are visible in this photograph, as well as the SA 'Horst Wessel' fahnen.

Above: The leader of the Steglitz RLB Ortsgruppe Wesemann delivers a speech during an indoor ceremony for the swearing-in of new RLB recruits.

Left: A view of the hall full of new recruits, some of whom are symbolically taking an oath on their RLB district flag. Note the emblems used on these early-pattern RLB flags, and the starburst and swastika emblem used on the post-1938 flags featured in the lower picture on page 23.

Air Raid Warning Service and Security and Assistance Service (Sicherheits-und Hilfsdienst)

The Security and Assistance Service was formed in 1935 under police direction in towns of the first category, ie, 106 of the largest German towns and cities which were regarded as the most vulnerable in the event of an air attack. It formed the mobile civil defence service for those towns. By 1939 the SHD was a conscripted force of men housed in barracks on a rota system, and allowed to sleep at home on alternate nights, air raids permitting. Service in the SHD was a form of 'reserved occupation' in that its members were exempted from having to serve in the Armed Forces. They were also exempt from physical training or rifle drill, though they were not permitted to pursue any other occupation whilst serving in the SHD.

In 1940 a mobile strategic reserve of some three or four battalions was formed to provide reinforcements in towns being heavily attacked. Each town having a Security and Assistance Service had to find a quota of men as a nucleus for these mobile battalions, which were self-supporting and capable of rapid transfer. Their equipment included pile-drivers, hydraulic jacks, cutting equipment and wrecking tools.

There were five branches of the SHD: 1. Decontamination Squads, 2. Fire Fighting

69

69 The Luftschutz Emblem

Right: Men of the Fire Protection Police, assisted by members of the Security and Assistance Service, dowse fires started the previous night by an RAF incendiary raid on Frankfurt on Main, October 1943.

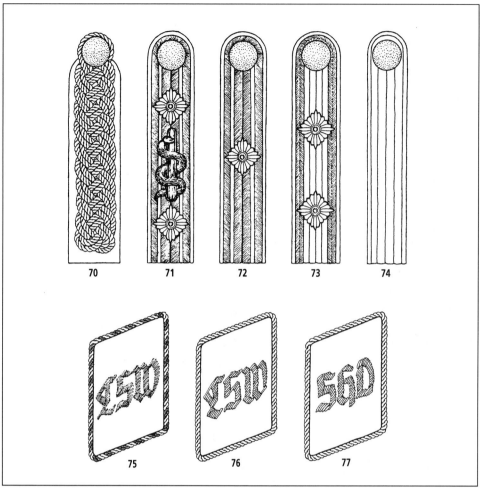

Shoulder-straps and collar patches for the Security & Assistance Service (SHD) and the Air Raid Warning Service (LSW).

70 SHD/LSW Abteilungsführer.
71 SHD/LSW Bereitschafts-führer (Arzt), medical branch.
72 SHD/LSW Oberzugführer.
73 SHD/LSW Stabsgruppen-führer.
74 SHD/LSW Mann.
75 Collar patch for lower ranks of the Luftschutz Warn-dienst, LSW Mann to LSW Stabsgruppenführer.
76 Collar patch for officer classes of the Luftschutz Warndienst, LSW Zugführer to LSW Abteilungsleiter.
77 Collar patch for officer classes of the Sicherheits u.Hilfsdienst. SHD Zugführer to SHD Abteilungsleiter.
The colouring of the shoulder-straps used by both the SHD and the LSW was a combination of dark green and silver. Metal rank stars were in white metal for lower and middle ranks up to SHD/LSW Stabs-gruppenführer, and in gilt metal for officer grades, including medical insignia, from SHD/LSW Oberzugführer upwards. The collar patches were in dark green cloth with silver-aluminium embroidered letters, either 'LSW' or 'SHD'. The piping to the patches was in silver and green twisted cording for lower and middle ranks, and in all-silver-aluminium twisted cording for SHD/LSW officer classes.

Units; 3. Repair Work Units; 4. Veterinary Service, and 5. Medical Units.

As a result of attacks on Lubeck and Rostock, an overhaul of the air protection organization came about, and in April/May 1942 the Security and Assistance Service was renamed the Air Protection Police, the 'Luftschutz-polizei'. This organization covered many of the areas previously dealt with by the SHD, such as fire-fighting and decontamination, rescue work and repairs, manning first-aid posts, operating first-aid squads and driving ambulances, rescuing and caring for pets and livestock whilst operating a veterinary service, and, finally, carrying out gas detection.

The administration of this service remained in the hands of Reichsführer Heinrich Himmler as head of the Order Police, although Göring was responsible operationally for this and all air protection services.

It should be noted that the voluntary Technical Emergency Service, the TeNo, the Todt Organization, hospitals, evacuation, Police, etc., were not part of the Air Protection Police Service, although they had to co-operate closely with it.

The mobile battalions of the SHD were transferred to the air force and renamed the Motorised Air Protection Battalions of the Luftwaffe. The battalions were confined to fire-fighting, rescue and debris-clearance duties, with decontamination and first aid playing only a minor role.

The training of the Air Protection Police was the responsibility of the local chief of the Order Police. The number of Air Protection Police allotted to a town was roughly proportional to the size of the population.

The Luftschutz Emblem
A wreath of oakleaves overlaid with a scroll bearing the word Luftschutz (Air

Right: Two youthful members of the SHD play their hose on fires started in the Reichs Capital during the night of 3/4 September 1943. The lad on the right is wearing a Czech steel helmet.

Protection), with a small swastika at its base and set between a pair of stylized wings, was the emblem chosen for the SHD and the Air Raid Warning Service (Luftschutz Warndienst), collectively referred to as the 'Luftschutz'. The emblem was worn on the front of the special civil-pattern RLB/SHD/LSW steel helmet as a transfer (decal) applied to the dark blue metal surface. As a machine-woven cloth badge it was worn over the right breast of certain uniforms and on the left upper arm of other uniforms of all three services. It was also used as a cap emblem.

When worn as a machine-woven badge, its colouring comprised a white design on darkish blue-grey material. When worn on the steel helmet as an applied transfer the emblem tended to be silver-grey on dark blue-grey, and when the badge was produced as a hand-embroidered bullion item

it was worked in silver-aluminium threads on dark blue-grey cloth.

Luftschutzwarndienst (LSW)

The Air Raid Warning Service was an important organization that acted in much the same way as Great Britain's Royal Observer Corps. Observers of the LSW kept watch from their vantage points during daylight hours for approaching aircraft, especially enemy aircraft. At all times, day and night, they analyzed incoming reports from other LSW posts, from the Police and from Flugmeldedienst units on the progress of enemy bomber formations over Germany. It was on their conclusions that the air raid warnings were sounded, alerting the local population of an impending air attack. They also worked in close unison with the Police authorities during the co-ordinating of air raid and post-air-raid services. The LSW

Left: An officer of the Luftschutzwarndienst (LSW-Zugführer), assisted by men from the Luftwaffe, listens anxiously for sounds of life amid the rubble of a destroyed Berlin building, 6–7 September 1943.

Right: Men of the German Red Cross (wearing arm bands), the SHD (foreground) and an officer of the Fire Protection Police carry the body of an air raid victim on a stretcher away from a badly damaged building whilst other rescue workers look on. Unidentified German town, 7 July 1943.

78   79   80   81   82

Sicherheits –und Hilfsdienst Specialist Arm Badges.
78 SHD Medical personnel (Sanitätsdienst)
79 SHD Decontamination squads (Entgiftungsdienst für im Gasspruren und Entgiften Ausgebildete).
80 SHD Fire Fighting personnel (Feuerlöschdienst).
81 SHD Repair and Maintenance personnel (Instandsetzungsdienst).
82 SHD Veterinary Service personnel (Veterinärdienst).

was also responsible for giving the 'all clear' signal.

SHD Specialist Arm Badges
Personnel of the five services of the SHD wore specialist badges on the left upper arm and occasionally on the left forearm of their uniform tunics. These specialist badges indicated the qualification held by the wearer. All badges were machine-woven in coloured threads. The badges were introduced during 1941.

SHD Medical personnel wore a badge consisting of a pale blue oval edged green displaying a white serpent and staff emblem. Personnel of the SHD Decontamination squads were distinguished by wearing a badge with the black Gothic letter 'G' on a green-edged yellow oval. Firefighting personnel of the SHD wore a red oval badge with green edging that displayed a white Gothic letter 'F'. SHD Repair and Maintenance personnel had a white Gothic letter 'I' on a green-edged brown oval badge, and the Veterinary Service personnel were distinguished by a white Gothic letter 'V' on a green-edged lilac oval.

Left: The gruesome but necessary task of recovering and removing the bodies of air raid victims from bombed buildings was frequently carried out by men of the Luftschutz. Here, in Berlin on 30 August 1943, men of the Fire Protection Police and the SHD are about to remove the burnt body of a woman to a collecting point where, before cremation or burial, her remains and the remains of all the other victims of the air raid will be put on display, hopefully for identification by surviving next of kin.

Right: Sounding the 'all clear'. A member of the Luftschutzwarndienst presses the button that electronically activates the sirens throughout a typical German town. The responsibility for ordering all siren warnings lay with the Chief of the Luftschutz Headquarters. He held the only key to the siren control box, and he alone had access to it. The precise moment of sounding all 'general alarm' air raid warnings and 'all clear' signals was noted by the assistant with a stopwatch. Note the Luftschutz emblem worn over the right breast pocket and the 'L.S. Warndienst' cuff-title on the left forearm. This item had silver-grey gothic lettering on a green band.

Left: The interior of the control room of the Bonn Air Raid Precaution Headquarters, October 1943.

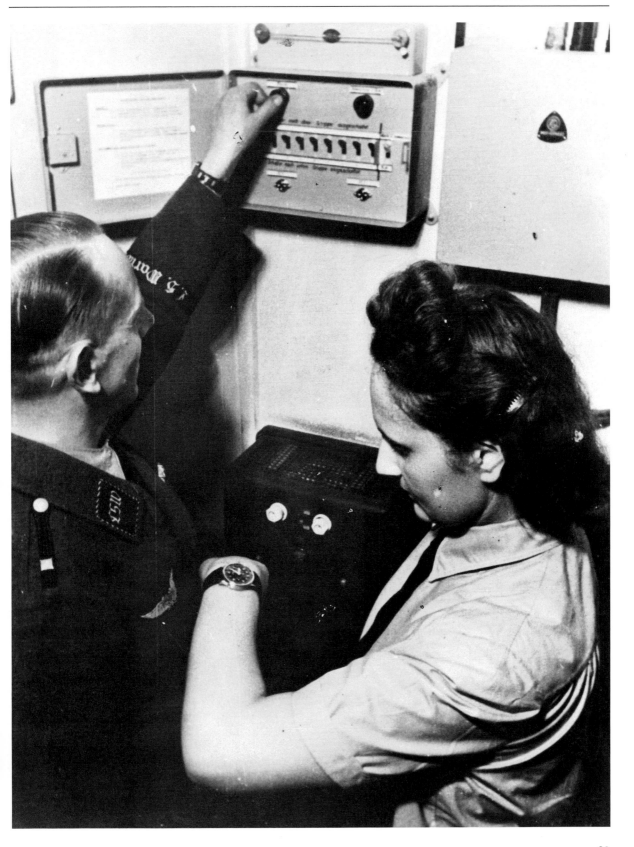

Top left: A Zugführer of the LSW receives a document from a female of the Luft-melddienst. Note the Luftschutz emblem on the upper left arm.

Lower left: An LSW-Mann acting as an observer scans the skies above the City of Bonn. The numbers one to twelve painted on the inside rim of the observation post were to assist the observers in reporting the sector location of approaching enemy aircraft.

Above: A mixed group of rescuers break for a well deserved glass of schnapps, Remscheid, August 1943.

Below: Men of the Berlin Sicherheits und Hilfsdienst parade with their firefighting appliances in front of the Reichs Sportsfeld, 22 July 1940.

2. THE LUFTWAFFE 1940–1945: FORMATIONS AND BRANCHES

Ranks and Appointments, 1935–1945. Introductory Notes

The lowest grade of Airman in the Luftwaffe was known as Flieger (flyer), Funker (signaller — air or ground signal units) or Kanonier (gunner — in anti-aircraft artillery units). Other junior rank terms existed especially just before and during the war years, being brought into use when new formations were raised, most of which had a military rather than a flying role. These are given in the listing of rank terms and appointments below.

A rifleman of the Grenadier Regiments or of the Guard Regiment of the Division 'Hermann Göring' was referred to as a 'Jäger' (literally 'Hunter'). NCOs bore the title 'Oberjäger'. These two rank terms originated from the early pre-war Landespolizeigruppe 'General Göring' (see Volume 1933–40, page 38). The same two terms were also applied to junior ranks and NCOs of the Luftwaffe-Jäger-Regimenter of the Luftwaffe Field Divisions, other than the 20 Luftwaffen-Felddivision and the Fusilierbataillone of the Luftwaffen-Felddivisionen. They had specific ranks introduced in July 1944 (see below).

Instructions were published in January 1943[1] whereby the rank term used by the lowest-grade of personnel of the Luftwaffen-Feldkorps and the Luftwaffen-Felddivisionen were to be changed from the normal Luftwaffe designation to the following:

a. Personnel of the Luftwaffe Infantry and Anti-Tank units were to be entitled 'Jäger'.
b. Personnel of the Luftwaffe Artillery and Anti-Aircraft Artillery units were to be called 'Kanonier.
c. Lowest-grade personnel of Luftwaffe Engineer units were to be known as 'Pionier'.

The two lowest rank terms used by members of the Fusilier Battalions of the Luftwaffe Field Divisions were 'Fusilier' and 'Oberfusilier'. From the rank of Gefreiter upwards the remaining ranks used within these formations were the same as those in Army Grenadier regiments.

Personnel of the Luftwaffe Jäger Regiments of the 20 Luftwaffe Field Division used rank terms appropriate to the cavalry.[2]

Instructions were issued in July 1943[3] stating that the cavalry rank terms of Reiter' (Trooper) and 'Wachtmeister' (the cavalry equivalent of Feldwebel — NCO) were to be used in place of the normal Luftwaffe designations.

The non-commissioned ranks from Sergeant to Warrant Officer in Flight (Flieger) and Signals (Nachrichten) branches of the Luftwaffe were known as Unterfeldwebel, Feldwebel, Oberfeldwebel and Hauptfeldwebel.

Anti-Aircraft (Flak-Artillerie) Sergeants, Sergeants-Major, Warrant Officers and Senior Warrant Officers were referred to as Unterwachtmeister, Wachtmeister, Oberwachtmeister and Hauptwachtmeister respectively.

Similar to the practice employed in the German Army, Generals in the Luftwaffe, other than Medical Generals and Officers of General Rank in the Corps of Engineers, were correctly referred to by their branch of service. Thus a General of Flying Troops was a 'General der Flieger', a General of the Anti-Aircraft Artillery arm was a 'General der Flakartillerie', a Signals General was a 'General der Luftwaffe-Nachrichtentruppe', and, finally, a General of Paratroop forces was known as a 'General der Fallschirmtruppe'.

Hermann Göring was the first officer of the Luftwaffe to be promoted to the rank of General Field Marshal, this honour being bestowed upon him by Adolf Hitler on 4 February 1938. Further promotions of other Luftwaffe officers to this senior rank took place after the Fall of France in August 1940. For further details see Volume 1933–40, page 79.

Hermann Göring was promoted to the unique and singular rank of Reich Marshal of the Greater German Reich by Adolf Hitler on 19 July 1940. Promotion to this newly created and extraordinary rank was the reward bestowed upon Göring for the part he had played in the development of the Nazi Party, the creation of the German Air Force and the victory in the West. For more complete details see page 263 in the section devoted to Hermann Göring.

Ranks and Appointments, 1935–45

Reichsmarschall des Grossdeutschen Reiches	Reich Marshall of the Greater German Empire

General Officers:

Generalfeldmarschall	General Field Marshal
Generaloberst	Colonel-General
General der Flieger	General of Flying Troops
General der Flakartillerie	General of Anti-Aircraft Artillery
General der Luftwaffe-Nachrichten-truppen	General of Air Force Air Signals Troops
General der Fallschirmtruppe	General of Parachute Forces
Generalleutnant	Lieutenant-General
Generalmajor	Major-General

Staff Officers:

Oberst	Colonel
Oberstleutnant	Lieutenant-Colonel
Major	Major

Field Officers:

Hauptmann/ Rittmeister	Captain
Oberleutnant	Senior Lieutenant
Leutnant	Lieutenant

Senior NCOs of Oberfeldwebel grade

Stabsfeldwebel/ Stabswachtmeister	Staff Sergeant Major
Hauptfeldwebel/ Hauptwachtmeister	Regimental Sergeant Major
Oberfeldwebel/	Battalion Sergeant
Oberwachtmeister	Major
Oberfähnrich	Senior Ensign

NCOs of Feldwebel grade

Feldwebel/ Wachtmeister	Company Sergeant Major

NCOs of Unteroffizier grade

Unterfeldwebel/ Unterwachtmeister	Sergeant
Fähnrich	Ensign
Unteroffizier	Lance-Sergeant
Oberjäger	Senior Rifleman

Other Ranks

Hauptgefreiter	Staff Corporal
Stabsgefreiter	Staff Corporal
Obergefreiter	Leading Corporal
Gefreiter	Corporal
Flieger	Airman
Kanonier	Gunner
Funker	Signaller
Jäger	Rifleman
Pioniere	Engineer
Sanitätssoldat	Medical Orderly
Grenadier	Rifleman
Fusilier	Rifleman

Shoulder-Straps and Collar Patches

Individual ranks were displayed on the Luftwaffe uniforms by means of collar patches and shoulder-straps. Other indications of rank or appointment were also used, but these methods (most of which are dealt with in Volume 1933–40) were either inconsistent or applied only to groups of ranks rather than to individual ranks.

Collar patches were worn in matching, mirror pairs. Shoulder-straps were worn one to each shoulder. The base cloth of the collar patches and the underlay cloth and the piping to the shoulder-straps worn by both officers and other ranks were in the arm-of-service colour (Waffenfarbe) appointed to be worn by the individual soldier (see the section on Waffenfarbe, page 51).

Shoulder-Straps and Collar Patches for Officers.

Reichsmarschall. (Figs. 83 to 90). In August 1940 Göring, in his capacity as Reichsmarschall of the Greater German Reich, wore for the first time the new insignia that went with his newly acquired

Left: Hermann Göring after his surrender to the American forces in May 1945. This clearly shows the shoulder-straps and the second-pattern collar patches for his rank of Reichsmarschall des Grossdeutschen Reich.

rank. The so-called first-pattern insignia consisted of a pair of collar patches and a set of shoulder-straps. The patches were described as having a silver brocade base with gold embroidered design. The right-hand patch displayed a hand-embroidered 'Wehrmacht style' eagle and swastika surrounded by a border of gold laurel leaves, the whole patch being piped in matt gold twisted cording. The left-hand patch had the same twisted cording and the same border of laurel leaves, but displayed a pair of crossed batons, presumably representing his new Reich Marshal's batons. The shoulder-straps had triple gold tubular cording mounted on an underlay of superfine white cloth. Displayed on the cording was an eagle and swastika (Wehrmacht style) surmounting a pair of crossed Field Marshal's batons. These were finely hollow-cast in gilt-coloured metal. Photographic evidence shows that these were manufactured as pairs, so that, when worn mounted on the straps, the heads of the eagles faced towards Göring's front. The shoulder-strap buttons were in pebble-finished gilt metal.

Göring continued to wear his new insignia until March 1941, when, it is believed for reasons of personal preference,

Luftwaffe Insignia of Rank, Collar Patches and Shoulder-straps, 1935–1945.

83, 84, 85 & 86 Reichsmarschall des Grossdeutschen Reiches, first pattern.

87, 88, 89 & 90 Reichsmarschall des Grossdeutschen Reiches, second pattern.

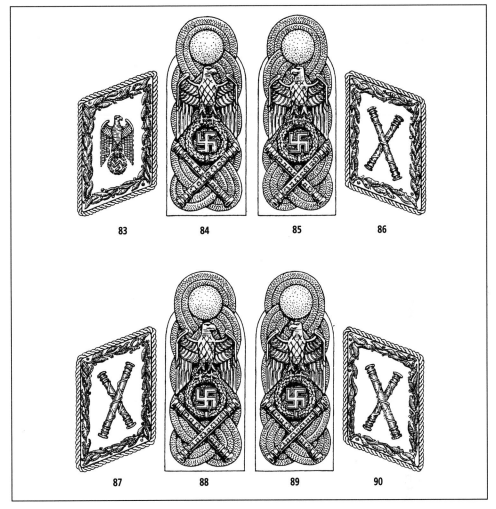

83   84   85   86

87   88   89   90

he had the right-hand collar patch changed to make it similar to the left-hand patch. This second-pattern set of insignia continued to be worn by Göring until the end of the war. (Figs. 87 & 90.) Towards the later part of the war Göring took to wearing a new and simplified style of uniform which carried shoulder-straps of a unique pattern. He wore this particular uniform when he presented himself to the Americans before being interned as a prisoner of war. Both the special shoulder-straps, as well as the uniform and cap, are illustrated and described on page 299.

Generalfeldmarschall. White background to collar patch and underlay to shoulder strap. Gold embroidered eagle and swastika, wreath and twisted collar-patch cording. Silver hand-embroidered crossed batons. Triple-plaited gold tubular cording on shoulder-strap, silver-alumini-

um metal crossed batons. Gilt metal pebble-finished button. (Figs. 91, 92).

Generaloberst. White background to collar patch and underlay to shoulder-strap. Gold embroidered eagle and swastika overlaying gold wreath. Gold twisted collar-patch cording. The shoulder-strap had gold-coloured tubular cording laid on either side of a single strand of silver-aluminium Russia braid. Shoulder-strap button in gilt pebble-finished metal. Rank stars were in silver-aluminium metal. (Figs. 93, 94).

General der Flieger, General der Flakartillerie, General der Luftnachrichtentruppe and General der Fallschirmtruppe. White background to collar patch, gold embroidered wreath and wings with twisted gold cording around patch. (Figs. 95 & 96). Shoulder-strap as described for Figs. 94.

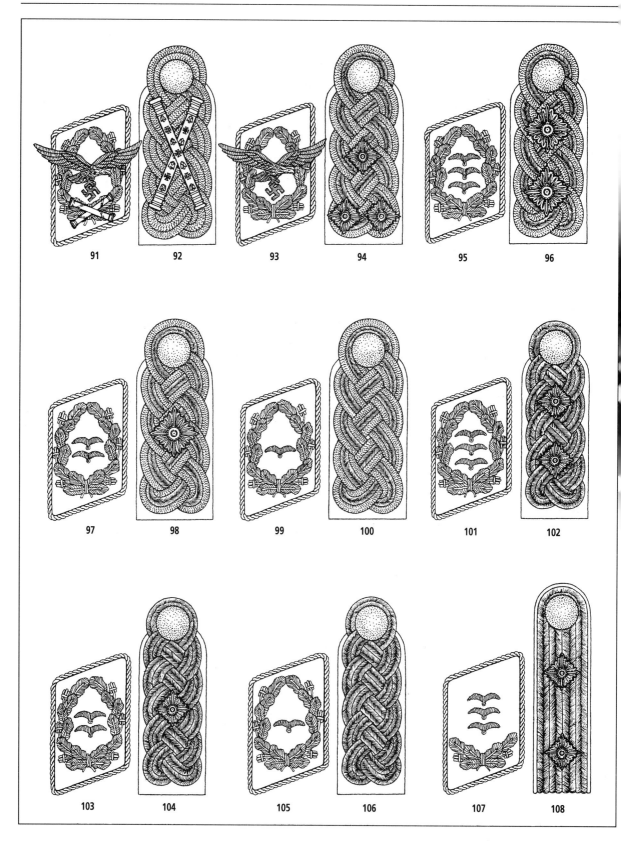

91   92   93   94   95   96

97   98   99   100   101   102

103   104   105   106   107   108

91 & 92 Generalfeldmarschall.
93 & 94 Generaloberst.
95 & 96 General der Flieger, etc.
97 & 98 Generalleutnant.
99 & 100 Generalmajor.
101 & 102 Oberst.
103 & 104 Oberstleutnant.
105 & 106 Major.
107 & 108 Hauptmann/ Rittmeister.

Right: Ritterkreuzträger, Generalleutnant Bülowius, Commander of a Flieger-Division, studies aerial reconnaissance photographs with Hauptmann Lange, holder of the Knight's Cross with Oakleaves and Commander of a Stuka Group somewhere on the Eastern Front, July 1943. The collar patches and shoulder-straps for a Generalleutnant are clearly shown.

Right: Major Bernhard Jope, former Condor Legion pilot and Commander of Kampfgeschwader 40 (Bomber Squadron 40), on the day the Führer presented him with the Oakleaves to his Knight's Cross, 24 March 1944. Major Jope, who survived the war to become a senior pilot with Lufthansa, was awarded the Knight's Cross (30 December 1940) for his achievement in sinking the 42,000-tonne liner *Empress of Britain* on his very first operational sortie, on 26 October 1940.

Generalleutnant. Construction and colouring of collar patch and shoulder-strap as described for Figs. 95 & 96 respectively.

Generalmajor. Construction and colouring of collar patch and shoulder-strap as described for Figs. 95 & 96 respectively.

The colour of the collar patches and the underlay to the officer rank shoulder-straps and the piping to the shoulder-straps for the remaining personnel were in the wearer's Waffenfarbe (see listing of arm-of-service colours on page 51).

Oberst. Wreath, wings and twisted cording to collar patch in silver-aluminium. Shoulder-strap with double-entwined strands of silver-aluminium Russia braid. White metal, pebble-finished shoulder-strap button. Rank star in gilt aluminium metal. (Figs. 101 & 102).

Oberstleutnant. Construction and colouring of collar patch and shoulder-strap as described for Figs. 101 & 102.

Major. Construction and colouring of collar patch and shoulder-strap as described for Figs. 101 & 102.

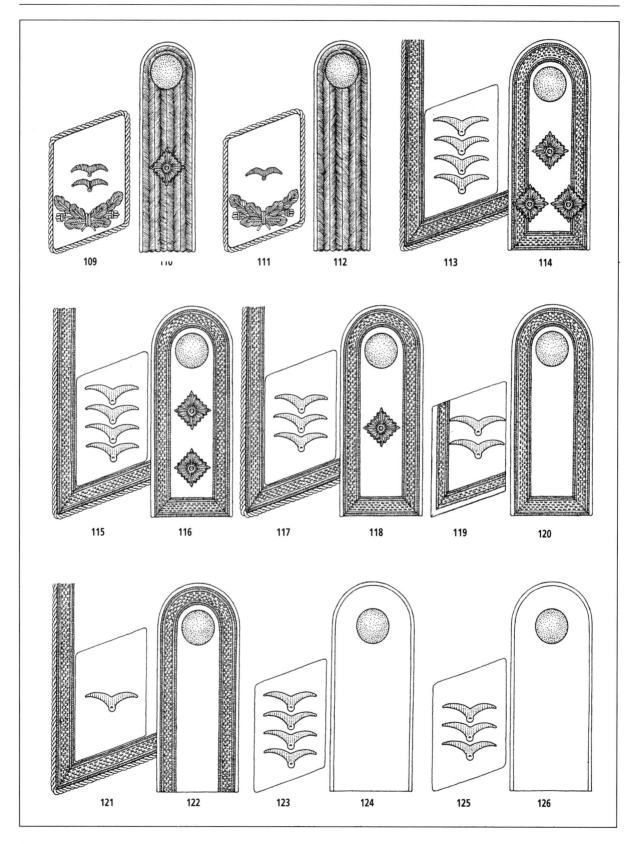

109   110   111   112   113   114

115   116   117   118   119   120

121   122   123   124   125   126

109 & 110 Oberleutnant.
111 & 112 Leutnant.
113 & 114 Stabsfeldwebel, etc.
115 & 116 Oberfeldwebel, etc.
117 & 118 Feldwebel, etc.
119 & 120 Unterfeldwebel, etc.
121 & 122 Unteroffizier, etc.
123 & 124 Hauptgefreiter, etc.
125 & 126 Obergefreiter, etc.

Right: Oberleutnant Herbert Bartels, a 20-year-old officer from Pomerania and Commander of a AA Battery from a Flak Regiment, received his Knight's Cross for his action in the Crimea. His unit destroyed 20 Soviet tanks and stopped the attempted breakthrough of a Soviet infantry regiment.

Hauptmann/Rittmeister. (Figs. 107 & 108). Half-wreath and wings in silver bullion embroidered threads. Collar patch piped in twisted silver aluminium cording. Two strands of silver-aluminium Russia braid to shoulder-strap. Gilt metal rank stars, white metal pebble-finished shoulder-strap button. (Figs. 109 & 110).

Oberleutnant. Construction and colouring of collar patch and shoulder-strap as described for Figs. 107 & 108.

Leutnant. (Figs. 111 & 112). Construction and colouring of collar patch and shoulder strap as described for Figs. 107 & 108.

Insignia of Rank for NCOs

Senior NCOs of Oberfeldwebel Grade. All NCOs from Stabsfeldwebel etc. down to Unterfeldwebel etc., were distinguished, depending on the type of uniform worn, by the wearing of either flat, silver-aluminium 1cm-wide braiding or flat, blue-grey cotton

braiding, also 1cm wide, around their collars and on their shoulder-straps. Special copper-brown rank braiding was used on the shoulder-straps and collar of the tan-coloured tropical uniform and matt, blue-grey rank braiding was used on the reed-green uniforms. For further details see page 62.

For collar patch, shoulder-strap, collar braiding and piping worn by Stabsfeldwebel, Stabswachtmeister, Sanitäts-Stabsfeldwebel, Stabsfeuerwerker and also those personnel with the appointment of Hauptfeldwebel or Hauptwachtmeister see Figs. 113 & 114. The collar patch, as explained, was in the wearer's arm-of-service colour with the 'wings' in white metal. The shoulder-strap was in blue-grey uni-

form cloth and carried white-metal rank stars. Piping was in the appropriate Waffenfarbe and was of either wool cloth or smooth, woven piping with selvedge set into the strap as part of the manufacturing process. The 1cm-wide flat braiding was of the pattern peculiar to the Luftwaffe (see Figs. 170–178 in Volume 1933–40, page 73, for an example of German Army rank braiding pattern by way of contrast). As well as being displayed on the shoulder-strap, it was also worn around the lower edge of all tunic collars. Stitched along the edge of the collar was a length of twisted wool piping in the colour of the wearer's arm of service.

For collar patch and shoulder-strap for an Oberfeldwebel, Oberwachtmeister, Ober-

Right: A Feldwebel from a Flak unit enjoys field rations.

fähnrich, Sanitätsoberfeldwebel, Ober-feuerwerker und Unterärzt and also for those personnel with the appointment of Hauptfeldwebel or Hauptwachtmeister see figs. 115 & 116. For construction and colouring of collar patch, shoulder-strap, collar braiding and piping see description for Figs. 113 & 114 above.

NCOs of Feldwebel Grade. For collar patch and shoulder-strap for Feldwebel, Wachtmeister, Sanitätsfeldwebel and Feuerwerker, see figs. 117 & 118. For construction and colouring of collar patch, shoulder-strap, collar braiding and piping see description for Figs. 113 & 114 above.

NCOs of Unteroffizier Grade. For the collar patch (of the type worn on the

Greatcoat collar before collar patches were abolished on this garment — see page 122 of this volume — and the shoulder-strap for Unterfeldwebel, Unterwachtmeister, Fähnrich and Sanitätsunterfeldwebel, see Figs. 119 & 120. The collar braiding worn by NCOs on the collar of the tunic was not worn on the Greatcoat. Instead, before it was abolished, the collar patch of the appropriate rank (four, three, two or single wings) was combined with an L-shaped length of 0.5cm-wide silver-aluminium flat braiding stitched along two edges of the patch, and as these patches, like all other Luftwaffe patches, were worn in mirror pairs, this narrow braiding ran along the outer and lower edge of both patches. Shoulder-strap worn without

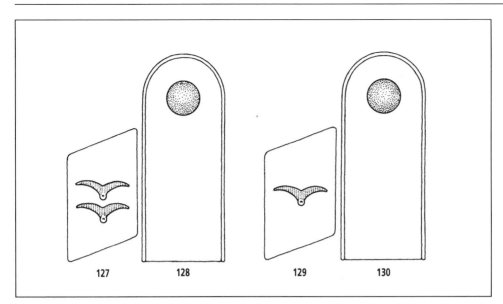

127 & 128 Gefreiter, etc.
129 & 130 Flieger, Funker, Kanonier, Pionier, Reiter, Grenadier, Fusilier, etc.

127   128   129   130

Below: A Gefrieter from a Luftwaffe Engineer Unit proudly shows his child to a nurse of the German Red Cross.

rank star was as described for Fig. 114 above.

See Figs. 121 & 122 for Collar patch and shoulder-strap for Unteroffizier, Sanität-sunteroffizier and Oberjäger, the latter for Parachute Troops and Rifle, Anti-Aircraft and Guard Battalion personnel from Regiment 'General Göring' and both Brigade and Division 'Hermann Göring''. For construction and colouring of collar patch, shoulder-strap, collar braiding and piping see description for Figs. 113 & 114 above.

Insignia of Ranks for Other Ranks

For collar patch and shoulder strap for Hauptgefreiter and Sanitätshauptgefreiter, see Figs. 123 & 124, plain blue-grey uniform cloth shoulder-strap with coloured piping. Appropriate-coloured twisted cording (not illustrated) was worn around the lower edge to the collar on the Tunic and Flight Blouse (not on the Greatcoat).

For Obergefreiter and Sanitätsgefreiter, see Figs. 125 & 126. Collar patch and shoulder-strap construction were as described for Figs. 123 & 124 above.

For Gefreiter and Sanitätsgefreiter see Figs. 127 & 128. Collar patch and shoulder-strap construction and colouring were as described for Figs. 123 & 124 above.

For Flieger, Kanonier, Funker, Sanitätssoldat, Pionier, see Figs. 129 & 130, had collar patches and shoulder-strap of form and colouring as described for Figs. 123 & 124 above.

For the ranks of Jäger, Fusilier, Grenadier and Reiter the construction and

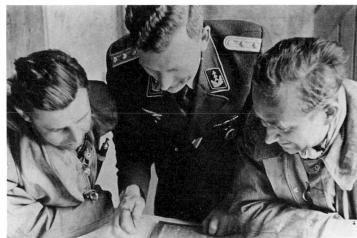

Above, upper right and right: Luftwaffe Administration Officials, specialists in meteorology, performed a very important function within all flying units. The success of flying operations depended on their meteorological findings and weather predictions.

Right: The distinctive Death's Head collar patches worn by men of the Panzer units from the Division 'Hermann Göring'. Shown here is Ritterkreuzträger Oberleutnant Karl Rossmann, Battery Commander of the 16 Motorised Flak Regiment 'General Göring', who received his Knight's Cross on 12 November 1941.

colouring of the shoulder-strap was as for Fig. 124 and the collar patch was as described in the footnote.[A]

Collar patches and shoulder-straps of the type worn by personnel of the Hermann Göring Brigade, Division and Corps, as well as by the Luftwaffe Field Divisions, the Death's-head collar patches worn on the black Panzer uniform, the shoulder-straps worn on the tan tropical uniform and shirts and the shoulder-straps worn on the reed-green fatigue uniform are described and in some cases illustrated in the appropriate section of this book.

Special Troop Service Officers of the Luftwaffe (Truppensonderdienst)

The start of 1944 saw the creation of a new section of the Wehrmacht. By an order issued by the Führer and promulgated in the Allgemeine-Heeres-Mitteilungen, Nr. 109 dated 24 January 1944, the Truppensonderdienst or Special Troop Service was created to operate within the framework of the three branches of the German Armed Forces.

This Special Troop Service was divided into two distinct sections: 1) The Administration Services of the Special Troop Service (Verwaltungsdienst im TSD) responsible for all provisions, clothing, housing and billeting of troops together with their service pay and allowances; and 2) The Armed Forces Judicial Branch of the Special Troop Service (Wehrmachtrichter im TSD) responsible for the military discipline of all members of the Wehrmacht and their followers.

The personnel of these two professions were further sub-divided into:
a) Active Officers of the TSD (Offz.i.TSD)
b) Reserve Officers of the TSD (Offz.d.Res.i.TSD), and
c) Officers awaiting Posting (at Disposition) of the TSD (Offz.z.V.i.TSD)

Subsequent orders issued to the Air Force in March 1944 explained that as from 1 May those Luftwaffe personnel previously employed within the non-technical administrative services of the Luftwaffe, these being the Paymaster Service and the Legal Service, were to be transferred into the new TSD. With this transfer these Luftwaffe administration officials became officers of the Special Troop Service and they were therefore soldiers under the terms of

German military law, enjoying the same rights and having the same responsibilities as fellow officers in Luftwaffe troop service. However, their powers of authority only extended within their area of service responsibility.

Uniforms of the TSD

The officers of the Luftwaffe TSD wore the same style and patterns of uniforms as Luftwaffe officers in troop service. This included all forms of head-dress, protective clothing and camouflage items. As with the Luftwaffe proper, the distinctions between TSD officers of General rank and other TSD officers was observed, General officers wearing gold coloured insignia, cap cords, breast eagles etc., and the remaining officers wearing silver-aluminium items. The lapel facings on the greatcoat and their kleinen Rock and the broad stripes and piping on the trousers and breeches worn by the TSD officers of General rank were in the appropriate arm-of-service colour of light blue (TSD Administration branch) or wine-red (TSD Judicial branch). These last subjects are dealt with elsewhere in this volume.

Interestingly, the decision regarding a finalised form of uniform for officers of the TSD was held in abeyance by the clothing authorities until after the war, something that did not happen.

Insignia of the TSD

The pattern for the insignia of rank worn by these officers followed the same style as used within the Luftwaffe. A distinction was made between the TSD officers of the Administrative service and the Judicial branch. Administration officers of the Luftwaffe TSD were distinguished by wearing light blue as their arm of service colour and wore a Caduceus emblem (Merkurstab) on their shoulder straps (see Fig. 190), whilst the Judicial officers of the Luftwaffe TSD displayed wine-red as their Waffenfarbe and carried a short 'Roman' sword (Rolandschwert) on their shoulder straps (see Fig. 192).

Illustrations of the collar patches and shoulder straps of the nine rank grades of Luftwaffe TSD Administration officer personnel are shown here (Figs. 131 to 148). The colour of all the collar patches and the underlay to all the shoulder straps was

Luftwaffe Officers in the Specialist Troop Service.
131 & 132 Generalsoberstabsintendant im TSD.
133 & 134 Generalstabsintendant im TSD.
135 & 136 Generintendant im TSD.
137 & 138 Oberstintendant im TSD.
139 & 140 Oberfeldintendant im TSD.
141 & 142 Oberstabsintedant im TSD.
143 & 144 Stabintendant im TSD.
145 & 146 Oberzahlmeister im TSD.
147 & 148 Zahlmeister im TSD.

A. The pattern of collar patches worn by these personnel was a pair of mirror rhomboids of coloured cloth in the wearers appropriate Waffenfarbe, stiffened with an inner lining of canvas and mounted with a single white metal wing to each patch.

As from April 1936 all personnel of the Regiment 'Hermann Göring' below officer rank had, prior to January 1943, worn white collar patches edged in either rifle green or bright red cloth piping. Jäger green was worn around the patches of the Rifle Troops of the Regiment whilst bright red was used by the troops of the Regiment's anti-aircraft battalions. This changed in January 1943 when a new system of displaying arm-of-service colour was introduced into the Division 'Hermann Göring', see page 55.

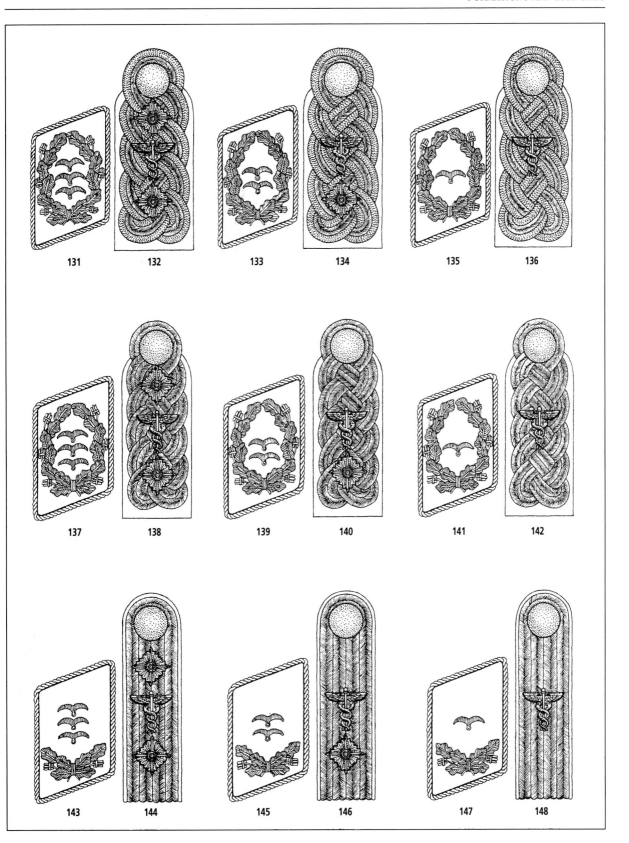

131   132   133   134   135   136

137   138   139   140   141   142

143   144   145   146   147   148

Equivalent Ranks of Officers of the Administrative TSD, Judicial Branch of the TSD and Luftwaffe Officers in Troop Service:

Administrative TSD ranks	Judicial TSD ranks	Luftwaffe ranks
Generaloberstabsintendant	—	General der Flieger
Generalstabsintendant	Generalstabsrichter	Generalleutnant
Generalintendant	Generalrichter	Generalmajor
Oberstintendant	Oberstrichter	Oberst
Oberfeldintendant	Oberfeldrichter	Oberstleutnant
Oberstabsintendant	Oberstabsrichter	Major
Stabsintendant	Stabsrichter	Hauptmann
Oberzahlmeister	—	Oberleutnant
Zahlmeister	—	Leutnant

light blue. The colour and quality of the embroidery work and the twisted cording on the patches and the braiding used on the straps was the same as that employed by equivalent ranks within the Luftwaffe proper. This was true of the metal rank stars and the Caduceus emblem.

Fig. 131 & 132: The collar patch and shoulder strap for the Luftwaffe Administrative TSD rank of Generaloberstabintendant im TSD, the equivalent of a General der Flieger

Figs. 133 & 134: Collar patch & shoulder strap for the Luftwaffe Administrative TSD rank of Generalstabsintendant im TSD, the equivalent of a Luftwaffe Generalleutnant.

Figs. 135 & 136: Collar patch & shoulder strap for the Luftwaffe Administrative TSD rank of Generalintendant im TSD, the equivalent of a Luftwaffe Generalmajor.

Figs. 137 & 138: Collar patch and shoulder strap for the Luftwaffe Administrative TSD rank of Oberstintendant im TSD, the equivalent of a Luftwaffe Oberst.

Figs. 139 & 140: Collar patch and shoulder strap for the Luftwaffe Administrative TSD rank of Oberfeldintendant im TSD, the equivalent of a Luftwaffe Oberstleutnant.

Figs. 141 & 142: Collar patch and shoulder strap for the Luftwaffe Administrative TSD rank of Oberstabsintendant im TSD, the equivalent of a Luftwaffe Major.

Figs. 143 & 144: Collar patch and shoulder strap for the Luftwaffe Administrative TSD rank of Stabsintendant im TSD, the equivalent of a Luftwaffe Hauptmann.

Figs. 145 & 146: Collar patch and shoulder strap for the Luftwaffe Administrative TSD rank of Oberzahlmeister im TSD, the equivalent of a Luftwaffe Oberleutnant.

Figs. 147 & 148: Collar patch and shoulder strap for the Luftwaffe Administrative TSD rank of Zahlmeister im TSD, the equivalent of a Luftwaffe Leutnant.

There were no NCOs or Men employed in the Special Troop Service.

It can be seen that there were fewer Judicial Luftwaffe Officers of the TSD than their Administrative TSD counterpart. They only had two grades of General officer and four grades of officers. Wine-red badge cloth was used for their collar patches and as underlay to their shoulder straps and the straps themselves all carried the short, bronze-coloured 'Roman' sword.

Rank Insignia worn on Protective Flight Clothing and Camouflage Clothing by Officers of the TSD.

The system employed by officers of the TSD was similar to that used by Luftwaffe officers in troop service. The chart of rank insignia as worn on protective flight clothing is shown on page 134 of this volume. Reference to the above table of equivalent ranks will indicate the Special Troop Service rank and by comparing this with the normal Luftwaffe officer rank it is a simple matter of identifying the precise rank badge worn by each of the nine grades of Luftwaffe TSD officers.

Secret Field Police (Geheime Feld Polizei-GFP)

Personnel who served in the Luftwaffe section of the Secret Field Police were, in the main, recruited from the Gestapo. Their principal duties consisted of:

a. the pursuit and arrest of persons

Luftwaffe Secret Field Police Insignia of Appointment: Collar Patches and Shoulder-straps.
149 & 150 Oberfeldpolizeidirektor.
151 & 152 Feldpolizeidirektor.
153 & 154 Feldpolizeikommissar.
155 & 156 Feldpolizeiinspektor.
157 & 158 Feldpolizeisekretär.

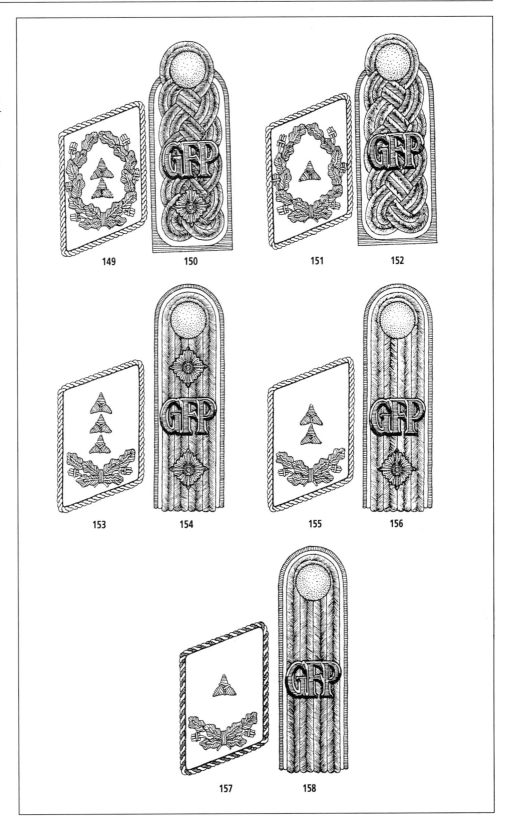

Left: This cuff-title was introduced as a sealed pattern on 16 September 1938 to be worn on the field blouse and greatcoat by members of the Secret Field Police. It was a 4.3cm wide band of black material with silver woven gothic lettering 'Geheime Feldpolizei'. Its possible that this same title was also worn by Luftwaffe personnel of the Secret Field Police when in Air Force uniform.

suspected of being traitors, spies and saboteurs;

b. the detection and arrest of persons suspected of graft and corruption as well as deliberate damage to Luftwaffe property;

c. the combatting of enemy propaganda;

d. the general execution of all security protection measures;

e. acting as security advisers, principally to the Intelligence Officer of the Luftwaffe unit with whom they were operating, and

f. the gathering and assessment of facts used by Luftwaffe courts in courts-martial cases.

Officials of the GFP wore the uniform of the Luftwaffe Wehrmachtbeamten, but with certain distinctive features. The colour of their collar patches and the primary arm-of-service colour displayed on their shoulder-straps was dark green. They were distinguished by the use of a secondary colour (Nebenfarbe) of wine red on their shoulder-straps. Gilt metal shoulder-strap insignia was displayed on the centre of their straps in the form of the Roman letters GFP, and was worn by these officials of all ranks. Illustrations of the five grades of GFP officials are shown here. With the exception of the double-coloured underlay to the shoulder-straps and the gilt-metal shoulder-strap cipher, all of the straps and rank stars illustrated were of the same quality, colour and construction as those used by Luftwaffe officers of equivalent rank. Collar patches are as described.

Figs. 149 & 150: The collar patch and shoulder-strap for the GFP appointment of Oberfeldpolizeidirektor, an official of the highest service level (Beamte des höheren Dienst), equivalent to the rank of a Luftwaffe Oberstleutnant. The collar patches were edged in gold-coloured twisted cording with silver-aluminium full wreath and two triangular rank stars.

Figs. 151 & 152: Insignia for the GFP appointment of Feldpolizeidirektor, an official of the highest service level and equivalent to the rank of Major. Collar patches were, as before, edged in gold-coloured twisted cording with silver-aluminium full wreath and a single triangular rank star.

Figs. 153 & 154: Insignia for the GFP appointment of Feldpolizeikommissar, an official of the executive service level (Beamte des gehobenen Dienst), equivalent to the rank of a Luftwaffe Hauptmann. The dark green collar patches had a half-wreath and three triangular rank stars as well as the twisted cording in aluminium-silver.

Figs. 155 & 156: Insignia for the GFP appointment of Feldpolizeiinspektor, an official of the executive service level and equivalent to the rank of Oberleutnant. Collar patches were, as before, edged in silver-aluminium twisted cording with a silver half-wreath and two triangular rank stars.

Figs. 157 & 158: Insignia for the GFP appointment of Feldpolizeisekretar, an official of the middle grade level (Beamte des mittleren Dienstes), equivalent to the rank of Leutnant. Dark green collar patches with silver-aluminium half-wreath and a single triangular rank star, but with alternated dark-green silk and silver-aluminium twisted cording.

In addition to the above insignia it is possible (but has not been established) that the Luftwaffe Secret Field Police personnel may have been eligible to have worn the Geheimefeldpolizei formation cuff-title. Luftwaffe Secret Field Police officials were also permitted to wear civilian clothing or any form of uniform necessary in pursuance of their duties. They also had power of command over all NCOs and Other Ranks.

3: BADGES AND ACCOUTREMENTS: WAFFENFARBE

Arm of Service (Waffenfarbe): Wartime Development and Use

Arm-of-service colours were employed extensively throughout the German Air Force. The German word 'Waffenfarbe' (literally 'arm (of service) colour') was used to denote the system whereby selected colours were used on items of uniform dress, insignia of rank and various military accoutrements, usually as facing colours or more frequently as piping, to indicate the wearer's branch of the force.

Luftwaffe arm-of-service colours is a subject that links both volumes of this work, so it is advisable to refer to the information published in Volume 1933–40 (pages 111 to 129) in order to understand the pre-war development of the Waffenfarbe system. It is also worth comparing the main listing set out in Volume 1933–40, starting on page 114, with the listing given here.

The wartime extension of this system saw little in the way of major changes, with the exception of the colours introduced to be worn by personnel of the 'Hermann Göring' Division, the Luftwaffe Field Corps Divisions and the Secret Field Police of the Luftwaffe. These formations are dealt with as separate entries.

The listing of Waffenfarbe and shoulder-strap insignia given in the table is mainly based on information published in a number of official sources. I have added certain wartime introductions into this list, whilst at the same time giving their source of reference.

*All entries in this list that differ from the information that can be found in the list of Waffenfarbe that was originally published in *Anzugordnung für die Luftwaffe (L.A.O.)* dated 27 November 1935 and revised to 1 April 1938 (see Volume 1933–40, page 114) are indicated by an asterisk.

Luftwaffe Waffenfarbe Regulations, 1939/40 to 1945

Serial	Arm-of-service, etc.	Arm-of-service colour	Secondary colour	Shoulder-strap insignia and remarks
1	Officers of General rank	white	—	Medical officers of General rank wore the Aesculapius insignia.
2	Air Ministry, permanent staff personnel	colour according to their arm-of-service *	—	RLM insignia * [A]
	Air Ministry supernumerary personnel attached to the following services:			
a	Flight Standby section of the RLM	gold yellow	—	RLM insignia [A]
b	Main Photographic Library Department of the RLM	gold yellow	—	RLM insignia [A]
c	Main Moving Film Library Department of the RLM	gold yellow	—	RLM insignia [A]
d	Signals Intelligence Detachment of the High Command of the Luftwaffe (Ob.d.L.) * [B]	golden brown	—	OL Insignia *

Serial	Arm-of-service, etc.	Arm-of-service colour	Secondary colour	Shoulder-strap insignia and remarks
e	All other RLM supernumerary personnel	the colour of their parent unit	—	—
3	Air Fleet Commands and Regional Air Commands	gold yellow	—	—
4	Flight Divisional Commanders	gold yellow	—	—
5	(Struck out)	—	—	—
6	Commanders of Air Force Instruction Divisions	Officers wore the colour of their parent unit.	—	L insignia
		NCOs and Men wore the colour of their economic troop unit	—	L insignia
7	General Staff officers	carmine	—	—
8	Regiment 'General Göring' c	white	—	—
9	Flying personnel (troops)	gold yellow	—	—
10	Air Force Guard Battalion Berlin, permanent staff personnel	gold yellow	—	LW insignia
11	Anti-Aircraft Artillery	bright red	—	number of wearer's unit
11a	Fortress Artillery *	bright red *	—	F insignia worn above the wearer's unit number. * D
12	Air Signals troops	golden brown	—	—
13	Instruction troops of the Luftwaffe	colour of their parent unit	—	L insignia
14	Reconnaissance Instruction Group Jüterborg	gold yellow	—	AL insignia
15	Medical officers, medical candidates, NCOs and Men, including Air Ministry medical personnel	dark blue	—	Aesculapius insignia worn on the shoulder-straps by medical officers and medical candidates.
	Fähnenjunker and Fähnriche (Sän.)	colour of their parent unit	—	—
16	Ordnance Officers of all services including the Air Ministry	bright red	—	W insignia
17	Artificers of all services including the Air Ministry	gold yellow * E	—	—
18	Replacement Depots of the Luftwaffe			
a	Air Material Groups	gold yellow	—	—
b	Air Material Bureaux	gold yellow	—	—
c	Air Parks	gold yellow	—	—
d	Principal Air Munitions Institutions	gold yellow	—	—
e	Air Munitions Institutions	gold yellow	—	—
f	Air Fuel Depots	gold yellow	—	—
g	Air Signals Material Depots	gold yellow	—	—
h	Anti-Aircraft Artillery Material Depots	gold yellow	—	—
19	Reich Air Inspectorate — Air Traffic Control	light green	—	—
20	(Struck out)	—	—	—

Serial	Arm-of-service, etc.	Arm-of-service colour	Secondary colour	Shoulder-strap insignia and remarks
21	Officers and Medical officers awaiting posting (at disposition)	colour used as for officers according to their arm-of-service*	—	Roman numerals in aluminium metal worn by these officers of Regional Air Commands. Aesculapius insignia in aluminium coloured metal worn by Medical Officers awaiting posting, Officers a.D posted to the Air Ministry wore RLM in place of Roman numerals
22	Retired Officers and Retired Medical Officers	colour used as for active officers according to their arm-of-service		Medical Officers of the Reserve and Lower Grade Doctors of the Reserve wore the Aesculapius; Landwehr Officers wore the roman numeral of their Regional Air Command in oxidised metal. Medical Officers of the Landwehr and Lower Grade Doctors of the Landwehr wore the Aesculapius insignia in oxidised metal
a	Reserve Officers		light blue	
b	Landwehr Officers			
23	Schools (Staff Personnel)			
a	Air War Academy	gold yellow	—	Initials KA
b	Anti-Aircraft Artillery School	bright red	—	Initials FAS
c	Air Signals School	golden brown	—	Initials NS
d	National School for Air Traffic Control	light green	—	Initials LS
e	Air Warfare School	gold yellow Officers wore the colour of their original parent unit. Officer Candidates of the Flak Artillery and Air Signals Troops wore the colour of their original parent unit	—	Initials KS
f	Higher Air Force School	gold yellow	—	Initials HS
g	Air Force Sports School	gold yellow	—	Initials SS
h	Driving School	gold yellow	—	Initials KRS
i	Ordnance Schools of the Luftwaffe * F	gold yellow *	—	Initials WS *
j	Artificer's Schools of the Luftwaffe * G	gold yellow *	—	Initials FS *
k	NCO Preparatory Schools * H	Officers, NCOs & Men wore the colour of their original unit *	—	Initials UVS *
l	NCO Schools * I	Officers, NCOs & Men wore the colour of their original unit*	—	Initials US *

Serial	Arm-of-service, etc.	Arm-of-service colour	Secondary colour	Shoulder-strap insignia and remarks
m	Flight Ordnance Technical Schools * ᴶ	gold yellow *	—	Initials WS *
n	Anti-Aircraft Artillery Ordnance Technical School of the Luftwaffe * ᴷ	bright red *	—	Initials WS *
24	National Institution for Air Defence	bright red	—	Initials RL
24a	Maritime Instruction Flying units * ᴸ	gold yellow *	—	Initials SL *
25	Economic Inspectors and all assigned Luftwaffe personnel	a) Officers wore the colour of their arm-of-service. b) NCOs & Men wore the colour of their economic troop unit	—	—
26	Soldiers of the Luftwaffe assigned to Defence Replacement Inspectorate		—	—
27	a) Garrison of the Air Force Training Areas (excluding Wustrow)	gold yellow	—	—
	b) Garrison of the Air Force Anti-Aircraft Artillery Training Areas (including Wustrow)	bright red	—	—
28	Staff Band Masters, Senior Band Masters and Band Masters	Colour of unit to which assigned	—	Lyre insignia
29	Air Force Construction Units *	black *	—	—

A. Reference to Volume 1933–40, page 130, under the heading 'Metal and Embroidered Shoulder Strap Insignia' (see also page 133) will show that there were two patterns of RLM insignia. The second pattern, consisting of the gothic letters 'RLM', was introduced on 10 September 1939 to supersede the former pattern by the final date of 1 April 1940. This changeover was announced in Luftwaffen-Verordnungsblatt Nr.43, Part C, dated 25 September 1939, p.338, Order Nr.846 issued 10 September 1939.

B. On a date as yet unestablished, personnel of the signals Intelligence Detachment of the Reichsluftfahrtministerium became the Air Signals Detachment of the Oberfehlshaber der Luftwaffe. In place of their first pattern 'RLM' insignia they were instructed to wear the new 'OL' insignia. This changeover was closely linked with Hermann Göring in his capacity as both the Commander-in-Chief of the German Air Force (Oberbefehlshaber der Luftwaffe, abbreviated to 'Ob.d.L.') responsible to Hitler at the OKW as Commander-in-chief of the Wehrmacht and as the Reich Minister for Air Travel (Reichsluftfahrtministerium, abbreviated to RLM) responsible to Hitler as Reichs Chancellor and head of the civil government.

Officially, the designation 'OKL' (Oberkommando der Luftwaffe) was not applied until 1944; until then the official designation was 'Ob.d.L.'.

C. Extensive information on the use of white as the arm-of-service colour by troops of the Regiment 'General Göring' can be found in Volume 1933–40 as footnote 'D' on page 118.

In January 1943 these instructions were both added to and in some cases superseded by the introduction of special Waffenfarbe to be worn as part of the rank insignia (shoulder straps and collar patches) for the personnel of Division 'Hermann Göring'. This new information is dealt with in this volume on page 55.

D. Personnel of Fortress Artillery batteries were authorized to wear red as their arm-of-service colour and the letter 'F' above their unit number according to instructions published in Luftwaffen-Verordnungsblatt Nr.30 Part C, dated 25 July 1938, pp 217–218 Order Nr.659 issued 7 July 1938.

It should be noted that these instructions were promulgated two months after the revised edition of 'Anzugordnung für die Luftwaffe (L.A.O.)' for 27 November 1935 and revised 1 April 1938. For this reason this entry is not shown in my listing that appears in Volume 1933–40, pp.114–117.

E. Artificers of all services including the Air Ministry originally wore bright red as their arm-of-service colour. In September 1936 for reasons of economy this was changed to gold-yellow as per instructions published in Luftwaffen-Verordnungsblatt Nr.36 dated 7 September 1936, pp.457–459, Order Nr.1130 issued 1 September 1936 with a rider that the changeover had to be completed by 1 October 1936. For further information see Volume 1933–40 footnote 'H' on page 118.

F. The colour originally allocated to the personnel of Ordnance Schools of the Luftwaffe was bright red. This was changed to gold-yellow in September 1936 for reasons of economy as per instructions published in Luftwaffen-Verordnungsblatt Nr.36 dated 7 September 1936, pp.457–459, Order Nr.1130 issued 1 September 1936. The changeover had to be effected by 1 October 1936.

G. At a date as yet unestablished, but assumed to be sometime after 1 April 1938, personnel of the Artificer Schools of the Luftwaffe were authorised to wear the initials 'FS' as their branch insignia.

H. According to Luftwaffen-Verordnungsblatt, Nr.29, dated June 1941, p.482, Order Nr.745 issued 30 June, 1941 those officers, NCOs and men who had been posted to (Luftwaffe) NCO Preparatory Schools (Unteroffiziervorschulen) were to wear the uniform (and Waffenfarbe) of their original unit but with the letters 'UVS' on their shoulder straps. These letters were in the normal quality and colour for insignia worn by officers, NCOs and men.

I. Five months after publishing instructions regarding the wearing of the initials 'UVS' by Officers, NCOs and Men posted to Luftwaffe Unteroffiziervorschulen, new instructions were published countermanding what had previously been laid down.

Luftwaffen-Verordnungsblatt Nr.51, dated November 1941, p.1101, Order Nr.1946 issued 22 November 1941, stated that as a result of a change of title the command staffs of the NCO Schools of the Luftwaffe and the NCO Preparatory Schools of the Luftwaffe were in future simply to be known as the command staffs of the NCO Schools of the Luftwaffe. Their shoulder insignia 'UVS' was replaced by 'US' insignia.

J. Personnel of Flight Ordnance Technical Schools (Flieger-Waffentechnische Schulen) were instructed to use gold-yellow Waffenfarbe and carry the initials 'WS' on their shoulder straps as published in *Luftwaffen-Verordnungsblatt*, Nr.34, dated 18 August 1941, p.596, Order Nr.967, issued 6 August 1941.

K. Personnel of the Anti-Aircraft Artillery Ordnance Technical School of the Luftwaffe (Flak-Waffentechnische Schule der Luftwaffe) were instructed to wear bright red Waffenfarbe and carry the initials 'WS' on their shoulder straps as published in *Luftwaffen-Verordnungsblatt* Nr.34, dated 18 August 1941, p.596, Order Nr.967 issued 6 August 1941.

L. Personnel of the Maritime Instruction Flying units of the Luftwaffe were instructed to wear gold-yellow as their Waffenfarbe and to carry the letters 'SL' on their shoulder straps as published in *Luftwaffen-Verordnungsblatt* Nr.30, Part C, dated 25 July 1938, p.218, Order Nr.660, issued 15 July 1938.

Waffenfarbe for the Division 'Hermann Göring'

On 15 July 1942 Regiment 'Hermann Göring' had been enlarged and upgraded to Brigade strength and redesignated Brigade 'Hermann Göring'. Exactly three months later, on 15 October, the Brigade was enlarged once more to Divisional strength, receiving the title Division 'Hermann Göring'.

January 1943 saw the publication of the first set of instructions regarding the arm-of-service colours to be used by personnel of the newly-created Division 'Hermann Göring'.[1] This order did not affect Officers of General rank, General Staff Officers, Armed Forces Officials serving with the Luftwaffe and attached to the Division, Medical Officers and Medical personnel.

Officers of the Division were instructed to wear white collar patches that were edged (piped) with silver-aluminium, twisted cording, and white cloth underlay to their shoulder-straps. NCOs and Men of the Division were, however, distinguished by wearing various coloured edging to their white collar patches, as set out in the chart below. These instructions in effect abolished the previous red- and green-edged collar patches. Shoulder-straps were without exception piped white.

Waffenfarbe for NCOs and Men of Division 'Hermann Göring', January 1943

Serial	Formation	White Collar Patch with outer edging in:	Piping to Shoulder-straps
1	Grenadier Regiments	white (with narrow black dividing line)	white
2	Guard Regiment A	white (with narrow black dividing line)	white
3	Armoured Regiment	rose pink	white
4	Reconnaissance Battalions	rose pink	white
5	Anti-Tank Battalions	rose pink	white
6	Artillery Regiments	bright red	white
7	Anti-Aircraft Artillery Regiments	bright red	white
8	Führer Anti-Aircraft Artillery Detachment A	bright red	white
9	Engineer Battalion	black	white
10	Signals Detachments	golden brown	white
11	Supply Troops	light blue	white

A. Personnel of the Guard Regiment and the Führer Anti-Aircraft Artillery Detachment continued to wear collar patches on their greatcoats despite the regulations as promulgated in *Luftwaffen-Verordnungsblatt* for May 1942, page 789 Order Nr.1453, whereby the wearing of collar patches on the greatcoat by NCOs and Men of the Luftwaffe was to be discontinued from 1 October 1942, and by Officers and those other Luftwaffe personnel who purchased their own uniform garments from 1 April 1943. (See also page 122.)

Three months later, in April 1943,[2] the whole arrangement of arm-of-service colours for the personnel of the Division 'Hermann Göring' was changed to that set out in the chart below. Interestingly, the identifying colours were switched from around the collar patches to the piping and underlay on the shoulder-straps. No official explanation has been found for this change, but it is safe to assume that it was not introduced just for change's sake. It probably had something to do with production costs and morale. It did mean, however, that all ranks wore the 'universal' and very distinctive white collar patches, a feature that was to have certain disadvantages under combat conditions (see below), and officers who previously had not featured any arm-of-service colour could now be identified by their coloured shoulder-strap underlay.

Right: Oberleutnant (later Major) Werner Dörnbrack, from an instruction unit of a bomber squadron, photographed on the day he was awarded the Knight's Cross of the Iron Cross, 21 August 1941.

Waffenfarbe for Division 'Hermann Göring', April 1943

Serial	Formation	Collar Patch colour	Piping and underlay to shoulder-straps
1	Divisional Staff	white	rose pink
2	Grenadier Regiments	white	white
3	Rifle Regiments	white	rifle (Jäger) green
4	Guard Regiment A	white	white
5	Armoured Regiment	white	rose pink
6	Armoured Reconnaissance Battalions	white	gold yellow
7	Aircraft Operational Readiness Units	white	gold yellow
8	Artillery Regiments	white	bright red
9	Führer Anti-aircraft Artillery Battalion A	white	bright red
10	Engineer Battalion	white	black
11	Signals Battalions	white	golden brown
12	Supply Units (including Field Police and Administrative Services)	white	light blue
13	Replacement and Training Regiments of the Division 'Hermann Göring'	white	colour of the active unit

A. As with the previous order, personnel of both the Wachregiment and the Führer-Flakabteilung were instructed to continue wearing collar patches on their greatcoats, in contrast to the rest of the Luftwaffe, who from 1 October 1942 had theirs abolished; see page 122.

Two months later,[3] a single alteration was made to the April 1943 instructions when the arm-of-service colour for personnel of the Feldgendarmerie (Officers & Other Ranks) was added. The new instructions were given thus:

Additional Waffenfarbe for Division 'Hermann Göring', June 1943

Serial	Formation	Collar Patch colour	Piping & Underlay to shoulder-straps
12	Field Police	white	orange

Further changes took place when it was ordered that the white collar patches were no longer to be worn on the field uniform. Divisional order Nr.64 of 1944, dated 3 January 1944, instructed all ranks to remove their collar patches from those tunics worn as part of their field uniform. The removal was necessary on the grounds of concealment and camouflage. However, NCOs and Men were permitted to wear the small metal 'wings' normally mounted on the cloth of the collar patch, to be affixed directly into the collar of the tunic. As a further measure, all silver-aluminium NCO braiding worn on the field uniform was forbidden and had to be replaced by dull matt-grey cotton braiding.

Shoulder-Strap and Uniform Buttons

Metal buttons, including shoulder-strap buttons, were finished in one of three basic colours: Luftwaffe blue-grey painted finish,

were spray painted blue-grey in bulk at the factory. The dimpled finish imparted to the untreated metal buttons ensured that the sprayed-on paint adhered to the surface of the button longer than it would have done on a smooth surface.

Small, dish-shaped horn and composition buttons, usually in dark grey or dark brown, were used extensively in the manufacture of uniforms. These were seldom to be seen on the outer surface of garments, being used for pocket fastenings, braces, buttons and the like. Dish-shaped gunmetal buttons, of various diameters, were frequently used on certain items of equipment that required openings or attachments to be fastened by buttons, and the Zeltbahn (shelter triangle) in particular made extensive use of these. Because of their inherent strength they were frequently used on various items of protective clothing.

Buttons were ordinarily sewn on to garments, but removable buttons held by a split ring were used on clothing that required frequent washing. Further information on other aspects of buttons can be found in Volume 1933–40, pp. 129–30.

Shoulder-Strap Insignia

Metal Shoulder-Strap Insignia

Insignia displayed on the shoulder-straps was used throughout the Luftwaffe as a means of identifying a person as belonging to a particular formation, school, training group or being on the staff of an academy or important air force establishment. Almost universally ornate in design, some insignia were in the style of Old or Black Gothic lettering, others in copperplate lettering, but the majority were in an elaborate, floriated style peculiar to the Luftwaffe. Both Roman and Arabic numerals were used. A few insignia depicted objects.

Metal insignia was manufactured in two finishes: gilt for officers from Oberst down to Leutnant and silver-white for NCOs from Stabsfeldwebel, etc., to Feldwebel, etc. (Unteroffizier mit Portepee). Generals' insignia was in silver-aluminium of a quality superior to that used by NCOs. The insignia of officials of the Luftwaffe Judicial Department had a bronze finish, but their Roman short sword was, to my knowledge,

silver-aluminium and gilt-coloured pebble surfaced.

Blue-grey finished buttons were used in the manufacture of the padded and reversible camouflage winter uniforms. Those buttons that were visible on the white side of these garments were over-painted white. Visible buttons on tropical uniforms were usually of metal painted copper-brown. Coffee-brown plastic buttons were occasionally used.

Metal buttons, other than those with gilt finish, were made of a white aluminium-type metal. Those destined for use on the Service Uniform and the Field Uniforms

the only metal insignia that had this colour.

Embroidered Shoulder-Strap Insignia

Embroidered insignia when used was only worn by ranks from Unterfeldwebel, etc., down to Flieger, etc. There were two qualities of embroidery used: a) The official issue, machine chain-stitched type known as 'Kurbelstickerei' and b) the superior quality of embroidery used on privately purchased straps, where the insignia was either worked into the cloth of the strap by an operator using an Jacquard machine or by a skilled needlewoman hand-embroidering the design. The design was similar· to the corresponding metal insignia of the more senior grades, The colour of the thread used for the embroidery depended on the arm-of-service colour of the wearer.[A]

When shoulder-strap insignia were worn they were worn on both straps, but not all Luftwaffe personnel wore insignia. All metal shoulder-strap insignia was manufactured with two or more, but usually two, short prongs affixed to the underside. These were pushed through the braided cording and cloth underlay and bent flat to hold the insignia firmly in place.

The majority of shoulder-strap insignia were introduced before the outbreak of the Second World War. A few items were brought into use during the war years. This subject has been dealt with in detail in Volume 1933–40, starting on page 130. The various individual insignia are reproduced here again and represent as complete a list of all known insignia as is possible to discover. The evidence for the existence of these items has been gathered from official publications, in particular *Luftwaffen-Verordnungsblatt* and *Anzugordnung für die Luftwaffe*, etc., as well as metal insignia manufacturers' catalogues (Assmann & Söhne's among others), actual items in various public and private collections and finally, and to a limited extent, from contemporary photographs.

163 'A'. Gothic 'A' worn by personnel of the Luftwaffe Medical Academy. Introduced by an order dated September 1941[4]. Officers were required to wear a gold-coloured letter 'A' directly above a gilt metal Askulapstab on their shoulder-straps (Fig. 162). NCOs who wore a sidearm knot (Portepee), up to and including the appointment of Ensign

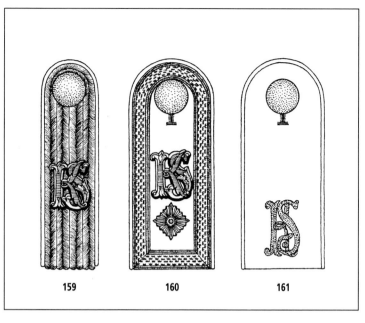

159   160   161

(Fähnriche) and Senior Ensign (Oberfähnrich) in the Medical Corps of the Luftwaffe were required to wear a white metal Gothic 'A' without the Askulapstab. NCOs and Men, including the appointment of Fahnenjunker in the Medical Corps of the Luftwaffe were distinguished by wearing just the Gothic letter 'A' in dark blue chain stitching outlined in light blue to emphasise the letter and without the serpent and staff emblem.

164 'AL'. Entwined letters 'AL' worn by personnel of the Reconnaissance Instruction Group Jüterbog (Aufklarungs-lehrgruppe Jüterbog).

165 'F'. Ornate letter 'F' worn by Fortress Anti-Aircraft Artillery (Festungs-Artillerie) personnel and usually over small Arabic numerals indicating the wearer's battalion number.[5]

166 'FAS'. Entwined and ornate copperplate style letters 'FAS'. Worn by personnel on the staff of an anti-aircraft school (Flakartillerie-Schule).

167 'FS' Ornate letters 'FS' worn by personnel of a War Ordnance School (Feuerwerkerschule).

168 'GFP' Roman letters 'GFP' worn by members of the Luftwaffe Secret Field Police (Geheime Feldpolizei der Luftwaffe). This insignia was introduced in November 1943. It was only produced in gold-coloured metal because the only persons entitled to wear it were Luftwaffe Officials

Examples of types of insignia worn on Luftwaffe shoulder-straps.
159 Gilt-metal shoulder insignia as worn on the shoulder-strap for a Leutnant.
160 White-metal shoulder insignia as worn on the shoulder-strap for a Feldwebel, etc.
161 Chain-stitched shoulder insignia as worn on the shoulder-straps by Luftwaffe ranks from Hauptgefreiter to Flieger, etc. This style of 'Kurbelstickerei' was executed in coloured threads corresponding to the arm-of-service piping used on the strap. The 'KS' insignia used to illustrate these three examples is that for an Aerial Warfare School (Luftkreigsschule).

A. Chain-stitched or embroidered insignia in black thread were outlined in white for emphasis. Dark blue, being difficult to distinguish against the blue-grey of the shoulder-strap cloth, was outlined in light blue thread.

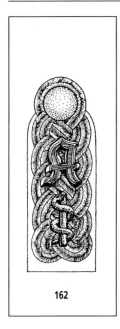

162

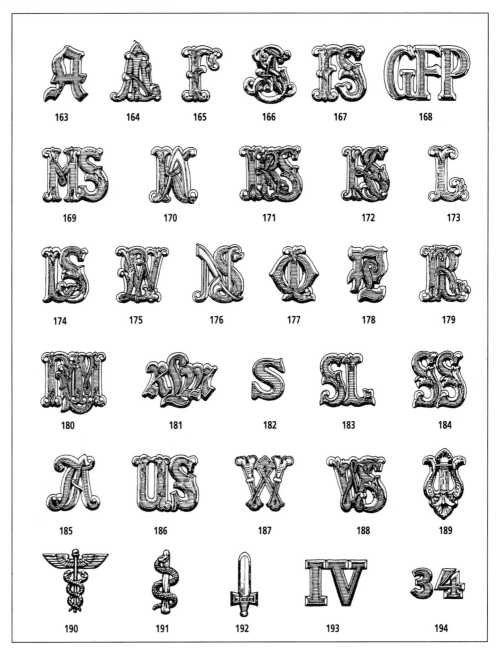

163   164   165   766   167   168

169   170   171   172   173

174   175   176   177   178   179

180   181   182   183   184

185   186   187   188   189

190   191   192   193   194

Shoulder-strap insignia
162 A with Aesculapius.
163 A.
164 AL.
165 F.
166 FAS.
167 FS.
168 GFP.
169 HS.
170 KA.
171 KRS.
172 KS.
173 L.
174 LS.
175 LW.
176 NS.
177 OL.
178 PL.
179 RL.
180 RLM.
181 RLM.
182 S.
183 SL.
184 SS.
185 TA.
186 US.
187 W.
188 WS.
189 Lyre.
190 Caduceus.
191 Aesculapius.
192 Sword.
193 Roman numeral.
194 Arabic numeral.

with Officer status (see p. 49 for GFP Ranks).[6]

169 'HS'. Ornate letters 'HS' worn by personnel on the staff of an Advanced Luftwaffe School (Höhere Luftwaffenschule).[7]

170 'KA'. Entwined letters 'KA' worn by personnel on the staff of the Air War Academy (Luftkriegsakademie).

171 'KRS'. Entwined letters 'KRS' worn by personnel on the staff of the Motor Transport School (Kraftfahrschule).

172 'KS'. Entwined letters 'KS' worn by personnel on the staff of the Aerial Warfare School (Luftkriegsschule).

173 'L'. Floriated letter 'L' worn by personnel of Instructional Units of the Luftwaffe (Lehrtruppen der Luftwaffe).

174 'LS'. Entwined letters 'LS' worn by personnel of the School of Air Traffic Control (Reichsschule für Luftaufsicht).

175 'LW'. Entwined letters 'LW' worn by Cadre personnel of the Guard Battalion of

Left: A Luftwaffe Gefeiter, an NCO Aspirant on the staff of an aerial warfare school, a member of an SA unit (right) and a Police Officer (left), stop and search a foreign worker they suspect of being an enemy agent. Berlin, August 1943.

the Luftwaffe (Berlin Garrison) (Stammpersonal des Wachbataillons der Luftwaffe).

176 'NS'. Entwined letters 'NS' worn by personnel on the staff of the Air Signals School (Luftnachrichtenschule).

177 'OL'. Entwined letters 'OL' worn by personnel of the Air Signals Intelligence Detachment of the Commander-in-Chief of the German Air Force, formerly of the RLM. (Luftnachrichtabteilung des Oberbefehlshaber der Luftwaffe). Exact date for the introduction of this new insignia has not yet been established, but is believed to have been some time in 1939-40.[A]

178 'PL'. Conjoined Gothic letters 'PL'. This cipher has been included here because it is believed to have been a Luftwaffe item. It is featured in the Assmann & Söhne catalogue, item 26078 on an illustrated page of insignia under the heading 'Wehrmacht-Luftwaffe'. However, no other evidence has come to light that can establish with certainty which formation used it. Although it resembles the style of insignia used within the Army, in particular the conjoined letters 'BL' for Artillery Observation Training Regiments and the conjoined letters 'PL' worn by personnel of Anti-Tank Instruction

A. The 'OL' insignia represented the already abbreviated form of 'Ob.d.L.' which in turn was the official abbreviation for 'Oberbefehlshaber der Luftwaffe', Commander-in-Chief of the German Air Force, namely Hermann Göring. Unlike the O.K.H. and the O.K.M. the Luftwaffe did not use the designation O.K.L. until 1944. Until then the official designation was Ob.d.L.

Battalions, no such insignia as illustrated here was used in the German Army, and it must be assumed that this item was used by an as yet unidentified Luftwaffe formation.

179 'RL'. Entwined letters 'RL' worn by personnel of the Institute for Air Defence (Reichsanstalt für Luftschutz).[8]

180 'RLM'. First-pattern insignia consisted of the ornate and entwined letters 'RLM'. Worn by permanent staff personnel of the Air Ministry (Reichsluftfahrtministerium-Planstellen) and by personnel of the following branch offices of the RLM who were directly subordinate to the Air Ministry:

(a) Flight Standby Section of the RLM (Flugbereitschaft des RLM)

(b) Main Photographic Department of the RLM (Hauptbildstelle des RLM)

(c) Main Moving Film Department of the RLM (Hauptfilmstelle des RLM), and before at least 1939–40

(d) Signals Detachment of the RLM (Nachrichtenabteilung des RLM) (See 177 'OL' above)

181 'RLM'. Second-pattern insignia consisting of conjoined Gothic letters 'RLM'. Introduced on 25 September 1939 to supersede first-pattern 'RLM' finally by 1 April 1940. Worn by all personnel of the Air Ministry (as listed at 180 above) other than General Officers, Officers of the General Staff and Medical Officers.[9]

182 'S'. Single, Latin-style 'S' worn by Reserve officers recalled to duty ('z.D') and by Luftwaffe Landwehr officers in the Maritime Air Force Command (Luftwaffekommandos (See)).[10]

183 'SL'. Ornate letters 'SL' worn by personnel of the Maritime Instruction Squadron (Lehrstaffel, See).[11]

184 'SS'. Floriated letters 'SS' worn by personnel on the staff of the Air Force Sports School (Luftwaffen-Sportschule).

185 'TA'. Conjoined letters 'TA' worn by personnel of the staff Air Force Technical Academy (Technische Akademie der Luftwaffe).

186 'US'. Ornate floriated letters 'US' worn by NCOs on the staff of Preparatory Schools (Unteroffiziervorschüler der Luftwaffe) and Schools for NCOs (Unteroffizierschüler der Luftwaffe). Introduced in November 1941. This insignia replaced the earlier insignia consisting of the letters 'UVS' (not illustrated because no specimen has yet been found) when these prepara-

tory schools underwent a change of title.[12]

187 'W'. Ornate letter 'W' worn by ordnance officers (Offiziere-(W)) (Not worn by NCOs or other ranks).

188 'WS'. Conjoined ornate letters 'WS' worn by personnel of the Ordnance Armourer School (Waffenmeisterschule). In August 1941 extended to personnel of the Aerial Technical Weapons School (Flieger-Waffentechnische Schulen) and the Anti-Aircraft Technical Weapons School (Flak-Waffentechnische Schule).[13]

189 'Lyre'. A Lyre worn by musicians holding officers' rank and also by musicians with the appointment of Musikleiter, see Volume 1939–40, p. 105.

190 'Caduceus'. Worn by Luftwaffe officers of the Forces Special Service (Offiziere im Truppensonderdienst – TSD). This insignia was introduced in May 1944.[14]

191 'Askulapstab'. (The Rod of Aesculapius). Worn by Medical personnel.[15]

192 'Judicial sword' (Rolandschwert). A short-bladed, bronze-coloured sword, the blade-tip pointing towards the shoulder-strap button. Worn by judiciary administrative officials and later by judicial officers of the TSD legal section.

193 Roman numerals. Both large (illustrated here) and small-size Roman numerals were worn by a selected number of Luftwaffe troops; the large size usually being worn alone, the smaller numerals in conjunction with another emblem or cipher.[16]

194 Arabic numerals. These were normally used to indicate the number of a particular regimental formation, which in the case of the Luftwaffe was very often the regimental number of an artillery unit. Both large and small (illustrated here) numerals were used for the same reasons as given in 193 above.

Slip-on Shoulder-Strap Titles

As explained in Volume 1933–40 (p.135), the wearing of slip-on titles on the shoulder-straps was not as widespread as in the Army. Those that were used tended to be for Flak units. The blue-grey cloth loops were approximately 3cm deep and wide enough to fit over the average shoulder-strap. The insignia displayed on these loops was usually in red chain stitching, showing the number of the wearer's anti-aircraft artillery regiment.

The only wartime instruction that I have come across regarding these slip-on titles was issued in January 1943.[17] Armed forces officials in preparatory service, undergoing instruction to become Flying Engineers, were ordered to wear a narrow loop of pink badge cloth at the base of their shoulder-straps to differentiate them from war establishment Flying Engineers.

Collar and Cuff Rank Braiding

The subject of rank braiding used on the collar and cuffs of the Uniform Tunic, the Service Tunic and the Flight Blouse, and on the collar patches worn on the Greatcoat, all of which were for certain grades of non-commissioned officers, has been dealt with in Volume 1933–40, pp. 135–9.

The practice continued throughout the Second World War without change to the instructions first laid down in May 1935, except that collar patches worn on the Greatcoat by all ranks were abolished from 1942–3 as an economy measure.[18]

The distinctive double rings of 1cm-wide silver-aluminium braiding to be worn as 'Special Badges of Appointment', originally by senior NCOs with the rank of Oberfeldwebel and Oberwachmeister, and later extended to those senior NCOs with the rank of Hauptfeldwebel and Hauptwachtmeister, were introduced shortly after the establishment of the Luftwaffe in 1935.[19] These distinctions were required to be worn on those blue-grey items of Luftwaffe clothing in the following manner:

1. On the Service Tunic and the Uniform Tunic two-stripe sleeve rings of flat aluminium NCO braiding worn around the cuffs, set apart at a distance of 0.5cm from each other and 0.5cm from the upper edges of the turn-back cuffs.
2. On the Flight Blouse around the forearms, at a distance of 0.5cm from each other, two stripes of flat aluminium NCO braiding, the lower stripe positioned 10cm up from the bottom edge of each sleeve.

The wearing of triple sleeve rings on the fatigue uniform worn by these NCOs was contained in instructions published in *Luftwaffen-Verordnungblatt* Nr. 18, dated 11 June 1935, p.116, Order Nr. 256, issued 27 May 1935. These instructions also dealt with the subject of Service Rank Insignia worn on the Denim Blouse, Overalls of Black Denim both lined and unlined, and the Protective Coat of blue-grey rubberized material for motorcyclists. These subjects can be found in this book under their appropriate headings.

Additional instructions were issued in 1939[20] regarding these special badges of appointment. Senior NCOs with the rank of Hauptfeldwebel or Hauptwachtmeister and acting Hauptfeldwebel (Hauptfeldwebeldiensttuer) or acting Hauptwachtmeister (Hauptwachtmeisterdiensttuer) were to wear, as a distinction from the ranks of Oberfeldwebel and Oberwachtmeister, the double stripes of NCO-patterned braiding on the cuffs of their cloth greatcoat in addition to the wearing of these stripes on their blue-grey tunic and blouse.

Order Nr. 2132, issued on 1 September 1942 and published on p.1267 of the *Luftwaffen-Verordnungsblatt* for 14 September 1942, stated that for the duration of the war the quality (and colour) of rank braiding was to be changed from 1cm-wide flat, silver-aluminium (silber-aluminium tresse) to 1cm-wide flat, dull, blue-grey rayon braiding (Zellwollborte).

This introduction affected the collar and shoulder-strap braiding and the double-stripe cuff braiding worn by personnel of NCO grade.

The order was also directed at those troops who wore chevrons on the left upper arm of their Service Tunic (Tuchrock), Uniform Tunic (Waffenrock), Flight Blouse (Fliegerbluse) and Greatcoat (Mantel).

The wartime use of light khaki-tan clothing for tropical climates brought into use rank braiding of a dull copper-brown colour. This type of rank braiding was worn by the above mentioned NCOs on the forearms of their cuff-less tropical jacket in the same manner and the same position as worn on the blue-grey Flight Blouse.

Any cuff-title worn by an NCO holding any of these special appointments was required to be positioned directly above the upper edge of the topmost sleeve ring.

Rank Chevrons, 1938–45

Rank chevrons were introduced into the Luftwaffe on 4 March 1938.[21] They were worn on the Service Dress Tunic, the Uniform Tunic, the Flight Blouse and the Greatcoat. They were positioned on the

Left: General der Flakartillerie von Schröder presents Iron Crosses to members of the Hamburg anti-aircraft gun crews on 9 August 1943. The silver-aluminium braiding worn as double cuff-stripes, as rank braiding around the collars of the various Flight Blouses and on the shoulder-straps of these NCOs is clearly seen.

Luftwaffe Rank Chevrons, 1938–1945.
195 Stabsgefreiter, introduced 4 February 1944.
196 Hauptgefreiter, superseded by chevrons for Stabsgefreiter.
197 Obergefreiter.
198 Gefreiter.

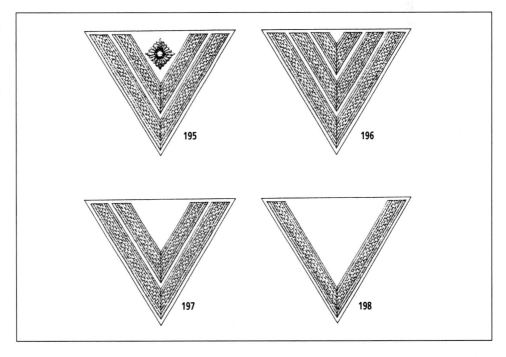

upper left sleeve of these garments midway between the elbow and the point of the shoulder. Initially (1938–44) there were three grades of rank chevron: a single chevron for a Gefreiter and a Sanitätsgefreiter, a double chevron for an Obergefreiter and a Sanitätsobergefreiter and triple chevron badge for a Hauptgefreiter and a Sanitätshauptgefreiter. All were made from strips of 1-cm wide Luftwaffe-pattern silver-aluminium 'Tresse', and normally sewn on to a triangular backing of blue-grey cloth.

On 4 February 1944 the chevrons indicating the rank of Hauptgefreiter were replaced by a new badge consisting of two chevrons with a woven rank star set into the space formed by the angle of the inner chevron (Fig. 195). This new badge was introduced when the new rank of Stabsgefreiter was initiated to supersede the rank of Hauptgefreiter.

Left and right: Gefreiter and
Obergefreiter rank chevrons.

Trade and Specialist Badges

Trade and Specialist badges, the bulk of which had been introduced before the war

and the few that were brought into use during the war, have been extensively covered and illustrated in Volume 1933–40 (pages 145 to 159).

Trade and Proficiency Badges
199 Administrative NCO (Unteroffizier and Feldwebel).

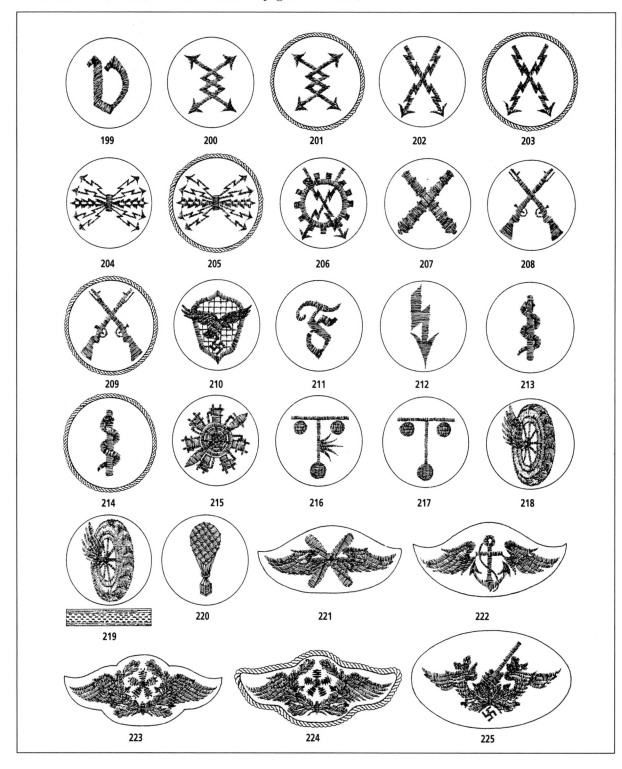

199   200   201   202   203

204   205   206   207   208

209   210   211   212   213

214   215   216   217   218

219   220   221   222

223   224   225

200 Air Signals personnel with qualification as 'B' Class telephone operators.
201 Qualified NCO telephone operator.
202 Air Signals personnel with qualification as 'B' Class teleprinter operators.
203 Qualified NCO teleprinter operator.
204 Air Signals personnel with qualification as 'B' Class radio operators.
205 Qualified NCO radio operator.
206 Air Signals equipment administrator.
207 Armourer NCO in the anti-aircraft artillery and Regiment 'General Göring'.
208 Armourer NCO in flying and air signals units.
209 Senior armourer NCO in flying and air signals units.
210 Motor vehicle driving personnel.
211 Ordnance personnel.
212 Signals personnel in flight and anti-aircraft units (non-air signals units).
213 Medical personnel with the exception of NCOs.
214 Medical personnel. Status unestablished.
215 Aircraft equipment administrator.
216 Searchlight equipment administrator.
217 Unidentified badge, thought to have been worn by personnel connected with searchlight units.
218 Motor transport equipment administrator.
219 Motor transport equipment administrator candidate.
220 Air Force balloonist.
221 Flight personnel, but worn only by those persons not entitled to wear a pilot's, observer's or radio operator's metal (or cloth) qualification breast badge.
222 Military seagoing boat personnel.
223 Flight technical personnel.
224 Flight technical personnel with more than one year's service.
225 Anti-aircraft artillery personnel.

Above: An NCO Direction Finding operator operating radio direction finding apparatus.

Below: Paratroopers being presented with Iron Crosses. The Oberfeldwebel awaiting his turn wears the trade badge for an Ordnance NCO.

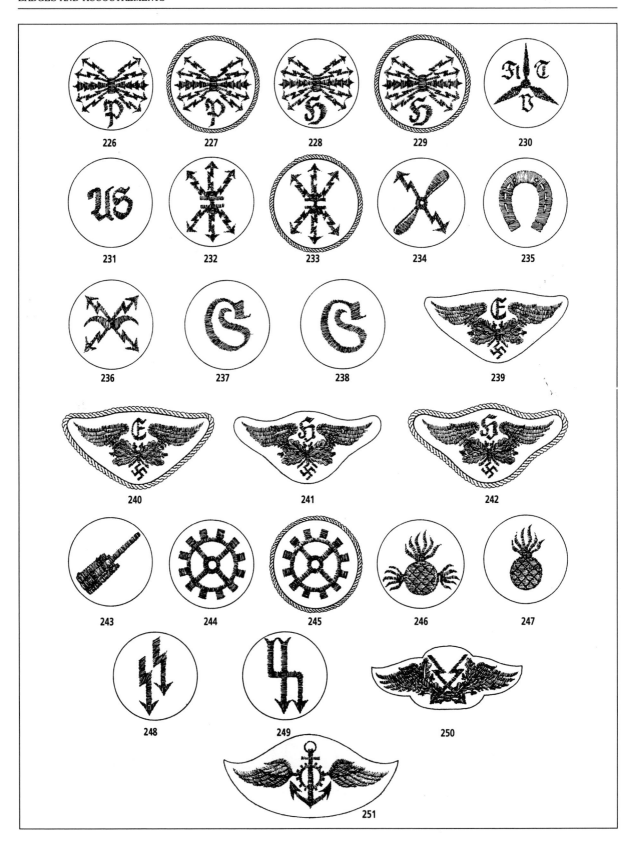

226

227

228

229

230

231

232

233

234

235

236

237

238

239

240

241

242

243

244

245

246

247

248

249

250

251

Trade and Proficiency Badges

226 Direction-finder operator.
227 NCO direction-finder operator.
228 Sound-locator operator.
229 NCO sound-locator operator.
230 Graduate from the Preparatory Training School for Aviation Engineers.
231 Student of a Luftwaffe school for NCOs.
232 Qualified radio instructor.
233 Senior qualified radio instructor.
234 Aircraft radio mechanic with 'B' Class proficiency.
235 Farrier.
236 Air raid warning service personnel.
237 Motor transport NCO storeman.
238 Horse-drawn transport NCO storeman.
239 Rangefinder crew member.
240 Rangefinder crew member with more than one year's service.
241 Anti-aircraft artillery sound-locator crew member.
242 Anti-aircraft artillery sound-locator crew member with more than one year's service.
243 Anti-aircraft artillery gun crew member.
244 Thought to have been for Air Force technical artisan.
245 Thought to have been for Air Force master technical artisan.
246 Heavy aerial munitions armourer.
247 Aerial bomb armourer.
248 Unidentified badge, thought to be for either signals or radar operator.
249 Unidentified badge, thought to be for either signals or radar operator.
250 Unidentified badge.
251 Unidentified badge, thought to be for helmsman of military seagoing boats.

Above: German Luftwaffe prisoners captured east of the Rhine are brought into US lines at Friedrichsfeld on the press Jeep of US war correspondent Fred Ramage (pointing). The Feldwebel on the bonnet of the Jeep wears the badge indicating that he served as a member of the Luftwaffe anti-aircraft artillery. The narrow line around the oval badge seems to be similar to the twisted gold piping worn on certain badges (see Volume 1933–40, pages 153 and 155) to identify a person who had served for at least one year in a particular trade.

Below: An Obergefreiter on the staff of the School for Air Traffic Control wears the trade badge for a motor vehicle driver.

Left: An unusual combination of 'trade' badges. This close-up shows a member of the Division 'Hermann Göring' working on the engine of an assault boat. On the left forearm of his Fliegerbluse he wears a naval specialist badge for a ship's diver above the Luftwaffe trade badge for military seagoing boat personnel.

Below: The crew of a Luftwaffe air-sea rescue launch. The Gefreiter on the far right wears on his upper left arm the Army badge for a helmsman of an assault boat and, below that, on his left forearm, the Luftwaffe trade badge for military seagoing boat personnel.

Qualification Badges

Those qualification badges that had been introduced before the war, with the obvious exception of those that had been made obsolete, continued to be awarded and worn by qualifying Luftwaffe troops. No new badges were introduced during the war other than the War Badges of the Luftwaffe, but these were not considered to be Qualification Badges.

The popularity of the flying jerkin that was brought into use after the start of the war (see page 173) may well have been responsible for the increase in the wearing of the cloth versions of these Luftwaffe qualification badges. The increasing shortage of metal was also a factor in the plethora of these cloth badges. A cloth version of a metal badge could be purchased by an individual on proof of his qualification. Unlike the metal items, once sewn to a garment a cloth badge was unlikely to become dislodged and lost with the resultant additional expense on the part of the wearer in having to purchase a replacement.

For details of the qualification badges of the Luftwaffe, see Volume 1933–40, pages 159 to 163.

Right: Two officers, both of whom wear the Qualification Badge for a Luftwaffe Pilot, celebrate the four million air kilometres flown in two years by the Field Post Air Mail service, in the course of which seven million kilogrammes of service mail was delivered between the German homeland and the various battle fronts.

Above left: An Unterfeldwebel, a veteran of Crete and the Eastern Front, wears, amongst other awards, the Luftwaffe qualification badge for a radio operator/air gunner.

Left: A veteran of Narvik, a former paratrooper and a member of a dive-bomber squadron, wearing the Luftwaffe qualification badge for a parachutist.

Above: Captured German Air craft in an airworthy condition were taken to RAF Duxford. Here they were flown by experienced RAF pilots who assessed the aircraft's performance passing on the data to the Air Ministry. This 'Flying Circus' was commanded by Fl. Lt. Lew Lewendon, shown here wearing an interesting war time copy of the Luftwaffe pilot's badge. 7 March 1944.

Operational Flight Clasps

By the start of 1941 the progress of the war in the air was such that the Luftwaffe authorities decided to introduce the first of a series of special badges both to reward and acknowledge the flying activities of aircrews and officials performing different types of air missions.[22]

Initially, each of the first three Flight Clasps to be introduced were awarded to personnel flying various types of aircraft fulfilling a set number of operational squadron functions.

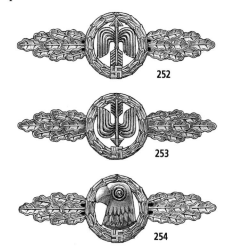

Operational Flying Clasps: the January 1941 first series of Flying Clasps.
252 Fighter, Long-Range Day Fighter and Air-to-Ground Support Squadrons.
253 Level-flight Bomber, Dive-Bomber, Transport and Glider Squadrons.
254 Reconnaissance, Air-Sea Rescue and Meteorological Squadrons

Persons eligible for any of these three grades of clasps were: pilots, observers, bomb aimers, wireless operators, flight mechanics, air gunners and Luftwaffe war correspondents. Administration Officials of the Luftwaffe and members of the Luftwaffe Corps of Engineers and the Corps of Navigational Experts were also eligible.

The number of operational flights required to have been flown by these persons in order to be eligible for any one of three grades of the three existing clasps were:

a. 20 operational flights were rewarded with a bronze clasp
b. 60 operational flights were rewarded with a silver clasp
c. 110 operational flights were rewarded with a gold clasp.

An operational flight was counted as one which penetrated to a minimum of 30km behind enemy lines, or one in which the enemy had been engaged. When over water the flight had to exceed 100km from the nearest friendly coast. This distance was reduced to 30km if the flight entered the airspace over an island or land mass held by the enemy. Operational flights of more than four hours' duration were counted as double if at least half of that time was spent over enemy territory (an island or a land mass). Flights of over eight hours' duration were counted as triple.

All eight awards, each in their three grades, were similar in overall design. They all had a circular wreath of laurel leaves with a small swastika set square at the base of the wreath. On either side of this wreath was placed a sprig of nine oak-leaves. Each clasp had a central motif set on the laurel wreath, which identified the clasp as being for a particular operational function.

The Flight Clasps were also produced in cloth. Officers wore hand-embroidered bullion versions, whilst those available to be worn by NCOs and Men were produced in appropriately coloured threads. All cloth Flight Clasps had to be purchased by the individual; they were not provided by the Luftwaffe.

By the summer of 1942 it was found necessary to expand the system by redesignating the existing Flight Clasps and at the same time introducing new ones to acknowledge a greater range of operational flying activities. The institution of all the following Operational Flight Clasps was announced in the *Luftwaffen-Verordnung-blatt* on the dates shown below. The number of flights needed to qualify for a bronze, silver or gold clasp remained the same as before.

Day fighter (Tagjäger) squadrons. Clasp instituted 30 January 1941.[A] Central motif was a winged arrow pointing upwards.

Heavy, Medium and Dive-Bomber (Kampf- und Sturzkampfflieger) squadrons. Clasp

A. After 28 January 1943[23] Day Fighter squadrons stationed near the English Channel Coast were permitted to calculate the following flights towards the award of the Day Fighter Operational Flying Clasp:
a) Three ship escort flights each with a minimum of 30 minutes duration.
b) Three fighter engagements each with a minimum of 30 minutes duration and within a minimum distance of 50 km from a friendly coast line.
c) Responding to three general alarms (scramble take-offs) each with a minimum of 30 minutes duration over water or a minimum distance of 50 km from a friendly coastline.

instituted 30 January 1941. Central motif was a winged bomb pointing downwards.

257

Reconnaissance, Air-Sea Rescue and Meteorological (Aufklärer, Seenotflieger-Verbände und Wetter-Erkundungs) squadrons. Clasp instituted 30 January 1941. Central motif was an eagle's head, facing left.

In 1944 personnel of Sea-Mine Locating units were made eligible for this clasp by instructions published in *Luftwaffen-Verordnungsblatt* and issued on 31 May 1944.[24] Three sea-mine locating flights were classed as the equivalent of one operational flight, provided the duration of each flight was no less than 30 minutes. Flights that had been made after 1 January 1944 were retrospectively accumulated towards the necessary total required.

258

Transport and Glider (Transport und Luftlandeflieger) squadrons. Clasp instituted 19 November 1941. Central motif was a stylized version of the Luftwaffe eagle and swastika, facing right.

259

Long Range Day fighter and Air-to-Ground Support (Zerstörer und Schlachtflieger) squadrons. Clasp instituted 26 May 1942. Central motif was a winged arrow pointing downwards. After 12 April 1944 this clasp was only worn by personnel of Long Range Day Fighter (Zerstörer) squadrons. A new clasp was instituted for Air-to-Ground Support squadrons at the same time, see Fig. 262.

260

Short-Range Night Fighter (Nahnachtjäger) squadrons. Clasp instituted 14 October 1942. Central motif was a winged arrow pointing upwards within a black laurel wreath.

261

Long Range Night Fighter and Night Intruder (Fernnachtjäger) squadrons. Clasp instituted 14 October 1942. Central motif was a winged arrow pointing downwards within a black wreath.

262

Air-to-Ground Support (Schlachtflieger) squadrons. Clasp instituted 12 April 1944. Central motif was two crossed swords, hilts to base of wreath.

By the summer of 1942 the accumulated numbers of operational flights being made by many aircrews began to outstrip the existing requirements of 110 missions for a person to be eligible for the award of a Flight Clasp in gold. To rectify this situation, on 26 June [25] the Luftwaffe authorities introduced a small pendant device comprising a highly polished gold star set between clusters of laurel leaves, which was to be suspended beneath the wreath of the gold Flight Clasps. (Fig. 263). The addition of a pendant signified that the following minimum operational missions had been flown:

1. 500 missions by Fighter and Transport squadron personnel;
2. 400 missions by Dive-Bomber, Long Range Day Fighter and Air-to-Ground Support squadron personnel;
3. 300 missions by Bomber, Air-Sea Rescue and Meteorological squadron personnel;
4. 250 missions by Reconnaissance and Night Fighter squadron personnel.

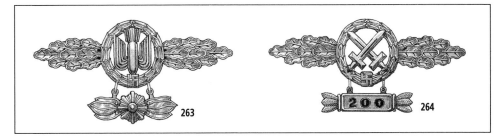

263 Flying Clasp with Star Pendant instituted in the summer of 1942 and here shown for Dive-Bomber Squadrons, gold Flying Clasp with pendant for 400 missions or Heavy and Medium level-flight Bomber Squadrons, gold Flying Clasp with pendant for 300 missions. Understandably, owing to much confusion as to the actual number of operational missions flown and represented by the Star Pendant, numbered Pendants were introduced in April 1944.

264 Flying Clasp with Numbered Pendant, here shown for Air-to-Ground Support Squadron, gold Flying Clasp with numbered pendant for 200 missions. Level-flight bombers were mainly the twin-engined Heinkel He 111 and Dornier Do 17, formed into Kampfgeschwader (KG) squadrons. The principal dive-bomber was the Junkers Ju 87, formed into Sturzkampf-geschwader (StG) dive-bomber squadrons. The principal fighter aircraft was the single-engined Messerschmitt Bf 109, formed into Jagd-geschwader (JG) squadrons. The principal aircraft in Zerstörergeschwader (ZG) destroyer squadrons was the twin-engined Messerschmitt Bf 110. The principal transport aircraft was the three-engined Junkers Ju 52, formed into Transportgeschwader (TG) transport squadrons. Many other makes and types of aircraft existed, some allocated to existing squadrons whilst others were flown by squadrons formed for specific purposes. However, as this work concerns the uniforms, clothing and insignia worn within the Luftwaffe, not the types of aircraft flown, it is left to the reader to search out references on German aircraft and their squadrons.

Right: An Oberfeldwebel pilot from a Transport Squadron enjoys a bunch of black-currants.

However, even this extension of the requirements was insufficient to meet the growing pressures of combat flying. There was also a certain amount of ambiguity, with the same star pendant being worn on different Flight Clasps for various totals of missions flow. All of this was overcome when, on 29 April 1944,[26] it was announced that a new form of pendant was to be introduced, presumably to replace the former pattern, but at least to reward future deserving aircrew.

The new pendant took the form of small golden tablet (bar) on which was displayed black numerals representing the appropriate minimum number of operational flights made by the recipient. These ranged from 200 (Fig. 264) to 2,000 in increments of 100. This new pendant was suspended, in the same manner as before, below the wreath of the Flight Clasp.

The pendant bearing the number 2,000 was awarded only once, to Oberst Hans Ulrich Rudel of Stuka fame, Germany's most decorated soldier of the period. His was the unique distinction of being the sole recipient of the Air-to-Ground Support Operational Flight Clasp in platinum and gold encrusted with diamonds, the pendant 2,000 testifying to his 2,000 aerial combat missions. Rudel received his award from the hands of Reichs-marschall Göring in April 1944.

Opposite page, top: A group of German fighter aces at the headquarters of Reichsmarschall Göring. Right to left: Oberstleutnant Dinert, Hauptmann Oesau, Oberstleutnant Mölders, Major Stork and an unnamed Oberstleutnant. Three of the five are wearing Operational Flying Clasps for time spent flying fighters.

Opposite page, bottom: Two of Germany's most successful night fighter aces, Major Streib (left) and Major Lent (right), both holders of the Knight's Cross with Oakleaves. July 1943.

Right: On 18 March 1943 Oberfeldwebel Haupt receives his Knight's Cross from the hands of the Führer for having successfully flown 350 bombing sorties against the enemy. Hung below his bomber Operational Flying Clasp is the first type of pendant, introduced on 26 June 1942, indicating that he had flown a minimum of 300 bombing missions.

War Badges

In Volume 1933–40, pages 159–63 dealt with the subject of Qualification Badges. These metal badges were the Air Crew Badge, the Pilot Badge, the Wireless-Operator/Air Gunner badge, the Combined Pilot-Observer Badge, the Air Gunner and Flight Engineer Badge, the Luftwaffe Paratroop Badge, the Glider Pilot Badge, the Army Paratroop Badge and the Airmen's Commemorative Badge.

Although most of these had been instituted before the outbreak of war, with the exception of the Air Crew Badge and Army Paratroop Badge they continued to be awarded throughout the war years. Cloth and bullion versions were available for private purchase by qualified recipients for wear on tunics, blouses or flight jerkins on occasions other than official parades.

The custom of awarding War Badges stemmed from the perceived need to recognize and acknowledge the work of those Air Force personnel who were called upon to operate Flak batteries, fight as infantry and man tanks and air-sea rescue launches. In some respects the introduction of these awards can be seen as reflecting the demise of the Luftwaffe proper.

As the war progressed, more and more anti-aircraft artillery was required to

Above: Hauptmann Gerlach, personal pilot to Generalmajor Kurt Student, was awarded the Knight's Cross of the Iron Cross for his part in the rescue of Benito Mussolini. A pilot with a transport squadron, Gerlach flew the Fieseler Storch that carried the Italian Dictator from his Gran Sasso hotel prison on 12 September 1943.

Right: An Oberstleutnant from the Division 'Hermann Göring' poses for his photograph. In addition to the Knight's Cross, the German Cross in gold and the Iron Cross First Class, he wears a Wound Badge in silver, the Luftwaffe Pilot's and the Fallschirmjäger Qualification badges as well as the Luftwaffe Ground Combat War Badge.

Left: Three highly decorated members of the same bomber crew, photographed in June 1944 on the Western Front. Left to right: Bomber Squadron Commander Oberstleutnant Hogeback with his Air Gunner, Oberfeldwebel Glasner, and his Wireless Operator, Oberfeldwebel Lehnart. All three wear the Bomber Operational Flying Clasp with the star pendant for having flown a minimum of 300 sorties. Oberfeldwebel Glasner wears the Krim (Crimea) campaign arm shield on his upper left arm, and the Kreta and Afrika with palms campaign cuff-titles on his left forearm. It is interesting to compare this photograph with that on page 93, as the order of precedence for wearing these campaign cuff-titles differs.

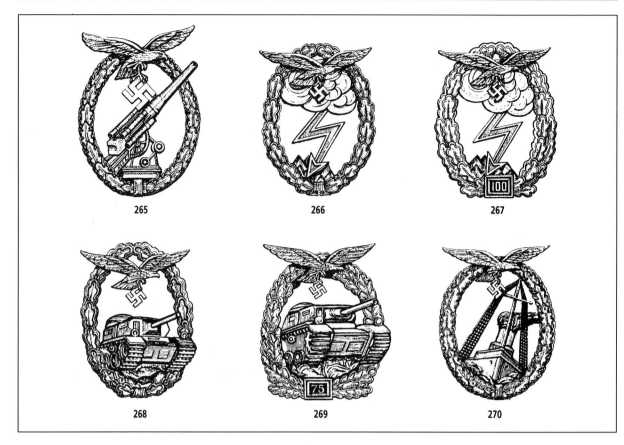

265   266   267

268   269   270

defend the increasing areas of conquest and occupation and, later, Germany itself. Entire divisions of ground combat troops were raised, many of the troops being redundant aircrews without aircraft and men of their supporting services and qualified paratroopers fighting as infantry. Tank crews were raised to serve in the Hermann Göring Panzer Division and, later still, the Fallschirm-Panzer Korps.

Anti-Aircraft War Badge of the Luftwaffe (Flak-Kampfabzeichen der Luftwaffe)

On 10 January 1941 Generalfeldmarschall Milch, in the name of the Reichsminister for Air Travel and Commander-in-Chief of the Luftwaffe, issued an order that introduced the 'Flak-Kampfabzeichen der Luftwaffe'.[27]

Although this pin-back badge was manufactured from silver-coloured base metal, it generally had the appearance of gunmetal grey. The design was a vertical oval of oakleaves bound around at its base. At the apex of the wreath was a Luftwaffe eagle in full relief, in an attitude of flight, its left talon clutching a swastika. The lower point of the swastika touched the recoil chamber of an 88mm anti-aircraft gun, the central design of the badge. The gun barrel was elevated to a 45-degree angle and pointed towards the right of the badge as viewed from the front, the muzzle extending beyond the wreath.

The badge was worn on the left breast pocket of the Tuchrock or Waffenrock or at a corresponding position on the Flight Blouse. It took precedence over any other military award but was positioned below the Iron Cross, First Class, if this decoration was worn.

The award of the badge was based on a points system, a minimum of sixteen points being required. The allocation of points to the crews of anti-aircraft batteries was made in the following way: (1) Four points were awarded to each gun crew member of a Flak battery if they succeeded, unaided, in shooting down an enemy aircraft. (2) Two points only were awarded to those members of a gun crew that co-operated with another battery in the destruction of an enemy aircraft.

Luftwaffe War Badges
265 The Anti-Aircraft War Badge of the Luftwaffe (Flak-Kampfabzeichen der Luftwaffe).
266 The Ground Combat Badge of the Luftwaffe (Erdkampfabzeichen der Luftwaffe).
267 The Ground Combat Badge of the Luftwaffe for 100 Engagements.
268 The Luftwaffe Tank Battle Badge (Panzerkampfabzeichen der Luftwaffe).
269 The Luftwaffe Tank Battle Badge for 75 Tank Engagements.
270 The Luftwaffe Sea Battle Badge (Seekampfabzeichen der Luftwaffe).

Above: This unnamed Feldwebel was a member of a Luftwaffe Flak unit believed to be connected with the V-2 rocket base at Peenemunde. He wears the Luftwaffe War Badge as an anti-aircraft artillery gunner, the Iron Cross First Class and a small semi-official unit badge.

the anti-tank role. They could be awarded the badge for participating in three successful engagements against land or sea targets. But the institution of the Luftwaffe Ground Combat Badge (see below) resulted in the Luftwaffe Anti-Aircraft War Badge being awarded only for anti-aircraft actions.

On 6 January 1945 an order proclaimed that females of the Flak-Waffen-Helferinnen-Korps, the Flak-Helferinnen and the RAD Flak-Waffen-Helferinnen serving with Luftwaffe anti-aircraft batteries and searchlight units were eligible to receive the War Badge.

The Ground Combat Badge of the Luftwaffe (Erdkampfabzeichen der Luftwaffe)

This badge was designed by Professor von Weech of Berlin and instituted on the order of Reichsmarschall Göring on 31 March 1942. It was introduced to reward those men of the Luftwaffe Field Divisions, including the Division 'Hermann Göring', who had distinguished themselves in ground combat (see page 222 for further details on these divisions).

The metal badge took the form of a matt-silver oval wreath of oakleaves with polished highlights, bound around at its base with a ribbon and surmounted by a silver-grey Luftwaffe eagle and swastika. On the more commonplace badges this eagle was frequently an additional casting riveted into place.

The central design consisted of a dark grey thundercloud from which was issuing a single bolt of lightning (represented by a black-painted, arrow-tipped zig-zag) striking earthwards, the ground represented by a range of pointed grey mounds directly behind the arrow tip. The badge was worn on the lower left breast of the tunic or blouse, below the Iron Cross, First Class, if this was worn.

The requirements stipulated that this badge would be awarded to:[28] (1) A soldier who had taken part in three separate military actions during front-line duty operating either infantry or artillery weapons, and this could include hand-to-hand combat. Medical personnel accompanying these combat units were also eligible. (2) Members of self-propelled artillery (Sturmgeschütze) units and parachutists who were engaged in

(3) Searchlight and sound-locator crews received one point for each first detection.

The prolongation of the war and the increase in the scale of enemy bombing raids brought about additional criteria for the award. It was given following five air defence actions even if these proved unsuccessful; after three actions if an aircraft were shot down; and the badge could be awarded to an individual for a single act of bravery or merit during air-defence operations. Battery commanders automatically received the badge when at least 50 per cent of the troops under their command had received it.

Luftwaffe 88mm Flak troops were frequently engaged in front-line combat on all fighting fronts as and when circumstances dictated, and were particularly deadly in three separate actions on three separate days.

The badge was automatically awarded to any person who also received a decoration in any of these actions, and it was awarded to the next-of-kin of any individual killed during the third of his combat actions. Any member of the Luftwaffe who had previously been awarded either the German Army's Infantry Assault Badge (Infanterie Sturmabzeichen), the General Assault Badge (Allgemeines Sturmabzeichen) or the Tank Battle Badge (Panzerkampfabzeichen) was required to surrender these in exchange for the Luftwaffe Ground Combat Badge.

The Luftwaffe Ground Combat Badge for Numbered Engagements

It rapidly became evident to the Luftwaffe authorities that the troops of the Luftwaffe Field Divisions were engaging in combat actions far in excess of the maximum number required for the award of the Ground Combat Badge. On 10 November 1944 instructions were issued introducing a series of four upgraded Ground Combat Badges, each badge of a higher grade than the last. In effect, this meant that there was a series of five badges, the original Ground Combat Badge being the Class 1 badge. All four of these new badges were similar in design and colouring to the basic class badge, although they were slightly larger, having a double wreath of oakleaves, and each of the new badges had a small black, framed tablet at the base of the wreath displaying the numbers 25, 50, 75 or 100. The 25-numbered badge was the 2nd Class, awarded for 25 combat engagements. The 50 badge (III Klasse) was for 50 engagements, the 75 badge (IV Klasse) was for 75 engagements and the 5th Class badge, displaying the number 100, was awarded for 100 or more engagements.

Although it is believed that these new badges were actually produced, it is just possible, owing to the late introduction of these awards, that these numbered, higher-grade Luftwaffe Ground Combat Badges were not actually awarded before the end of the war. So far, published documentation or contemporary photographic evidence has not been forthcoming.

Left: An unusual cloth badge, thought to have been worn by Flak crews either originating from Danzig or actually serving in the former Free State. This badge was almost certainly not an official issue.

Tank Battle Badge of the Air Force (Panzerkampfabzeichen der Luftwaffe)

The same order that announced the introduction of the higher grades of the Luftwaffe Ground Combat War Badge also introduced the special Tank Battle Badge for the Luftwaffe. The two versions of this badge, in black and in silver, both instituted on 3 November 1944, were not generally dissimilar to the silver and bronze Tank Battle Badges of the German Army.

1. The silver badge had a silver oakleaf wreath surmounted by a matt-silver Luftwaffe eagle and swastika. The central motif in black consisted of a Tiger tank emerging from the wreath. It was awarded to:

(a) Tank commanders, gunners, radio-operators and drivers for participation in three combat engagements on three separate days.

(b) Tank recovery and repair crews provided they were in the front-line and had been engaged by the enemy on three occasions on three separate days.

(c) Medical personnel attached to Luftwaffe armoured units which had been engaged on three occasions on three separate days.

2. The black badge which had a black wreath, matt-silver eagle and swastika and black Tiger tank. This was awarded to:

(a) Members of Luftwaffe Panzergrenadier formations who manned front-line positions and had been engaged in three actions on three separate days.

(b) Medical personnel attached to Luftwaffe Panzergrenadier units which were engaged in at least three actions on three separate days.

(c) Personnel of Luftwaffe Armoured Reconnaissance units if engaged in at least three combat actions on three separate days.

Tank Battle Badge of the Air Force for Numbered Tank Actions

On 10 November 1944, only a week after the institution of the Tank Battle Badge, a series of four, numbered Tank Battle Badges was brought into use. Similar in principle to the numbered Luftwaffe Ground Combat Badges, they were awarded for 25 engagements (II Klasse), 50, 75 and 100 or more engagements (V Klasse).

The design of these higher-grade badges was similar to the 1st Class Tank Battle Badge, but the wreath of oakleaves was more substantial, the Tiger tank slightly more prominent and each badge had a small black tablet at the base displaying the numerals 25, 50, 75 or 100 in gold.

Sea Battle Badge of the Air Force (Seekampfsabzeichen der Luftwaffe)

The German Navy had no functional aircraft carrier, and those spotter aircraft catapulted from major surface ships were crewed by Luftwaffe personnel, so the Luftwaffe had total control of all aircraft and personnel engaged in coastal and maritime operations.

On 27 November 1944[29] Göring instituted the Sea Battle Badge to recognize and reward the efforts of Luftwaffe personnel, officials and civilian specialists who manned the air-sea rescue launches, supply vessels and other surface craft. This proved to be the last of the war badges to be introduced before the end of the war.

The badge consisted of an oval-shaped wreath of gold-coloured oakleaves surmounted by an antique-silver Luftwaffe eagle and swastika. The central motif, in dark grey metal, featured the forward section of a steamship complete with mainmast and shrouds, heeling to port with smoke billowing from the funnel and waves breaking from the bows. The badge was intended to be worn on the lower left breast. Given its late introduction, however, it is doubtful if it was actually awarded.

It was to have been awarded to the following persons for specific periods of seagoing duty:

1. Masters and crews of supply and other surface craft for:

(a) Sixty days at sea in the North or East Seas, between 5 and 20 degrees longitude and south of the 60th degree of latitude, or

(b) Twenty days at sea in the Mediterranean, Aegean or Black Sea.

2. Masters and crews of air-sea rescue launches for:

(a) Twenty seagoing days with a minimum of one sea rescue attempt or a daily seagoing mission for the twenty days each of a duration of three or more hours.

(b) Ten seagoing days with a successful air-sea rescue, but a successful air-sea rescue mission counted as two seagoing days.

A day at sea was calculated as being of ten hours' minimum duration. Days with less than ten hours spent at sea were accumulated on an hourly basis, an example being 14 accumulated hours, constituting one sea day.

The Luftwaffe Sea Battle Badge could not be awarded for an action that entitled the participant to any one of the Kriegsmarine war badges.

The Luftwaffe Close Combat Clasp (Nahkampfspange der Luftwaffe)

On 3 November 1944 Göring instituted the Luftwaffe Close Combat Clasp for 'courageous participation in hand-to-hand fighting on the part of Air Force ground personnel'. The introduction of this Luftwaffe decoration[30] was undoubtedly influenced by the Army hand-to-hand combat clasp instituted two years earlier. The Luftwaffe set very similar criteria for the award of each their three grades. The design consisted of two clusters of oakleaves, one

each side of a narrow circular wreath of laurel leaves, identical with the design of the Operational Flying Clasp, except that there was no swastika at the base. The metal used for these oakleaves and wreath was bronze, silver or gold-coloured depending on the grade of the clasp. The central motif was a small silver Luftwaffe eagle and swastika set directly above a stick grenade crossed with a bayonet, both in silvered metal. The colour of the central motif was the same for all three grades. On the Service Tunic it was worn directly above the upper edge of the left breast pocket, and in a corresponding position on the Flying Blouse. If the recipient was wearing medal ribbons mounted on a ribbon bar or full medals the Clasp was worn 1cm directly above the ribbons.

The three grades were:

(a) Class I, bronze, 15 days' of close combat, reduced to 10 days if the receipient had been wounded during that time.
(b) Class II, silver, at least 30 days' of close combat, reduced to 20 days for wounds sustained during that period.
(c) Class III, gold, 50 days or more of close combat, reduced to 40 days for wounds received

Because the Luftwaffe Close Combat Clasp was instituted so late in the war it was decided to make its eligibility retrospective, as was already the case with the Army Clasp. Military service in Russia prior to November 1944 counted towards the award, eight months' service counting as 5 combat days, twelve months' as 10 combat days and fifteen months' as 15 combat days.

Those individuals who were awarded the gold Class III Clasp also received the additional privilege of 21 days' leave.[31]

The Roll of Honour Clasp of the Luftwaffe (Ehrenblatt Spange der Luftwaffe)

272

In July 1941 a special 'Roll of Honour' was created for the German Army (Ehrenblatt des deutschen Heeres), on which were recorded the names and heroic deeds of Ger-

man soldiers. The German Navy instituted a similar record in February 1943 when they created their own 'Honour Table' (Ehrentafel der deutschen Kriegsmarine) and German Air Force personnel who were deserving of the honour had their names recorded on an 'Honour List' kept by the Luftwaffe (Ehrenlists der deutschen Luftwaffe).

In 1943 the Oberkommand der Wehrmacht decided to award those armed forces members whose names had been recorded with a visible recognition of their deeds. On 30 January 1944 the Roll of Honour Clasp of the Army (Ehrenblatt Spange des Heeres) was instituted. The Navy followed on 13 May with their Honour Clasp (Ehrentafel Spange der Kriegsmarine) and the Honour Clasp for the Air Force (Ehrenblatt Spange der Luftwaffe) was instituted on 5 July 1944.

The Luftwaffe version consisted of a small, gilt-metal wreath of oakleaves containing a Luftwaffe eagle and swastika. The Clasp was worn on the ribbon of the Iron Cross 2nd Class when the ribbon was worn in the buttonhole on the front of the tunic. It was not worn on the ribbon of the Cross if the medal itself was worn. To be eligible for award of the Clasp, the recipient had to have been in possession of the 1st Class and 2nd Class Iron Cross. If the person had been awarded the 1939 Bar to his 1914 Imperial Iron Cross 2nd Class, he only wore the Roll of Honour Clasp on his medal ribbon, and not both insignia.

Members of the German Air Force who had been presented with either the Luftwaffe Goblet of Honour or the Luftwaffe Salver of Honour automatically received the Luftwaffe Roll of Honour Clasp.

Marksmanship Lanyards, 1936–45

The system of shoulder lanyards, introduced in the autumn of 1936, and awarded to personnel below officer status who were proficient in shooting, is explained fully in Volume 1933–40, pp.166–170.

The awarding of these marksmanship lanyards continued throughout the war years, but the practice may have declined out of necessity during the final months. Those persons who had been awarded lanyards continued to wear them on the appropriate items of dress as and when required to do so by regulations.

Right: Berlin in 1941. On a bright October day, on the corner of the Kurfürstendamm and the Joachimsthalerstrasse, two German airmen ask directions from a traffic policeman on point duty. The nearest airman is wearing a marksmanship lanyard second grade.

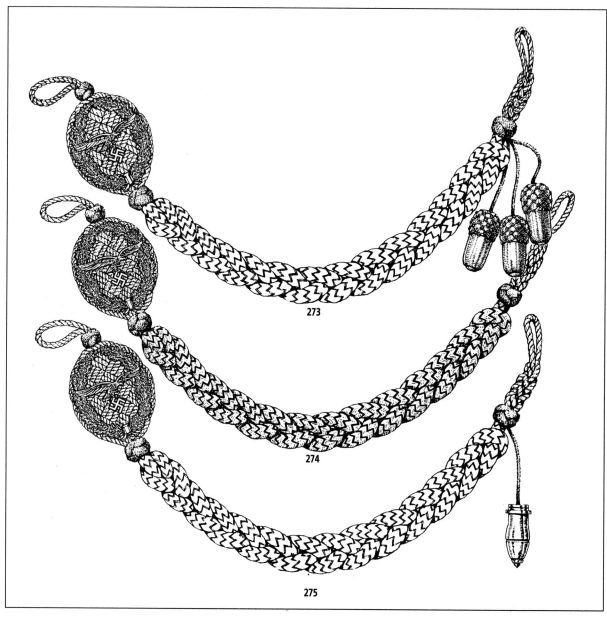

273

274

275

Marksmanship Lanyards
Introduced in 1936 to replace the earlier system of cuff stripes (see Volume 1933–40, pages 162 and 164–167), these lanyards came in twelve grades divided between three levels of achievement. Three of these grades are illustrated here.

273 Grade 4, the highest grade in the first level of achievement. A lanyard made from blue-grey silk cords interwoven with a latticework of bright silver-aluminium threads forming a pattern of small chevrons. The loops at each end of the lanyard and the plaited base to the dull silver metal plaque were of blue-grey silk flecked with bright silver-aluminium. The three ball-shaped sliders were formed of silver threads. The three acorns constructed from silver-aluminium metallic threads, when worn on a first-level-of-achievement lanyard, indicated that the wearer had reached the fourth grade in marksmanship from a unit other than an anti-aircraft unit.

Acorns manufactured form silver-aluminium or gold metallic threads were frequently used on marksmanship lanyards instead of the gilt or white-metal acorns as illustrated in Volume 1933–40, page 169. This was purely a manufacturer's choice.

274 Grade 5. A lanyard made from silver-aluminium cords interwoven with small chevrons of dark blue-grey silk threads forming patterns of zigzags. The loops and the plaited base to the bright silver metal plaque were of silver-aluminium and blue-grey threads interwoven in approximately equal amounts. The three sliders were formed of silver threads.

275 Grade 10. A lanyard made from blue-grey silk cords interwoven with a latticework of gold threads forming a pattern of small chevrons. The loops at each end of the lanyard and the plaited base to the gold-coloured metal plaque were of blue-grey silk flecked with gold threads. The three ball-shaped sliders were formed of gold-coloured threads. The gilt-coloured metal artillery shell distinguished this achievement level of lanyard as being for the 10th grade of marksmanship skill for a member of the Luftwaffe anti-aircraft artillery.

Officers' Dress Aiguillettes, Adjutants' Aiguillettes and Service Badge Cords.

276 The all-gold Dress Aiguillettes as worn by Luftwaffe officers, officials, etc., from the rank of Generalmajor upwards.

277 The matt-silver aluminium Dress Aiguillettes as worn by all grades of Luftwaffe officers, administration officials, officers of the Engineer Corps, and the Corps of Navigational Experts, plus Inspectors of Music and Bandmasters of all grades below the rank of Generalmajor.

278 The all silver-aluminium Duty Aiguillettes for wear by Luftwaffe officers appointed as adjutants. On those occasions when an adjutant was required to parade with the officers and men of his unit formed up for a full-dress parade, the adjutant wore Duty Aiguillettes, not Dress Aiguillettes, and most definitely not two patterns of aiguillettes worn together. It should be noted that the design shown here is the correct pattern for the Duty Aiguillette as worn by a Luftwaffe adjutant. The pattern featured as illustration 492 on page 170 in Volume 1933–40 was shown in error. That drawing actually showed the pattern of Duty Aiguillette as worn by an adjutant in the State Police Regiment 'General Göring' (see Fig. 73, page 40 of Volume 1933–40) and an adjutant in the Deutscher Luftsport-Verband (see Fig.15, page 15 of Volume 1933–40).

279 The all-yellow service badge cords (Dienstabzeichen) worn by Luftwaffe officers and NCOs, both male and female (see also page 243), when on duty and engaged in specific tasks, among which were Duty Officer (Offizier von Dienst) and Duty NCO for the Day (Unteroffizier von Tagesdienst).

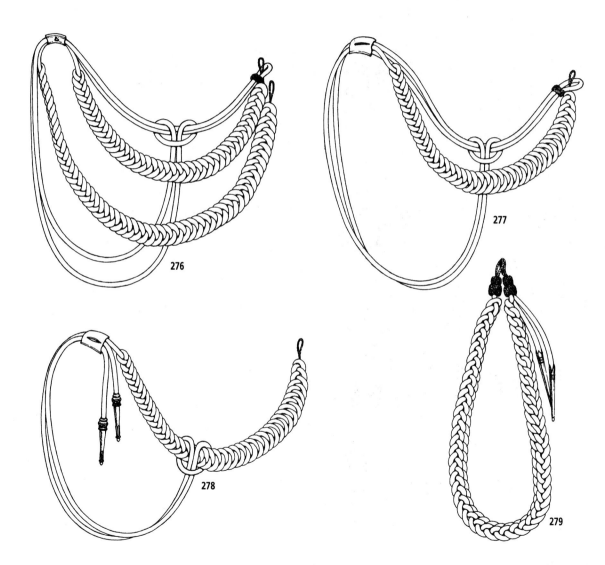

Aiguillettes and Service Badge Cords

The three patterns of officers' Aiguillettes and the Service Badge Cords have been illustrated and written about in detail in Volume 1933–40, pp.170–2. All of these items continued to be worn on appropriate occasions throughout the war years. Illustrations of these accoutrements are shown again here.

Above: A presentation ceremony for the award of the Iron Cross, 2nd Class. The inspecting officer talking to the men he has just decorated is accompanied by his Adjutant who is distinguished by the duty cords worn on his right shoulder.

Left: Men of the Luftwaffe operate an unidentified piece of apparatus believed to be associated with a Flak battery. The Unteroffizier on the far left, as Duty NCO for the Day, wears the all-yellow Service Badge cord.

Gorgets (Ringkragen)

The two patterns of Standard-Bearers' gorgets, the Luftwaffe gorget and the gorget for the Regiment 'General Göring', described in some detail in Volume 1933–40, pp.173–176, continued to be worn on those ceremonial occasions when they were obligatory, even during the last months of the war.

The gorget for the Flag- and Standard-Bearers of the NSFK is described on page 17 of this book.

Other gorgets existed for units of the Luftwaffe or units associated with the Luftwaffe. These were:

Right: The Luftwaffe standard-bearer's gorget. Interestingly, both of the NCO bearers are wearing their carrying sash inside its foul-weather protective cover.

1. The duty gorget of Army pattern worn by members of Luftwaffe and Paratroop Field Police Units;
2. The duty gorget of Luftwaffe pattern worn by members of Luftwaffe and Paratroop Field Police Units;
3. The duty gorget worn by members, including Luftwaffe personnel, of Feldjägerkorps units.

All three gorgets were of the same dimensions, of similar appearance, and made from the same quality metal. The half-moon plates and the chain links had a matt-silvered finish, and the raised metal scrolls were painted a darkish field-grey. The lettering on these scrolls, the eagle and swastika emblems and the pebble-surfaced bosses all had a luminous paint finish. Other features of these gorgets and the method of wearing them were very similar to the gorgets described in Volume 1933–40.

There is ample contemporary photographic evidence showing the Army Feldgendarmerie gorget being worn by Field Police units of the Luftwaffe Field Divisions, the Fallschirmjäger units and the Field Police of the Hermann Göring Division. The use of the duty gorget displaying

Far left: Luftwaffe Feldgendarmerie and Feldjägerkorps Duty Gorgets.
280 Army-pattern Field Police gorget.
281 Luftwaffe-pattern Field Police gorget.
282 Gorget for personnel of Feldjägerkorps units, including Luftwaffe troops.

Right: The Luftwaffe-pattern Feldgendarmerie duty gorget, worn by mounted members of a Luftwaffe Field Police unit somewhere in southern Ukraine.

Left: The Army-pattern Feldgendarmerie duty gorget, worn by a Fallschirjäger member of the Luftwaffe Field Police on traffic duty somewhere on the Russian Front.

the Luftwaffe-style eagle and swastika emblem in place of the Army-pattern eagle was undoubtedly introduced at a much later date, and photographs do exist of it being worn by Luftwaffe Field Police. The Feldjägerkorps gorget was not a Luftwaffe item, but Luftwaffe personnel assigned to these units would have worn it when on official duty.

A description of the purpose of the Feldjägerkorps units can be found on page 66 in the author's book *German Army Uniforms and Insignia, 1933–1945*.

Musicians' 'Wings' (Swallows' Nests)

As far as I am aware, there was no wartime development beyond that established prewar in the use of 'Swallows' Nests' (Schwalbennester), the colloquial name given to the decorative items worn by musicians, bandsmen and drummers and fifers on

Right: Musicians from Regiment 'General Göring' parade through a deserted street of what is believed to be a French town. They all wear the distinctive silver braiding on white cloth 'Swallows' Nests' peculiar to this regiment.

both shoulders of the Luftwaffe Service and Uniform tunics. It may have been possible that, depending on circumstances, these Musicians' Wings were used less frequently during the war years than had been the case in peacetime. The subject of these Swallows' Nests is fully dealt with in Volume 1933–40, on pages 140 to 145.

Bayonet Knots, Sword Knots and Dagger Knots

Little, if any, development of the systems employed for the wearing of these items took place during the war. As with other items of decoration, it is quite evident that the use of these knots declined the closer Germany came to defeat.

Personnel who wore sidearms and their appropriate knots when war was declared continued to do so on those occasions when they were required to be worn. But wartime recruits, particularly towards the end, may not have been issued with the coloured Faustriemen for wear on their bayonets. Losses of these decorative items due to enemy bombing no doubt added to shortages of these knots (as well as many other non-essential items for that matter).

Bayonets continued to be issued to troops right up to 1945. Generals, officers and NCOs required to wear swords or daggers were still able to purchase them even during the later stages of the war.

The subject of Personal Side-Arms and their Accoutrements has been covered in Volume 1933–40, pp.176–185.

Cuff-Titles

These can be divided into four distinct groups:
1. Commemorative Honour cuff-titles were worn by personnel of units carrying the name of a famous personality or location. These were known as 'Errinerungsband'.
2. Great War Honour Titles refered to as 'Kriegserinnerungsband' were those items specially introduced to commemorate former Air Arm service during the Great War. Named after squadron commanders, they were among the first to be introduced into the new Luftwaffe.
3. Formation Titles, worn by personnel of certain élite or specialist formations, displayed the name of the unit or formation.
4. Campaign Titles, indicating a specific period of active service in a theatre of war.

All the Commemorative Honour cuff titles, the Great War Honour titles and most of the Formation titles were introduced before September 1939. These have been dealt with in Volume 1933–40, pp.185-195. The first of the Campaign titles for wear by Luftwaffe personnel, the 'Kreta' title, was introduced in October 1942.

It was not unusual for a member of the armed forces to have been awarded more than one campaign cuff-title, which in the case of the Luftwaffe tended to be the 'Kreta' and 'Afrika' titles. When this occurred, and as both titles were worn on the left forearm, the earlier award took precedence and was worn above the other.

Below: The Luftwaffe 'Afrika' campaign cuff-title, worn by an unidentified Hauptmann, a member of a fighter squadron serving in North Africa.

Below: Feldmarschall Erwin Rommel accompanied by army, air force and parachute officers during what is thought to be a tour of inspection of German defensive measures along the Atlantic Wall. The Luftwaffe/Fallschirmjäger officers are wearing both the 'Afrika' with palms and 'Kreta' campaign cuff-titles. When this photograph is compared with that on page 79, it will be seen that there was a misunderstanding regarding the correct order in which these two titles were to be worn.

Right: The campaign cuff-title awarded to those personnel, including Luftwaffe and Fallschirmjäger troops, who had taken part in the fighting for the island of Crete.

Campaign Cuff-Title 'Kreta'.

Instituted on 29 September 1942, on the orders of the Führer[32] to reward those personnel of the three armed forces who had participated in the battle for the British-held Mediterranean island of Crete. It was officially described as a 'white cuff band (Armelband) with gold-yellow edging and lettering 'Kreta' with two palms'. In fact, although the cuff-title was of off-white cloth, 3.3cm-wide, the 0.3cm-wide border on both the upper and lower edging was in gold-coloured Russia braid, and the gold-yellow Roman lettering 'KRETA' was flanked on each side by acanthus leaves.

The title was worn on the left forearm, 1cm above the turnback cuff of the Uniform Tunic, the Service Tunic and the Greatcoat, and at a corresponding position on the left forearm of the Flight Blouse. No distinction was made between the title worn by officers and that worn by the rank and file.

The requirements for the award of the 'Kreta' cuff-title were:

(a) For troops (including glider crews) to have made a parachute descent or a glider-borne landing on Crete between 20 and 27 May 1941[33].

(b) For crews of reconnaissance aircraft, fighters, heavy bombers, dive-bombers and long-range day fighters who must have taken part in operations over Crete or Cretan waters before 27 May 1941.

(c) For Naval personnel who had been on active service off Crete on 19 May 1941.

The final date on which the 'Kreta' cuff-title could be awarded was set at 31 October 1944.[34]

Formation Cuff-Title 'Afrika'.

On 25 February 1942 Reichsmarschall Göring, in his capacity as Commander-in-Chief of the Luftwaffe, ordered all Air Force personnel stationed in Africa to wear a dark blue cuff-title bearing the name 'AFRIKA'.[35]

The title was described as a 3.3cm-wide, dark blue, plain material band without edging and with the word 'AFRIKA' in block capital letters. This was embroidered in silver-aluminium for officers and officials of equivalent officer rank and in matt-grey cotton for NCOs, administrative officials of NCO rank and other ranks. The title was worn on the right forearm approximately 16cm from the lower edge of the tropical uniform sleeve and at the equivalent height on the blue-grey Service Tunic, which was in effect 1cm above the turn-back cuff. The regulations governing the right to wear this title were extended to embrace:

(a) All members of Luftwaffe units and formations stationed in North Africa.
    Those personnel who were required to fly on missions to or over Africa were not classed as being 'stationed in Africa' and were not eligible to wear the cuff-title.
(b) Personnel who had been wounded in Africa and transferred to military hospitals in Europe.
(c) Troops in Europe on leave from Africa; these were permitted to wear the cuff-title on their blue-grey uniform.

The dark-blue 'Afrika' cuff-title was required to be removed when Luftwaffe units were transferred out of the African theatre or when individuals were transferred to other units not stationed in Africa.

Campaign Cuff-Title 'Afrika' with Palms.

On 15 January 1943, Generaloberst von Brauchitsch, Chief of the Army General Staff, ordered that the Army unit cuff-title 'Afrikakorps' and the Luftwaffe 'Afrika' title were to be replaced by a new title displaying the single word 'AFRIKA' flanked on each side by a representation of a palm tree.

The new 3.3cm-wide title was made of soft camelhair material, light khaki-brown in colour with 0.3cm-wide silver-grey cotton Russia braiding along the upper and lower edging. The silver-grey Roman lettering 'AFRIKA' was flanked on each side by a stylized five-frond palm tree in silver-grey.

This title was considered the equivalent of a campaign award and could be worn by eligible personnel from all three services, the SS and the NSDAP[36]. It was worn on the left forearm, 1cm above the turn-back cuff of the Service Tunic and Greatcoat and in a corresponding position on garments without cuffs.

Eligibility to wear the cuff-title required:

(a) A minimum of six months' service in North Africa, waived if the individual had been wounded within that theatre on land or in the air during that time.
(b) Being invalided out of the theatre as the result of contracting an illness after having served a minimum of three months.

Personnel flying missions to or over Africa were not classed as being stationed in Africa and were not eligible to wear the cuff-title.

Units or individuals transferred out of the African theatre were required to remove the cuff-title.

In January 1944 it was announced[37] that anyone who had been awarded a decoration in the North African theatre, regardless of length of service, was automatically eligible to wear the 'Afrika' with

Right: The 'Kurland' campaign cuff-title, worn by an unnamed Luftwaffe Hauptmann, who, on hearing that Germany had capitulated, flew his aircraft to Copenhagen Airport on 10 May 1945 and surrendered to the British. This comparatively rare campaign cuff-title was instituted on 12 March 1945 and awarded to all German personnel who had served with Army Group Courland, encircled in the Latvian pocket in October 1944 and cut off from the rest of the German forces until the final capitulation. It proved to be the last award introduced for German forces in the Second World War.

Upper left: The formation cuff-title for those Luftwaffe troops serving in the North African theatre of operations. The version shown here was for men and NCOs.
Lower left: The campaign cuff-title awarded to German forces serving in North Africa.

Campaign Cuff-Title 'Kurland'.

October 1944 found German troops in Latvia separated from the rest of the German Army, apart from air transport, and encircled in a defensive pocket around Courland, attempting to resist the advance of superior Soviet forces. Army Group Courland remained cut off from the main body of the Wehrmacht until the final capitulation of all German troops at the beginning of May 1945.

At the suggestion of Generalfeldmarschall Ferdinand Schörner, Commander-in-Chief of the Army Group Courland, a campaign cuff-title based on a design submitted to the Führer's Headquarters was approved on 12 March 1945. Owing to the desperate situation both in Germany and in Latvia, supplies of this award could not be flown into the Courland Pocket. Instead, the cuff-titles were produced locally from suitable materials. A weaving mill at Kuldiga (Goldingen) was selected for the production of these titles, and initially only hand looms were available. Later the cuff-titles were produced on a mechanically operated weaving machine. Local housewives who possessed sewing machines were engaged as out-workers to perform the finishing-off work. Distribution of the many thousands of these awards is thought to have started at the end of April 1945 and continued right up to May 1945.

No precise details of the qualifications required for a person to be eligible for this award have so far come to light. In their classic work,[A] Littlejohn and Dodkins list the following conditions for a person to have been a recipient of this cuff-title:

(a) To have participated in three engagements in the Courland pocket as a combatant (one being sufficient if the recipient was wounded), or

(b) To have served a minimum of three months, calculated from 1 September 1944, as a non-combatant with Army Group Courland.

Palms cuff-title. These decorations were specifically noted to include the Iron Cross, the German Cross in Gold, the Luftwaffe Honour Goblet and the Luftwaffe Salver of Honour.

On 6 May 1943 Hitler decreed that the service time requirement be reduced from six to four months for personnel who had fought in the final phase of the Africa campaign.[38]

The cuff-title ceased to be awarded to members of the Luftwaffe after 28 August 1944, unless the recipient had been a prisoner of war, had been missing in action or a person temporarily confined to hospital[39] having contracted an infectious disease and was likely to return to his unit.

Below right: The Campaign cuff-title awarded to German armed forces personnel, including the Luftwaffe, who formed the Army Group Courland. This item, formerly in the collection of the late Colonel Clifford M. Dodkins, is believed to be an original title.

A. *Orders, Decorations, Medals and Badges of the Third Reich (Including the Free City of Danzig)* by David Littlejohn and Colonel C.M. Dodkins. Page 136. (See also Bibliography).

Führerhauptquartier

Führerhauptquartier

283 First-pattern yellow on black 'Führerhauptquartier' cuff title.
284 Second-pattern silver on black 'Führerhauptquartier' cuff title.

However, as the photograph on page 95 shows, the wearing of this cuff-title was also extended to Luftwaffe personnel. There must have been certain requirements governing the award of this title to Air Force troops, probably similar to those that applied to the Luftwaffe Afrika cuff-title.

Original Kurland titles that have survived the war are normally 4cm high. They are made from material that is variously described as being off-white, silver-grey and silver-grey-white in colour. The original intention was to have had these titles woven from silver-aluminium threads with black cotton detailing, but shortages of suitable materials meant that this was not possible. The block lettering 'KURLAND' was in black cotton, as was the unusual design of the top and bottom edging. On the left of the lettering was a small shield bearing the emblem of the Grand Master of the Order of Teutonic Knights, and the small shield on the right of the lettering displayed an elk's head in profile, the arms of the town of Mitau, the principle town in Courland.

Formation Cuff-Title 'Führerhauptquartier', 1st and 2nd patterns.
This formation cuff-title was worn as a distinction by military personnel entrusted with the personal safety of the Führer and

Left: The 'Hermann Göring' formation cuff-title for NCOs and Men. Here it is worn on the right cuff of a member of the Division 'Hermann Göring' killed in a night attempt to infiltrate Allied outposts around the Anzio beachhead, Italy.

the security of all personnel at the Führer's Headquarters. So, although not a Luftwaffe cuff-title, it was worn by Luftwaffe personnel assigned to guard duty at the Headquarters, a task they shared with troops from the Army's 'Grossdeutschland' Regiment, and the manning of Flak cars on special trains.

In September 1939 the 7th Light Anti-Aircraft Battery from Regiment 'General Göring' was detached from the Regiment to serve as escort to the Commander-in-Chief of the Luftwaffe, Hermann Göring, and Foreign Minister Joachim von Ribbentrop and

provide air defence for the Führer's Headquarters.

In mid-1942 the Battery was expanded to Battalion strength and entitled IV.Führer-Flak-Abt./Flak-Regiment 'Hermann Göring'. Men from this unit manned the Flak wagons protecting the private trains used by Hitler, Ribbentrop and Göring.

The first pattern Führerhauptquartier cuff-title was a machine-woven item with yellow edging and Gothic lettering, all on a black band. A specimen I examined was identical in manufacture, size, quality and colouring with the 'Reichsbahndirektion' cuff-titles worn by certain railway personnel. The lettering of the 'FHQ' title was without a hyphen.

The second pattern, introduced on 15 January 1941[40] was a black cloth band with silver Russia braiding stitched along both edges and having hand-embroidered lettering in Sütterlin script in silver-aluminium thread.

Both patterns of this cuff-title were worn on the left forearm and the quality of manufacture was the same for officers and rank and file.

Other variations have been recorded,[41] all of which differ to varying degrees from those described above, most noticeably in the use of a hyphen between the words 'Führer' and 'Hauptquartier'.

Formation Cuff-Title 'Hermann Goring'

The early summer of 1942 saw the expansion of Regiment 'General Göring' to that of Brigade strength. Personnel of this new Brigade continued to wear the 'General Göring' cuff-title as described and illustrated in Volume 1933–40, pp.189–90. On 15 July the formation was redesignated Brigade 'Hermann Göring' and its personnel were issued with a new cuff-title bearing the title 'Hermann Göring'. On 22 May 1942 an order had been promulgated[42] to the effect that these Luftwaffe personnel's cuff-title be changed no later than late August 1942.

The new cuff-title was produced first with Gothic lettering, and shortly afterwards with block letters. As usual there was a differentiation for officers, NCOs and other ranks. Regulations governing the method of wearing the new cuff-title also followed standard Luftwaffe practice. It

Below: The 'Herman Göring' formation cuff-title for officers. Here it is worn by a young Leutnant captured in Italy and photographed on his way to a prisoner-of-war camp in England.

Left: An unidentified Hauptmann; a Knight's Cross holder and member of the Kampfgeschwader 53 'Legion Condor'.

Right: Major Adolf Galland speaks with the Führer, Adolf Hitler, on 20 October 1940. As Kommodore of JG 26, Major Galland wears the 'Jagdgeschwader Schlageter' cuff-title.

Right: The 'Kriegsberichter der Luftwaffe' formation cuff-title, worn by a war correspondent officer (Leutnant).

Upper left: The Division 'Hermann Göring' formation cuff-title as worn by the rank and file.

Lower left: The Division 'Hermann Göring' formation cuff-title for officers.

was worn by all ranks on the right forearm, 1cm above the turn-back cuff of the Service Tunic and Greatcoat, and 16cm up from the bottom edge of the right sleeve of the cuff-less Tropical Tunic and Flight Blouse.

It should be noted that NCOs holding the appointment of Hauptfeldwebel or Hauptwachtmeister wore their Luftwaffe cuff-title, regardless of pattern, on the appropriate forearm, directly above their double rings of NCO sleeve braiding.

Commemorative Honour Cuff-Title 'Jagdgeschwader Udet'

Ernst Udet was an internationally famous stunt pilot and aviator. He was one of Imperial Germany's top fighter aces, flying in Jagdgeschwader Nr.1 under Rittmeister Manfred von Richthofen and achieving a score of 62 aerial victories, an achievement second only to that of the 'Red Baron' himself and recognised by the award of the Order Pour le Mérite.

After the war, Udet became a commercial and stunt flyer, travelling extensively to Africa, Greenland, the United States and other countries, but in 1934 he was persuaded by his wartime comrades Göring and Lörzer to accept the honorary position of Vice-Commandant of the German Air Sports League (DLV). Udet entered the Luftwaffe on 1 June 1935 with the rank of Oberst, and on 10 February 1936 he was

Right: The Geschwader Mölders Formation cuff-title is worn here by Leutnant (later Oberleutnant) Oskar Romm. Born on 18 December 1919 at Haindorf/Isergebirge, 'Ossi' Romm won his Knight's Cross as an Oberfeldwebel on 29 February 1944, after 76 air combat victories. On 27 September 1944 he shot down three Liberator bombers in one single attack. He was seriously wounded in a crash on 24 April 1945, by which time he had flown 229 missions, 54 fighter-bomber sorties with 92 victories (including 82 in the East and 8 four-engine bombers). He had been nominated for the Oakleaves.

Left: The 'Kriegsberichter der Luftwaffe' formation cuff-title, worn by a junior NCO (Unteroffizier).

appointed Inspector of Fighters and Dive-Bombers. This appointment did not last very long, for on Hitler's insistence Göring was obliged to appoint Udet Chief of the Technical Office of the Luftwaffe. A year later he was promoted to Generalmajor. In 1938 he became Chief of the Office for Special Supply and Procurement (Generalluftzeugmeister), a position he held until his death.

Unfortunately for the Luftwaffe, Ernst Udet did not understand the intricacies of political manoeuvring and personal pres-sures; nor was he particularly talented in the field of aircraft development and production planning. Generaloberst Ernst Udet committed suicide on 17 October 1941. He had been depressed for a considerable time, and was convinced that Erhard Milch as Secretary of State for Air Travel and Inspector General of the Air Force was attempting to oust him from his position as Generalluftzeugmeister. The truth of his suicide (a pistol shot to the head) was obscured from the public. The official explanation for his death was 'an accident which had occurred whilst testing a new weapon'. Udet was given a military State Funeral in the Reichs capital on 21 November 1941 (see Volume 1933–40, pages 196 and 236).

The Commemorative Honour cuff-title 'Jagdgeschwader Udet' was introduced by order of the Führer and Supreme Commander of the Wehrmacht. Instructions were issued on 20 December 1941[43] for it to be worn by all ranks of Jagdgeschwader Nr.3. The 3.3cm-wide dark blue cloth band had the gothic-lettered inscription worked in silver-aluminium hand-embroidered threads for officers and in matt-grey cotton for NCOs and other ranks. The cuff-title was worn just above the turn-back cuff on the right sleeve of the Service Dress and tan Tropical Jacket by all ranks, and in a corresponding position on the white Summer Tunic and the blue-grey Flight Blouse by officers.

Commemorative Honour Cuff-Title 'Jagdgeschwader Mölders'

This title was appointed to be worn by members of Jagdgeschwader 51 on 20 December 1941, less than a month after the death of Oberstleutnant Werner Mölders. Mölders, a highly respected fighter pilot and holder of the Oakleaves with Swords and Diamonds to his Knight's Cross, tragically died in an air crash on 22 November 1941. He was returning to his squadron after attending the state funeral of Ernst Udet on the previous day when the Heinkel He 111 in which he was a passenger crashed in bad weather near Breslau-Gandau. Like Udet, he too was afforded a military State Funeral, held in Berlin on 28 November 1941 (see Volume 1933–40, pages 220 and 237).

Affectionately known to his subordinates as 'Vati' (Daddy), Mölders flew more than

300 missions, during which he achieved 115 air victories: 14 in Spain, 68 on the western front and 33 in Russia. His name and memory lives on today: a squadron of the present-day German Luftwaffe bears his name as 'Geschwader Mölders'.

The Second World War cuff-title was very similar in colour, quality and size to all other Luftwaffe Commemorative Honour titles as described in Volume 1933–40, pages 190–193, and as described above for the 'Jagdgeschwader Udet' title. It was intro-

duced by order of the Führer and Supreme Commander of the Wehrmacht, and instructions for its wear were issued on 20 December 1941.[44] It was worn on the right forearm.

Other Luftwaffe Cuff-Titles

Rumours abound of the existence of two other Luftwaffe cuff-titles, both of which would fall within my definition of Commemorative Honour Titles. These were 'Jagdgeschwader Galland' and 'Jagdgeschwader Lutzow'.

Left: This very unusual photograph shows an unidentified Luftwaffe Hauptmann, a veteran of Spain, wearing a Leibstandarte-SS 'Adolf Hitler' cuff-title. It is possible that he was attached to the Führer Headquarters as a pilot, probably as Hitler's personal pilot, and as such came under the jurisdiction of the SS.

Right: The 'General Göring' formation cuff-title worn on both the blue-grey Luftwaffe tunic (Generalmajor Conrath, holding papers) and the black Panzer uniform.

A. In October 1941 it was announced[45] that the High Command of the German Armed Forces had agreed that those persons serving within the Armed Forces (and that included the Luftwaffe) who were members of the Reichs Arbeits Dienst, the German Labour Service or RAD, would be issued with yellow arm bands bearing the words 'Deutsche Wehrmacht' for so far and as long as their units were operating

The first title most definitely did not exist. Those Commemorative Honour titles that were introduced into the Luftwaffe were without exception named after deceased persons, and Adolf Galland survived the war. The second title was worn by actors taking the parts of Luftwaffe personnel belonging to a fictional fighter squadron that featured in a wartime German film.

Armbands

Those armbands worn by personnel of, or attached to, the Luftwaffe that are know to have been in use prior to the Second World War have been dealt with in Volume 1933–40, pp.196–8. With only a very few exceptions all of these pre-war armbands continued to be used from 1940 to 1945, but certain armbands were introduced after the outbreak of war and these are given here.

An armband worn on a military uniform indicated that the wearer held a special but temporary appointment, or was fulfilling a particular role. When worn on civilian clothing it indicated that the wearer was officially employed or engaged in a military or ancillary role.

Generally, armbands were not the property of the individual, but were issued as and when required and then handed back to the issuing unit. When circumstances permitted, armbands were stamped with the cachet of the issuing unit in indelible marking ink. Not only did this form of marking serve to identify an armband as being the property of a particular issuing unit, but, for security reasons, it also reduced the possibility of fake or stolen armbands being used by unauthorised persons, the hand stamp on the armband having to correspond with the written authority carried by the wearer.[A]

Air Defence Leader of the Air Force (Luftschutz Leiter der Luftwaffe)

A white armband, 10cm-deep, with a 1cm-wide strip of blue tape along the top and bottom edge and in the centre a Luftwaffe

outside the frontiers of Germany and were employed within the framework of the German Armed Forces. These arm bands were marked with the Wehrmacht service stamp of the issuing unit, and lists of those persons to whom the arm bands were issued were required to be kept up to date and on file. Permission to wear this arm band had to be noted in the paybook of each RAD member.

eagle and swastika machine-woven in black. It is assumed that this, and the following armband, were the equivalent of the army versions. According to Adolf Schlicht[A] the army versions, introduced by Order Nr. 410 published in *Allgemeine-Heeresverordnungsblatt*, dated 15 August 1942, were worn by Air Defence and Deputy Air Defence Leaders who, as designated army district leaders, were responsible for the air defence of their district.

Deputy Air Defence Leader of the Air Force (Stellvertreter des LS-Leiters der Luftwaffe)

This was similar to the armband described above but had an extra strip of 1cm-wide blue tape positioned vertically on each side of the eagle and swastika.

Deutsche Luftwaffe (Aircrew)

A bright yellow armband on which was printed a large Luftwaffe eagle and swastika detailed in black, directly above the legend 'DEUTSCHE LUFTWAFFE' which was printed in black block capitals.

This item was introduced late in the war[46] in the endeavour to identify aircrew, mainly pilots, of aircraft shot down over Germany. Incidents were recorded of aircrew of downed Luftwaffe aircraft being fired on and in some instances killed by angry or overzealous civilians who mistook them for enemy 'Terrorflieger'. The armband was worn on the upper left arm.

Deutsche Luftwaffe (Auxiliaries)

A white linen armband on which was printed a large Luftwaffe eagle and swastika, detailed in blue, directly above the legend 'Deutsche Luftwaffe' printed in blue, upper and lower case Gothic lettering.

This item was worn on the left upper arm by civilian personnel attached to Luftwaffe auxiliary organizations such as the Heimatflak.

Armed Forces Interpreter (Wehrmachtdolmetscher)

The extent of the German territorial conquests and the increasing numbers of foreigners serving with the German forces made it necessary for the Wehrmacht to employ interpreters.

Selected Luftwaffe personnel underwent extensive instruction at an armed forces school of languages to become fluent in one or more foreign languages. Once they had achieved the required standard they were issued with a pink armband bearing the legend 'WEHRMACHTDOLMETSCHER' in black lettering. The pink linen armband was 7cm deep and was worn on the upper left sleeve.[47]

Air Defence Guards (Luftschutz Personnel)

Luftschutz Ordnungs-und Absperrdienst personnel who were assigned to air defence guard duty wore on the left upper arm a dark blue armband bearing a machine-woven letter 'O', 7.5cm high.

Left: The Red Cross armband worn by three Parachute PoWs riding in the back of a Willys Jeep, Italy.

A. Adolf Schlicht, assisted by John R. Angolia, writes authoritatively on all aspects of the uniforms of the German Army in his three-volume work entitled *Uniforms & Traditions of the German Army, 1933–1945*. See Bibliography for further details.

4. UNIFORMS

Steel Helmets

Several distinct models, or patterns, of steel helmets were worn within the Luftwaffe at various times. The first two models, the M1917 and the M1935, were mentioned in Volume 1933–40, pages 199 to 204. The period between 1939 and 1945 saw the introduction of the Model 1942 helmet for universal wear. Certain innovations and adaptations of protective helmets for crews of aircraft were also brought about. These are described in the appropriate section of this book under Flight Clothing and Equipment.

The Model 1917 Helmet

The Model 1917 Steel Helmet was used by personnel of the Luftwaffe before January 1936 for the simple reason that no other pattern of helmet was available. In January 1936 the Model 1935 Helmet was introduced, and after a short period of time, when the new helmet became available in sufficient quantities, it superseded the Model 1917. However, the early patterns were not entirely abandoned. Instances have been noted when Model 1917 helmets were distributed during the war to home front personnel, doubtless because there were insufficient modern helmets.

The Model 1935 Helmet

First introduced into the Luftwaffe in limited numbers in January 1936, this pattern was designed as an improvement on the earlier helmet. The 'Stahlhelm 35', to give it its official designation, had better protective properties and was less of a hindrance to the wearer than the previous model. It allowed for better sighting when firing weapons or operating optical equipment, and it was easier to hear when wearing this model, owing to the shallowness of the side

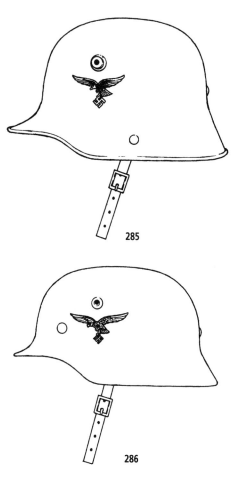

285

286

protections or 'aprons' when compared with the M17 helmet.

The helmet was painted both externally and internally with a matt, blue-grey finish which served to prevent rust forming and also acted as an anti-glare agent. All helmets were produced with the Luftwaffe national emblem on the left side, facing forward, and the German national colours in the shape of a shield on the right side. After 12 June 1940 the black, white and red shield transfers (decals) were no longer

applied to newly manufactured helmets. The new Model 1935 helmet was produced and distributed throughout the German Armed Forces until 1942, and it continued to be used for the remaining years of the war.

The Model 1942 Helmet

On 6 July 1942 the Chief of the Army Equipment Office of the OKH announced that from 1 August that year the inward crimping around the helmet rim was to be abolished. For reasons of economy, future production was simplified. The helmet shell was stamped out of one piece of metal without having the helmet rim crimped inwards around the edge. This gave the Model 42 helmet a much sharper appearance, and at the same time made it appear slightly larger around the apron.[A]

Colouring, Insignia and Covers for Steel Helmets

Steel helmets worn in the Luftwaffe before the war were manufactured with a matt, rust-protective blue-grey painted finish both inside and out. It was forbidden to alter this finish by polishing, repainting or applying grease to the surface. Wartime conditions modified these pre-war regulations, insofar that those troops serving in hot-climate countries and on the eastern front during the winter months frequently

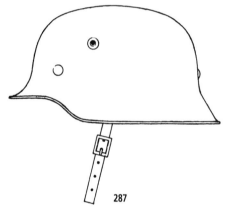

287 The Model 1942 steel helmet.

overpainted their blue-grey helmets a sand colour or applied a thick coating of white-wash, respectively, as a means of camouflage. The type of insignia carried on the helmet has been dealt with in Volume 1933–40, pp.199–200 and 204.

Helmet covers were not issued within the Luftwaffe, other than to Parachute and Field-Division troops. Information on the types of covers and methods of application can be found in this book under the appropriate headings.

Cloth Head-dress

The Uniform Peaked Cap (Schirmmütze)

The Luftwaffe Uniform Peaked Cap was worn by all ranks of all branches, including

A. Apart from the Luftwaffe insignia and the blue-grey colour of the external and internal paint finish, these steel helmets worn by personnel of the Air Force were in all respects the same as those steel helmets worn within the other branches of the Wehrmacht. Anyone wishing to read more of this subject is recommended to read *The History of the German Steel Helmet, 1916–1945 by Ludwig Baer* (see bibliography).

Left: The Commander-in-Chief of the Air Force, Generaloberst Göring, inspects the troops of a Luftwaffe Honour Guard drawn up in the forecourt of the new Air Ministry building in Berlin. The parade was held on 16 March 1935 to mark the reintroduction of military conscription, and the troops are wearing the newly introduced Model 1935 steel helmets, all of which have a high-gloss finish. This was forbidden later that year by instructions published in the handbook *Anzugordnung für die Luftwaffe (L.A.O.)*, L.Dv.422 Abschnitt A.

Right: Men of a static Flak unit wearing the Model 1935 steel helmet, with the second-pattern Luftwaffe national emblem displayed on the left side.

Right: Luftwaffe troops on the Eastern Front man an 88mm Flak gun. All three men wear M35 steel helmets overpainted in a light colour.

the Air Force Administrative Officials. It was prescribed to be worn by officers and NCOs with Service Dress and Undress Uniform, with Parade Dress by officers not actually engaged in a parade, and with Dress Uniform by officers and with Walking-Out Dress by officers, NCOs and men.

The cap was of the same basic design, shape and colouring for all ranks. It had a blue-grey cloth top and crown, a black artificial silk ribbed cap band[A] and a black patent vulcanised fibre peak, the edge of which had of a narrow ridge machine-stitched in position. Other cap distinctions depended on the wearer's rank. All men and NCOs[B] wore a black patent leather chin strap and black chin-strap buttons on their caps. The national emblem, the oak-leaf wreath and stylized wings were of silver coloured pressed aluminium metal. The cockade was also of white aluminium, but the coloured roundels were hand painted; red for the centre and black to the outer (see Volume 1933–40, Figs. 4 & 5). Piping used on the Uniform Peaked Cap was 0.2cm thick. It appeared around the crown of the cap and around the top and bottom edge of the black cap band, and was in the wearer's arm-of-service colour.

Luftwaffe officers, administration officials and officers of the Engineer & Navigational Corps, below the rank of General, wore the same style of cap. In place of the black chin strap they wore silver coloured cap cords held in position on the cap by small, silver coloured pebble-finished cap cord buttons. Their national emblem cap insignia was hand embroidered in silver-aluminium wire on to a backing of blue-grey material, while the stylized wings, the wreath and cockade were embroidered on to a backing of buckram-stiffened black material.

Officers' insignia was therefore sewn in position on the cap, while those of the men and NCOs were affixed to the material of the cap by metal prongs fitted to the back of the insignia.

Caps worn by officers, regardless of branch of service, were piped in silver coloured tubular piping 0.2cm thick around the crown to the cap and around the top and bottom edges of the black cap band.

Luftwaffe officers of General rank and above, as well as Engineer Officers and

Luftwaffe Administrative Officials with the equivalent ranks, wore caps with gold coloured cap cords, gilt metal cap-cord buttons and gold coloured hand-embroidered bullion cap insignia, and were piped with gold coloured tubular piping. However, in January 1943 instructions were issued[1] whereby all Officers, Medical Officers and Luftwaffe Administrative Officials including those of General rank or their Administrative equivalent were ordered to wear silver or gold coloured metal insignia on their Uniform peaked Caps in place of the metallic bullion hand-embroidered insignia for the duration of the war. The production of bullion cap insignia ceased

A. The black, artificial silk cap bands began to be introduced on new caps after September 1937. Prior to that date the cap bands were made of black ribbed mohair. The change-over, which was a gradual process, was announced in *Luftwaffen-Verordnungsblatt* Nr.40, dated 20 September 1937, page 523, Order Nr.1215 issued 13 September 1937.

Left: The Other Ranks Uniform Peaked Cap, worn by a Feldwebel captured during the fighting in Normandy, July 1944.

Right: US war correspondent photographer Edward Worth, covering the British Second Army in northern Europe, talks with German troops from all three services who had been ordered to leave Denmark after the capitulation of all German forces, 8 May 1945. The Luftwaffe officer in the centre of the photograph is wearing a privately purchased officers' peaked cap, the equivalent of the German Army Officers' Old Style Field Service Cap. This is an excellent example of the 'Luftwaffe Crush'. Also of interest is the Kriegsmarine minesweeper war badge he wears on his left breast pocket.

Far right: The white-topped summer cap for Luftwaffe and Fallschirmjäger officers.

B. Non-commissioned Officers of the rank of Oberfähnrich, Unterarzte and Oberfeuerwerker were permitted to wear the quality of cap normally worn by officers. Even though they were NCOs they displayed silver coloured cap cords and cap cord buttons. Their caps were piped in their arm-of-service colour. On those caps which they were issued with they wore the standard pattern pressed aluminium metal insignia (see Volume 1933–40, page 10, Figs. 4 & 5). On those caps that they were permitted to purchase for themselves they were allowed to wear officer's quality silver-aluminium, hand embroidered insignia as shown in Figs. 1 & 2 on page 10.

with immediate effect from the date of the order, but stocks of the embroidered insignia were required to be used up first.

The Summer Cap (Sommermütze)

The white-topped peaked cap — the 'Sommermütze' — was available to be worn before the war by all ranks of the Luftwaffe, the Luftwaffe Administrative Officials, Engineer Officers and Officers of the Corps of Navigational Experts. It was of fundamentally the same style both for officers and the rank and file personnel, and was very similar in appearance to the Schirmmutze — the Uniform Peaked Cap.

Like a number of non-essential items of dress, the Summer Cap, together with the white summer uniform for officers, ceased to be a required garment once the war had started. Persons were still permitted to continue wearing the cap, and it could still be purchased, but its official issue was suspended for the duration of the hostilities.

When it was used, the Summer Cap was permitted to be worn from 1 April to 30 September each year as part of the Luftwaffe Summer Uniform (see page 207 and page 227, Volume 1933–40), which in turn was worn as Walking-Out Dress, Undress Uniform or daytime Full Dress. However, as contemporary photographic evidence shows, the white-topped Summer Cap was

frequently worn by Officers when wearing the blue-grey Waffenrock, occasionally the Fliegerbluse and even the Tropical Uniform.

The Summer Cap was constructed in two parts: the body of the cap covered by the cap band plus the fibre peak, and the removable white cloth top. Because the Summer Cap was so like the Uniform Peaked Cap, practically all of the details regarding the cap insignia, the cap band, the chin strap or cap cords, the buttons and the piping were of the same type, size and colour when used on the Summer cap. The one noticeable and obvious exception to this was the removable white cloth top and the insignia thereon. There was no piping around the crown of the white cloth top. What is sometimes mistaken for white piping is just a raised seam of white cloth. The Luftwaffe version of the national emblem displayed on the front of the cap top consisted of a silver-aluminium metal pin-on badge for use by NCOs and Men. For officers this same insignia was embroidered in either silver-aluminium metallic or gold coloured bullion threads, depending on the wearer's rank. The embroidery of this badge was worked on to a backing of white material, stiffened with buckram and mounted with a pin brooch fastening. Both

the metal pin-on badge and the bullion and linen version were removable to allow the white top to be laundered.

The Flying Cap (Fliegermütze)

The Luftwaffe Fliegermütze was a form of cloth head-dress that existed from the day the Luftwaffe was formerly announced right through to the end of the war in Europe, despite the wartime introduction of the Luftwaffe Replacement Flight Cap — the Einheitsfliegermütze — which was intended to replace the Fliegermütze (see page 112).

For Men and NCOs the Fliegermütze was in plain blue-grey woollen cloth without piping to the upper edge of the curtain. the Luftwaffe version of the national emblem positioned in the centre of the upper part of the front to the cap was in grey cotton machine-stitched yarn, usually on a backing cloth of blue-grey material. Below the eagle and swastika and on the front of the lower section to the curtain was stitched a flat silk or cotton woven version of the Reichskokarde (see Volume 1933–40, page 10, Fig. 9).

The Fliegermütze worn by officers of the Luftwaffe up to and including the rank of Oberst (Colonel), as well as Administrative Officials, Engineer and Navigational Offi-

Right: The officers' Flight Cap, here worn by Hauptmann Weinrich, RKT.

Left: The Fliegermütze of the type worn by Men and NCOs. Two ground mechanics attach the nozzle of a hot-air generator to the underside of an aircraft engine. Pumping hot air around the engine assisted starting during cold weather.

288 The Luftwaffe Mountain Cap (Bergmütze), here shown for wear by ranks below officer grade.

trative Officials of equivalent rank was distinguished by gold coloured metallic piping to the upper edge of the curtain. The cap insignia was in gold coloured bullion threads worked on to a backing of blue-grey cloth. The cockade was of the same type as that worn by Air force Officers, but had a narrow outer circle in gold-coloured threads instead of silver-aluminium threads.

Personnel with the appointment of Oberfähnrich were permitted to wear their version of the Fliegermütze. This was distinguished from the Flight Caps worn by other NCOs by silver coloured officer-quality piping around the upper edge to the curtain, and at the same time displayed the Luftwaffe national emblem and the Reichskokarde of the quality normally worn by NCOs and Men.

Finally, the Fliegermütze worn by female members of the Luftwaffe were very similar in colour, shape and quality to those worn by their male counterparts, though no Reichskokarde was displayed on the cap.

The Luftwaffe Mountain Cap (Bergmütze)

Luftwaffe troops operating in mountainous areas and manning fixed positions such as Flak batteries, Air Signals units and weather stations were issued with certain items of specialist clothing normally associated with Army mountain troops but manufactured in blue-grey Air Force cloth. For details of this Luftwaffe mountain clothing see Volume 1933–40, pp.225 and 227.

These troops were also issued with a distinctive Mountain Cap, closely modelled on the pattern used in the German Army but made from blue-grey material. On the front of the cap was the Luftwaffe version of the national emblem, below which was a

cers, was invariably made from better quality blue-grey material than was the case with the caps issued to the rank and file. Officers' Flight Caps were distinguished by having 0.2cm thick silver-aluminium piping, either tubular or twisted cording, stitched along the upper edge of the curtain. The insignia displayed on the cap was usually of the silver metallic thread, hand-embroidered type, the cockade being of the padded or raised hand-made pattern (see Volume 1933–40, page 10, Fig. 7).

The Flight Cap for use by Luftwaffe Generals and above and by Air Force Adminis-

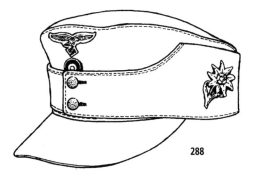

288

cloth Reichskokarde. The curtains of the cap were fastened at the front by two 0.12cm-diameter blue-grey-finished buttons. Although it was not an official Luftwaffe emblem, the metal Edelweiss as worn on the left side of the Army Bergmütze was occasionally worn in a corresponding position by Luftwaffe troops on their Mountain Caps, though this practice was officially forbidden.[2]

In 1943 instructions were issued[3] with regard to the wearing of the Bergmütze by officers and armed forces officials with officer rank. They were ordered to wear 0.3cm-thick silver-aluminium or gold-coloured piping (according to the wearer's rank) around the crown of the cap. Generals and officials of general's rank wore gold-coloured national emblem and cap buttons.

The Luftwaffe Replacement Flight Cap (Einheitsfliegermütze)

In September 1943 a new form of headdress was introduced, to be worn by all personnel of the Luftwaffe.[4] In place of the Flight Cap (Fliegermütze) and the Moun-

tain Cap (Bergmütze), a new cap referred to as the Replacement Flight Cap (Einheitsfliegermütze) was to be used for the duration of the war. Of blue-grey cloth, it had a cloth-covered peak and was similar in general style and manufacture to the Army Replacement Field Cap. The Luftwaffe national emblem and Cockade worn on the front of the cap was either machine-stitched or machine-woven in matt-grey threads (matt-gold for Generals, etc.) on to a backing of blue-grey cloth. Officers and Armed Forces Officials, etc. with grades equivalent to officers were distinguished by silver-aluminium piping set into the seam

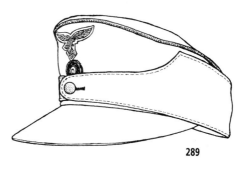

289

Below left: The Luftwaffe Einheitsfliegermütze, worn by Feldwebel Ernst Meinecke, who was taken prisoner in the Wurzburg area by troops of the US Seventh Army.

Below right; Generalleutnant Gundell after he and a number of other high-ranking German officers were taken into custody by troops of the US Seventh Army following the declaration of Germany's unconditional surrender. The General wears the two-button version of the Luftwaffe Replacement Flight Cap. He was the holder of the Knight's Cross of the War Merit Cross with Swords.

289 The Luftwaffe single-button Replacement Flight Cap (Einheitsfliegermütze), here shown for wear by officer ranks.

Flight Caps of the former pattern were to be worn until stocks were exhausted. The average price of the new Replacement Flight Cap was set at 3.19 Reichmarks.

Luftwaffe Footwear

Black leather Marching Boots, lace-up shoes and Officers' Riding Boots

The footwear worn by NCOs and Men was either black leather Marching Boots (Schaftstiefel or Marschstiefel) or black leather lace-up shoes (Schnurstiefel). Those NCOs who were permitted to buy their own clothing (which included footwear), as well as Officers, Armed Forces Officials and Engineer Officers, wore Riding Boots (hohe Stiefel). Riding Breeches worn with Riding Boots and Flying Trousers (the long blue-grey cloth trousers) worn with Marching Boots were worn with Field Dress, Service Dress, Reporting Dress and Parade Dress. Long blue-grey slacks (Tuchhose) and black leather lace-up shoes were worn with Walking-Out Dress and on certain full-dress occasions.

The Flying Service Dress (not to be confused with the Protective Flight Suits) was

Above: Luftwaffe troops and paratroopers from a Luftwaffe Field Division take the opportunity for a cigarette and a short rest during a lull in the fighting somewhere in France. A good selection of the various types of footwear is shown in this photograph. The paratrooper in the foreground is wearing ankle boots, the man resting on the wooden door has issue marching boots, the paratrooper seated next to him wears side-lace-up jump boots, and the young paratrooper standing to the right is wearing mountaineering boots.

290 The leather riding boot.

in the crown of the cap. Generals and Armed Forces Officials in the rank range of Generals had gold coloured piping to the crown.

These new-style caps were issued to all NCOs and Men. Those persons responsible for obtaining their own clothing against allowances were required to purchase the Replacement Flight Cap from the Luftwaffe Clothing Department. They were not, however, allowed to wear either this Replacement Flight Cap or the Mountain Cap when wearing Walking-Out Dress. The September 1943 instructions also added that, if the peak of the new cap got in the wearer's way when he was working with machinery or operating equipment, it was permissible for the cap to be worn back to front.

The former Flight Caps worn by Rank and File personnel were to be used as work caps for the duration of the war, each NCO and man receiving one cap. The Luftwaffe Mountain Caps and the officer-quality

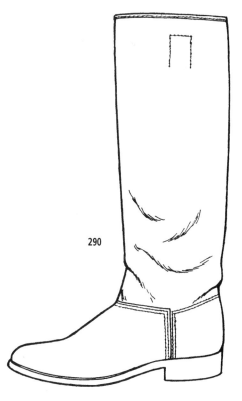

290

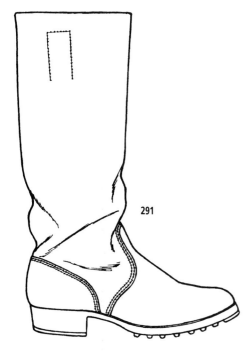

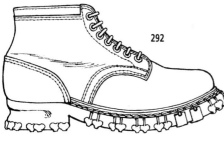

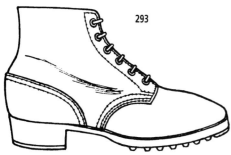

Mountain Boots and Ankle Boots

Luftwaffe or Fallschirmjäger troops operating in hilly or mountainous countryside were issued with special Mountain Boots of the same pattern as those used by the Gebirgsjäger of the German Army. The heavy-duty leather soles were hobbed and had cleats around their edge.

The black leather ankle boots were produced in an effort to conserve stocks of leather. They were usually worn with issue canvas gaiters.

Mention and details of other types of Luftwaffe and Fallschirmjäger footwear can be found in this volume under Flying Boots, page 170; Fallschirmjäger Jump Boots, first and second patterns, page 193; Tropical footwear, page 211; and Cold Weather Guard Boots, page 234.

Gloves

Gloves of the type authorized before the war continued to be worn on appropriate occasions during the war.

Details of the different types of glove and the system of marking hand sizes of

291 The black leather marching boot.
292 The mountain boot.
293 The black leather ankle boot.

generally worn with the Flying Trousers and lace-up shoes, although Marching Boots and/or riding boots worn with breeches were also permitted.

Further information on the various types of Luftwaffe footwear can be found in Volume 1933–40, on page 212.

Left: The soles of the marching boots, showing the hob patterning.

Right: A signaller operating a portable radio. He wears a single woollen glove of the pattern issued to NCOs and Men throughout the Luftwaffe.

Below: The pattern of waistbelt and buckle for NCOs and Men of the Luftwaffe. Rudolf Harbig, the celebrated 1936 Olympic 4 x 400-metre bronze medal winner, is seen on arrival at the Gare du Nord before taking part in a grand sports event at Colombes stadium, Paris (see also Volume 1933–40, page 251).

woollen knitted gloves are given in Volume 1933–40, pp. 214–15.

Information about the pattern of gloves issued to Fallschirmjäger and aircrews, and mittens worn with the reversible winter uniform are given in this volume under their respective subject headings.

Waist-belts and Buckles

The brocade waist-belt as worn pre-war by General Officers and Administrative Officials of equivalent rank and by officers and officials of officer grade below General rank was discontinued in September 1939. This was undoubtedly an economy measure, and contemporary photographs seem to indicate that the withdrawal instruction was universally observed. Details of the brocade belt are given in Volume 1933–40, p. 215.

For the duration of the war officers continued to wear the leather service belt with its two-pronged, open claw buckle and the rank and file continued to wear the leather waist-belt and metal box buckle. Details of these items are given in Volume 1933–40, pp. 215–17.

The leather cross-strap that was worn with, and helped to support, the officers' leather service belt had been discontinued shortly after September 1939. Göring, however, continued to wear a cross-strap with his Generalfeldmarschall's and Reichs-marschall's uniforms.

The design of the eagle on the belt buckle worn by the rank and file, dating from May 1935, was altered slightly with the introduction of the new-style Luftwaffe national emblem, whose eagle had more pronounced and outswept tail feathers.

Wartime shortages of leather brought about the introduction of webbing for a variety of equipment straps, including waist-belts. This quality of equipment tended to be used by troops, including Luftwaffe personnel, serving in North Africa, Sicily and Italy. The olive-green (Army) and blue-grey (Luftwaffe) coloured webbing was particularly suitable in a hot climate where leather, unless treated, has a tendency to dry out and crack, so its introduction was fortuitous.

Luftwaffe Field-Division troops in Normandy and Europe used canvas webbing equipment of necessity. Metal parts of their equipment, particularly belt buckles, were usually painted a darkish blue-grey.

Tunics and Flight Blouses

The pre-war introduction of the Service Tunic (Tuchrock), the Uniform Tunic (Waffenrock) and the two patterns of Flight Blouse (Fliegerbluse), one for officers of all

grades, the other for NCOs and other ranks, has been dealt with in some detail in Volume 1933–40, pp. 217–225.

The Service Tunic was intended to be replaced by the Uniform Tunic in November 1938, but the transition was of necessity a gradual one and the Service Tunic was still being worn during the war years.

The Uniform Tunic was the standard issue garment for all entrants after November 1938, and continued to be issued until the end of the war.

294 The Tuchrock (Service Tunic), here shown for an Unteroffizier.

Above: The officer's pattern of dark brown leather service belt and silver-grey two-pronged buckle. The wearing of the matching leather supporting cross-strap was discontinued shortly after the outbreak of war.

295 The Waffenrock (Uniform Tunic), here shown for a Hauptfeldwebel/Hauptwacht-meister.

Below: Major Hans Ulrich Rudel, Group Commander of a Dive-Bomber Group, with a Squadron Doctor, Stabsarzt Dr B. This photograph was taken in April 1944, shortly after Rudel had been awarded the Diamonds to his Knight's Cross Oakleaves and Swords. The Stuka ace wears the Tuchrock (Cloth Coat), while his companion wears the pre-war version of the officers' Fliegerbluse.

Far right: A Fallschirmjäger Hauptmann, taken prisoner in Italy, wearing the Waffenrock buttoned closed at the neck.

Since its introduction in 1935, the Flight Blouse (Fliegerbluse) had proved a popular item, and although it was meant to be replaced by the ubiquitous Uniform Tunic, it continued to be worn up to 8 May 1945.

The pre-war pattern of Officers' Flight Blouse continued unaltered throughout the war years, although superior quality cloth and the addition of flaps to the side pockets proved increasingly popular.

The Flight Blouse for NCOs and other ranks underwent a slight modification in December 1940, when side pockets were added to all newly issued garments. Troops who possessed the old pocketless version were required to wear it unaltered until it

296

was no longer serviceable, and stocks of this blouse had to be exhausted before unit clothing stores were allowed to order the new version.

On 1 October 1940[5] the Luftwaffe eagle and swastika was ordered to be displayed on the right breast of the Flight Blouse for NCOs and other ranks. Hitherto it had been devoid of this emblem, but the onset of the war and the need for personnel to be easily identifiable brought the insignia into

297

296 The pre-war-pattern Flight Blouse for officers. This style continued to be worn by those officers who possessed the garment even after the new pattern Officer's Fliegerbluse with side pocket flaps had been introduced. Here shown for an Oberleutnant.

Left: The post-1940 Fliegerbluse for an officer, here worn by a Paratroop Leutnant taken prisoner in Italy.

Right: Unteroffizier Heintze and Gefreiter Hübner (foreground) photographed whilst on leave from North Africa. Both men wear the Fliegerbluse correctly buttoned at the neck, mainly to display their neck order (see also the photograph on page 219). Arnold Hübner was born at Schubin on 14 July 1919, and served as a ground gunner in the Luftwaffe on the German home front and in North Africa, France and southern Germany. He rose to become a Leutnant, and was decorated with the Iron Cross 1st Class on 17 June 1941, and the Knight's Cross on 7 March 1942. The 'Afrikakorps' cuff-title is just visible on his right forearm.

Far right: Broad white stripes, one of the distinguishing marks of a Luftwaffe General officer. Generaloberst Keller, Commander of a Fliegerkorps, clearly shows the double white stripes and white piping worn on officers' breeches.

297 The Flight Blouse for officers, late pattern as used during 1939–45, here shown for a Sonderführer (R) ranking as a Luftwaffe Oberst.

298 The Flight Blouse for NCOs and Men, post-1940 pattern, here shown for a Flieger.

Far right: A Fallschirmjäger taken prisoner during the American advance towards Brest, 22 September 1944. This picture clearly shows the deterioration in the quality of material used for the wartime manufacture of garments, in this case the Luftwaffe Flight Blouse.

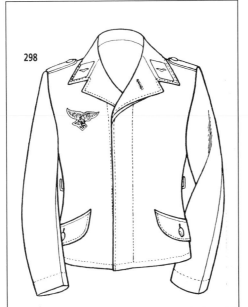

use. The eagle was required to be sewn on the right breast of the blouse in a position corresponding to that on the Service Tunic. Flight Blouses supplied after this date had the emblem already sewn on.

There was no further development of these garments during the remaining war years.

Trousers and Breeches:
General Officers' Coloured Broad
Stripes and Piping

Before 1943,[A] coloured cloth stripes and coloured piping were displayed on long cloth trousers and riding breeches worn by certain categories of officers:

1. General officers displayed white piping set into the outer leg seams, flanked on each side by a 4cm-wide white cloth stripe. These stripes were set apart from the white piping by a gap on each side measuring 0.4cm. In 1943[6] instructions were issued stating that generals, officers of the Luftwaffe General Staff and members of the Luftwaffe Corps of Engineers with ranks

equivalent to general were no longer required to wear the double, broad cloth braided stripes on the long cloth trousers (or, presumably on the breeches). The coloured piping, however, had to be retained. No mention was made in this order of the higher officials of the Judge Advocate-General's branch, or of the other higher officials in the other judicial services, but it is safe to assume that this economy measure also applied to them.

2. Armed forces officials with ranks equivalent to a Luftwaffe general had the same configuration of piping and stripes but in dark green cloth. Then, instructions promulgated by *Luftwaffen-Verordnungsblatt* Order Nr.187 issued in February 1940 stated that the dark-green piping and cloth braided stripes were to be changed to white piping and broad white stripes on the long cloth trousers (and presumably, on the riding breeches).

3. Officers of the Corps of Engineers with ranks equivalent to general had pink piping and pink cloth stripes.

4. Officers of the Luftwaffe General Staff

A. In October 1939 orders were published (*Luftwaffen-Verordnungs-blatt* Nr.47, dated 9 October 1939, p.357, Order Nr.875 issued 12 September 1939) approving the wearing of long cloth trousers without the broad white or carmine stripes by general officers and officers of the Luftwaffe General Staff. The order also extended to the trousers worn by Luftwaffe Administration Officials (dark green) and officers of the Luftwaffe Corps of Engineers (pink) with ranks equivalent to general.

Left: The broad white stripes and piping worn on the cloth trousers by General der Flieger Christiensen, Wehrmacht-befehlshaber for the Netherlands, seen in conversation with Reichsleiter Robert Ley.

Right: The result of wartime instructions abolishing the broad stripes, issued late in 1943, is clearly seen here. An unidentified Luftwaffe Generalleutnant, surrounded by other Police and Luftwaffe officers, watches intently as a listening device is activated in Berlin in September 1943. It is noticeable that only white piping is displayed on the General officer's breeches.

had carmine piping and broad cloth stripes.

5. From December 1939 instructions were issued[7] which allowed higher officials of the Judge Advocate-General's branch to wear Bordeaux-red coloured piping and broad cloth stripes.

6. These same instructions were extended to Luftwaffe higher officials of other judicial services, who were permitted to wear wine-red coloured cloth piping and stripes.

7. From January 1944 Truppensonderdienst officers of general's rank were required to wear coloured piping and broad cloth stripes to their trouser and breeches. Light blue was worn by General Officers of the TSD administration service, wine red by Generals of the TSD Judicial branch, dark blue by Generals of the TSD Medical section and dark green by TSD Administration General

8. Officials of generals' rank serving in the Building Administration Service (Bautechnisches Verwaltungswesen) were instructed in August 1944 to change the colour of their trouser piping and stripes from red to black.

Greatcoats and Guard Coats

The cloth Greatcoat, which formed part of the wardrobe of every member of the Luftwaffe, continued to be issued (or purchased) throughout the war years. It was intended to be worn during cold or inclement weather, other than for flying duties.

Details of its cut, colour, appearance and mode of wearing for all ranks including Armed Forces Officials are given in Volume 1933–40, pp. 235–8, as are details about the leather coats worn by officers, and notes on the raincoats and top coats of rubberized material.

Wartime development of the cloth Greatcoat was as follows:

1. In May 1942 instructions were issued[8] that the wearing of collar patches on the Greatcoat by NCOs and other ranks was to be discontinued as from 1 October 1942, and by officers and other personnel who purchased their own uniforms from 1 April 1943. All units were instructed to observe this ruling with the exception of the Luftwaffe Guard Regiment Berlin and the Führer-Flakabteilung of the Division 'Hermann Göring'.

2. General officers were distinguished by white lapel facings and collar piping to their Greatcoats. Administrative officials of ranks equivalent to generals had lapel facings and collar piping in dark green; those of the Engineer Corps wore pink.

Wartime introductions of new colours started in December 1939,[9] when senior officials of the Judge Advocate-General's branch were instructed to wear Bordeaux-red lapels and piping to their Greatcoat collars. Higher officials of other judicial services were required to display Greatcoat lapels and piping of wine red.

3. This was followed in April 1944 by further instructions[10] that extended the practice to certain officers of the 'Truppensonderdienst' (TSD).

Officers of General rank of the TSD with a career in administration were to wear lapel facings of light blue. Similar grade General officers of the TSD with a career in the judiciary were to wear lapel facings of wine red. Dark blue was to be used by TSD Medical Generals and dark green by TSD Administration Generals.

4. Finally, in August 1944,[11] black was ordered to be worn as the facing colour for the Greatcoat lapels and collar piping for construction officers of General's rank in the Luftwaffe.

Below left: The state funeral for Generaloberst Udet, 21 November 1941. Luftwaffe holders of the Knight's Cross form an escort to the war-flag-covered coffin borne on a gun carriage. Following the funeral cortege are Reichsmarschall Göring and other senior officers from the German armed services and paramilitary formations (see also Volume 1933–40, pp.196 & 236). The Unteroffizieren pall-bearers wear the Luftwaffe cloth Greatcoat.

Below: The state funeral of Oberst Mölders, 28 November 1941. Adolf Hitler and Generalfeldmarschall Erhardt Milch (right), accompanied by Reichsleiter Martin Borman (left) and SS-Gruppenführer Julius Schuab, Hitler's Chief Adjutant (behind Hitler), leave the forecourt of the Berlin Air Ministry (see also Volume

1933–40, pp.220 & 237). Milch wears the cloth greatcoat for a General of the German Air Force. The very distinctive white lapel facings contrast with the lapels of the cloth greatcoat worn by the senior Luftwaffe officer on the far left of the photograph.

Right: Generalmajor Neuffer (left) and Generalmajor Bassenge, two of a number of senior German and Italian officers who were captured when the Axis forces capitulated in North Africa. Generalmajor Neuffer wears the cloth greatcoat for a Luftwaffe officer, its dark blue-grey silk lining being evident. Generalmajor Bassenge wears the blue-grey rubberized raincoat for Luftwaffe officers.

Below: Oberst (later Generalmajor) Dietrich Peltz inspects the technical members of a fighter squadron somewhere on the Western Front. The officer behind Colonel Peltz, presumed to be the squadron commander, wears the blue-grey leather greatcoat for air force officers. The men being inspected all wear cloth greatcoats without collar patches, which dates the photograph as post-October 1942.

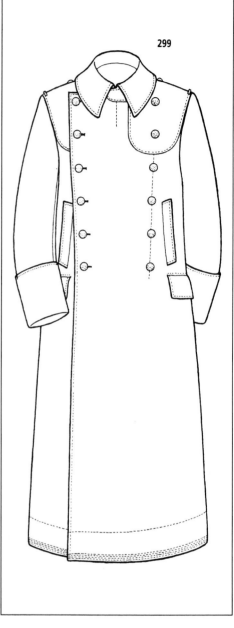

299 The special, heavy-duty Guard Coat with blanket lining, deep collar and side pockets.

The Guard Coat

Greatcoat development continued with what is believed to be the wartime introduction of the Guard Coat. This was similar in general appearance to the Luftwaffe Greatcoat as worn by the rank and file, but the Guard Coat was considerably bulkier. It had an extra-thick 'blanket' lining for additional warmth, a deeper-than-normal collar, which when turned up afforded the wearer better protection from the wind, and deep flannel-lined side pockets. The shoulders sometimes had an extra layer of cloth or were covered in leather, which protected those required to carry ammunition or heavy pieces of equipment and provided extra warmth.

Because this garment was cumbersome it was not suited for front-line combat duty. Its main use was by crews of fixed Flak or searchlight emplacements or by persons on guard duty, when warmth in cold weather was necessary and freedom of movement was not paramount.

Above: The heavy-duty, blanket-lined greatcoat, worn by Luftwaffe troops manning an observation post and scanning the skies for approaching enemy aircraft. The extra-thick guard coats, with additional pockets, were designed to be worn in very cold weather by troops in exposed static or semi-static positions. Note the guard boots worn by the man on the left.

Above right: An 88mm gun crew operating at night. All of the men wear the heavy-duty guard greatcoat for additional warmth.

Right: Generalleutnant G. Frantz and Generalmajor C. P. Kochy, both captured in North Africa, arrive at a special English prisoner-of-war camp for senior Axis officers in May 1943. Generalleutnant Frantz, an officer of the Flak branch of the Luftwaffe, wears an unofficial sheepskin jacket and a Luftwaffe sun helmet, while his companion wears the tropical version of the motor-cycle coat.

Left: General der Fallschirm-jäger Bernhard Ramcke, Commander of all German forces in the U-Boat fortress of Brest, is taken into custody as a prisoner of war of the US VIII Army Corps, 24 September 1944. Ramcke, the Fallschirmjäger officer who led the German Parachute invasion of Crete, wears a privately purchased short-length, double-breasted leather coat. Although he wears his shoulder-straps on this coat, it is an unofficial garment.

Luftwaffe Protective Work Uniforms

Special protective clothing was issued to those who had to undertake dirty or heavy-duty work.

On entering the Luftwaffe, recruits were issued with a heavy-duty fatigue uniform as part of their full complement of uniform items and equipment. This was a two-piece outfit in oatmeal-coloured herringbone twill or blue-grey denim. Its purpose was to avoid unnecessary wear and tear on the Service uniform during field training, barrack square drill, fatigue and barrack duties, and equipment, weapons and vehicle cleaning.

As early as July 1936 the economic situation within the German Reich regarding the provision of clothing and the supply of raw materials made it necessary for the Luftwaffe authorities to issue instruc-

Above: A paratrooper (wearing the motorcyclists' rubberized protective coat) and a soldier struggle to extricate a motor-cycle and sidecar combination from the muck and mire that passes for a dirt road, somewhere on the Eastern Front, 24 November 1942. The heat of summer and the wheels and tank treads of passing vehicles turned these dirt roads into tracks many inches deep in fine choking dust. The autumn rains turned the dust into quagmires of thick, cloying mud that was extremely difficult to drive through. The cold of the Russian winters brought its own difficulties. Whilst it froze the mud hard, the surface was deeply rutted and usually under a heavy blanket of ice and snow. Only spring brought any relief.

tions[12] concerning the need to protect articles of clothing, and in particular cloth clothing. The Service Tunic was to be used for training purposes only when absolutely essential. Black drill combination overalls were to be worn by crews of anti-aircraft artillery units. However, the authorities were cognisant of the Luftwaffe's image, and on occasions when troops were in the public eye they were to wear the Service tunic (Tuchrock), as laid down in *Anzugordnung für die Luftwaffe (LAO)* L.Dv, 422, section B, for the appropriate service they were undertaking. On manoeuvres, when marching, and when journeying in lorries through a populated area, the cloth uniform was always to be worn.

During the war years the two-piece fatigue uniform was also worn by troops when clearing rubble from bomb sites and sometimes, usually during summer months, by crews manning anti-aircraft batteries. Because of their light colouring these garments were unsuitable for ground combat.

Two-piece suits and one-piece overalls, both in dark blue-grey denim and black drill material, were also issued for troops who performed dirty and oily tasks, such as aircraft and vehicle mechanics, armourers and workshop personnel.

Insignia of rank was worn on all of these fatigue and protective work garments. These are fully described and illustrated on page 131.

The Reed-Green Two-Piece Denim Suit

In September 1943 it was announced[13] that suits of reed-green denim were to be introduced for the duration of the war. They consisted of a jacket and trousers of the same cut and manufacture as those used within the Army. This was undoubtedly an economy measure. By 1943 it was considered unnecessary for Luftwaffe personnel to wear blue-grey or cream coloured fatigues when they could quite easily wear the same-coloured fatigues as worn by other ground forces. The manufacturing and supplying of a single type of garment rather than a variety of different outfits made more sense, and being of a universal reed-green colour it had better concealment qualities than the lighter-coloured fatigues supplied hitherto. This last aspect was an important consideration in light of the number of Luftwaffe Fields Divisions that had been raised and were required to be equipped and supplied with uniforms suitable for ground combat.

Whilst it was of the same pattern as that worn in the Army, the reed-green jacket had a collar very similar in cut to the one used on the Luftwaffe Fliegerbluse. The trousers were also patterned on those worn in the Army, and had a built-in waist belt.

Officers and Beamte Officials of officer rank wore their normal pattern of shoulder-straps with the reed-green tunic, but the braiding of the straps was in matt-grey artificial silk rather than the standard silver-aluminium braiding. Normal arm-of-service colours were used.

NCOs and Men wore detachable shoulder-straps made from reed-green cloth, piped in the appropriate arm-of-service colour. Those straps worn by NCOs of Unteroffizier rank and above had shoulder-strap braiding in blue-grey artificial silk. This same colour and quality of 'Litzen' was worn as a 'chevron' on the leading edge of, and along the front portion to, the lower edge of the collar. When worn, cuff stripes were of the same braiding. Those soldiers entitled to wear arm rank chevrons also had blue-grey artificial silk braiding sewn to a triangular backing of reed-green denim.

No collar patches were worn on this jacket. The Luftwaffe national emblem was worn on the reed-green jacket in the same position as on the Tuchrock/Waffenrock. The eagle, however, was worked on to a base of reed-green material. Normal-pattern trade badges in blue-grey cloth were to be worn on the tunic.

The new reed-green denim suit was issued to all NCOs and Men, while those persons who had to clothe themselves were required to purchase it. The jacket cost 13.11 RM, and the trousers 9.43 RM.

The denim tunics and trousers of the former pattern, as well as jackets and trousers in light summer clothing, were to be withdrawn and returned to the Luftwaffe Clothing Department when the reed-green suits were issued. There were no special regulations governing their disposal.

Rank Insignia for use on Luftwaffe Protective Garments

From May 1935 to December 1937 a series of important instructions were issued covering the wearing of various types of rank insignia on a variety of protective garments. The first of these instructions was

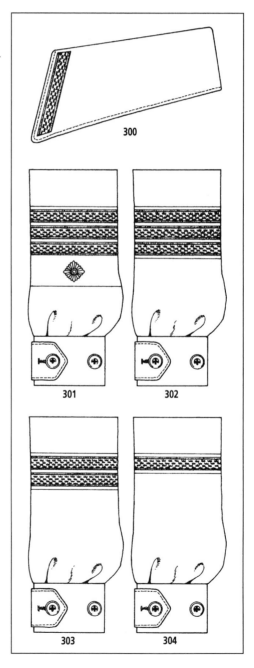

Rank Insignia for the blue-grey rubberized Motor-Cycle Protective Coat.
300 Collar insignia for all NCOs.
301 Cuff insignia for the rank of Stabsfeldwebel.
302 Oberfeldwebel and Oberwachtmeister in Troop Service, plus, at a later date, the ranks of Hauptfeldwebel and Hauptwachtmeister.
303 Oberfeldwebel and Oberwachtmeister.
304 Feldwebel and Wachtmeister.

Right: A youthful member of a gun crew wearing the one-piece black overalls, August 1944.

touched on in Volume 1933–40, but to show their full extent they are given here in their chronological order of issue.

On 27 May 1935 there were issued the first of a number of instructions[14] dealing with the subject of the wearing of service rank insignia by Luftwaffe personnel on a) the Denim Tunic, b) the Combination Overalls of black drill material, both lined and unlined, and c) the Protective Coat of blue-

grey rubberized material for use by motor-cyclists.

On the Denim Tunic and on the Combination Overalls of black drill material, both lined and unlined, the following insignia was to be worn:

All NCOs were distinguished by wearing a strip of 1cm-wide grey Luftwaffe rank braid down the front edge and around the base of their collar, 0.3cm from the edge (Fig. 306).

Far right:
305 The Combination Overalls of black drill material both lined and unlined, here shown with rank insignia for a Stabs-feldwebel or Stabswachtmeister.

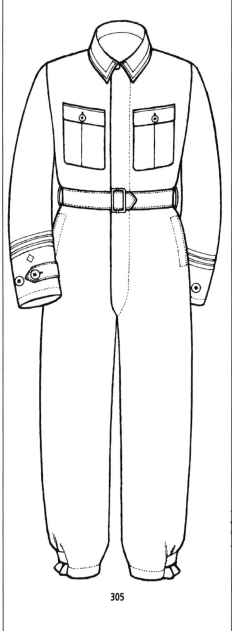

305

Left: Two armourers, both wearing the one-piece black fatigue overalls, load machine-gun ammunition into saddle and cylinder drums. The man in the background, being an NCO, wears braiding around his collar.

Below: A cheerful group of ground mechanics, all wearing the Luftwaffe Fliegermütze with the exception of the pipe-smoking man in the centre, who wears the black fatigue cap, part of the black fatigue uniform. Note that only the eagle and swastika, without the cockade emblem, was worn on the front of this cap.

Rank Insignia for the Denim Tunic and the Combination Overalls of black drill material both lined and unlined.

306 Collar insignia for all NCOs.

307 Cuff insignia for the rank of Stabsfeldwebel.

308 Oberfeldwebel and Oberwachtmeister in Troop Service, plus, at a later date, the ranks of Hauptfeldwebel and Hauptwachtmeister.

309 Oberfeldwebel and Oberwachtmeister.

310 Feldwebel and Wachtmeister.

311 Hauptgefreiter.

312 Obergefreiter.

313 Gefreiter.

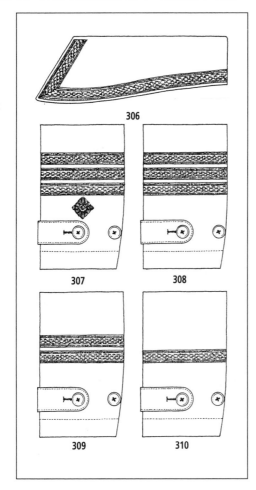

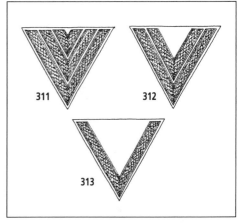

In addition, the following individual NCO ranks were marked: An Oberfeldwebel and Oberwachtmeister who was in Troop Service wore three sleeve rings of 1cm-wide Luftwaffe rank braiding on both forearms, with 0.5cm between each ring and with the bottom edge of the lower ring 10cm from the end of the cuff (Fig. 308). This particular distinction was also extended to those persons who held the appointment of Hauptfeldwebel and Hauptwachtmeister when these positions were introduced much later.

An Oberfeldwebel and Oberwachtmeister wore two sleeve rings of the same size on each forearm, quality and position as before (Fig. 309).

Right: The one-piece off-white fatigue uniform, worn by light-anti-aircraft gunners of the Luftwaffe protecting a motorized unit of the Waffen-SS advancing in Yugoslavia, 9 April 1941.

A Feldwebel and Wachtmeister wore single sleeve rings, 0.5cm wide and 10cm from the bottom edge of each cuff (Fig. 310).

Persons holding the rank of Unterfeldwebel and Unterwachtmeister displayed only the collar braid as an indication of their rank.

A Gefreiter wore a single arm chevron (Fig. 313), an Obergefreiter a double arm chevron (Fig. 312), and a Hauptgefreiter a triple chevron badge (Fig. 311). They were all positioned, point down, on the centre of the left upper arm. All chevrons were made of grey cotton braid with a distinctive pattern (not silver-aluminium). They were 1cm wide and had an outer edge length of 8cm and an inner angle of 60°. When worn as a double or triple

chevron badge, the chevrons were set 0.2cm apart.

(Fig. 307 shows the rank distinction as worn by a Stabsfeldwebel and Stabswachtmeister. These ranks were introduced later, long after the issuing of the 1935 orders, and their insignia was eventually added to the existing insignia.)

Officers were also distinguished when wearing the black drill Combination Overalls by displaying a form of insignia. All officers were instructed to wear a single 1cm-wide cuff-band of white material, previously introduced by L.D. Nr. 1667/33 dated 13 January 1934. The 1935 instructions do not state the precise position on the Overalls for this cuff-band, nor whether they were worn as a pair of bands.

Above: Three members of a Hamburg Flak battery photographed on the day they were presented with the Iron Cross 1st Class, August 1943 (see also photographs on pages 290 to 294). The very dirty off-white, one-piece fatigues worn by the gunner on the right contrast with the freshly laundered off-white fatigue jacket worn by some of the men in the background.

Above: Men of a Stuka squadron unload bombs from a lorry in readiness for arming their aircraft, August 1943.

On the Motor-Cycle Protective coat of blue-grey rubberized material, the rank insignia as described above was worn by all the ranks mentioned with just two exceptions:

All NCOs, regardless of individual rank, were distinguished from Other Ranks and officers by wearing a short length of Luftwaffe-pattern, dull-grey rank braiding along both leading edges to the collar of the Motor Cycle Coat (Fig. 306). The second exception was the position of the various sleeve rings. Unlike the two previous garments, the rings worn on the Motor-Cycle Coat were positioned on both forearms 15cm from the bottom of the cuffs. Because the coat was a rubberized waterproof garment, all insignia were required to be stuck to the surface of the coat with a rubber adhesive solution, and not stitched. According to the 1935 instructions, officers were distinguished when wearing the Motor-Cycle Coat by wearing two 1cm-wide and 15cm-long stripes of braid stuck to each arm 12cm from the point of the shoulder.

Rank Insignia for Flight Clothing

On 6 January 1936 further instructions were promulgated (issued December 1935)[15] setting out precise details for the wearing of new-style rank insignia on the three types of issue flight clothing, as well as on other protective garments. The badges, which took the form of stylized wings worn separately, in combination, or with one or more narrow rectangular bars, were positioned in the centre of both upper arms, midway between the elbow and the shoulder seam on the following garments: the Protective Flight Combination Clothing for Summer, the Protective Flight Combination Clothing for use over Land during Winter, the Protective Flight Combination Clothing for use over Sea during Winter, the Protective Coat in grey twill, formerly

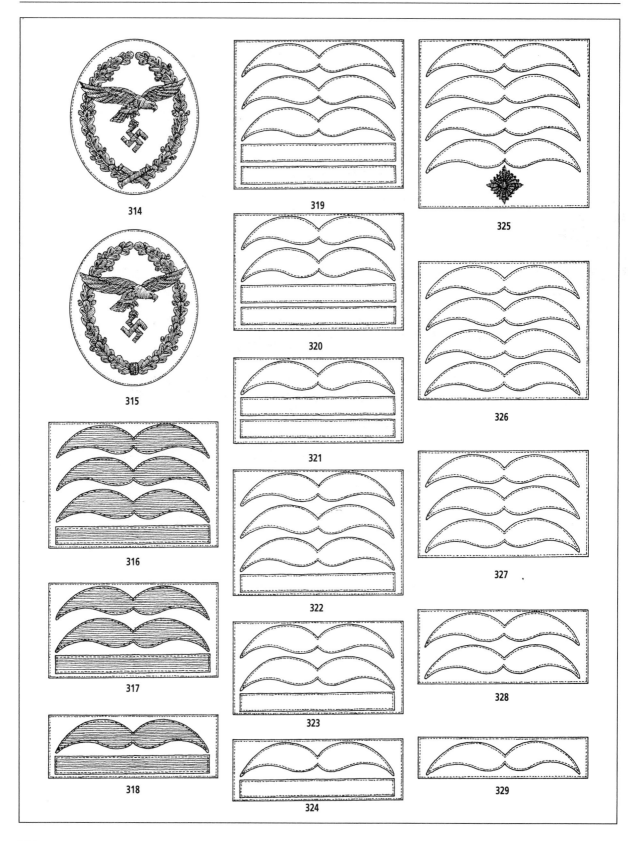

314

315

316

317

318

319

320

321

322

323

324

325

326

327

328

329

Rank Insignia for Flight Clothing, Protective Clothing, Coats and other Protective Garments.

314 Generalfeldmarshall.
315 Generaloberst.
316 General der Flieger, etc.
317 Generalleutnant.
318 Generalmajor.
319 Oberst.
320 Oberstleutnant.
321 Major.
322 Hauptmann.
323 Oberleutnant.
324 Leutnant.
325 Stabsfeldwebel.
326 Oberfeldwebel, Hauptfeldwebel and Oberfähnrich.
327 Feldwebel.
328 Unterfeldwebel and Fähnrich.
329 Unteroffizier

Right: Luftwaffe rank insignia worn on the flight jerkin by Hauptmann (later Major) Wilhelm Mortiz (left) and on an animal-skin coat worn by Major (later Oberst) Walther Dahl, Knight's Cross holder (11 March 1944), on the right. The badge for the Captain is in white on navy blue backing, one of the two standard-issue types of flight clothing rank badges. The badge worn by Major Dahl appears to be of a different colouring. This photograph was taken on 8 July 1944, ten days before Wilhelm Motitz was awarded the Knight's Cross. It also seems from the date of this photograph that Major Dahl is addressing the men of a special wing formed to combat the USAAF day bombers, of which he was appointed Kommodore. Known as JG zbV, and later redesignated JG 300, it had two 'Ram Groups' attached. On 26 January 1945 Dahl was appointed Inspekteur der Tagjäger (Inspector of Day Fighters).

referred to as the Denim Tunic, combination Fatigue Clothing (previously referred to as Combination Overalls) in black drill material, both lined and unlined, Motoring Protective Coat in blue-grey rubberized material, Anti-Gas clothing, Anti-Acid clothing, Rubber Clothing and Training Track Suits.

The chart of special rank insignia opposite shows the full extent of the development of this insignia. The original range of badges introduced in 1936 extended only up to the rank of General der Flieger etc. (Fig. 316), and did not include the item for wear by persons with the rank of Stabs-

feldwebel (Fig. 325). This rank, together with that of Generaloberst (Fig. 315) and Generalfeldmarshall (Fig. 314) was introduced when these ranks were created at a later date.

The dimensions of the individual badges were given as 10cm wide and, in the case of the stylized wings, 2cm high at their highest point. The bars, also 10cm wide, were 1cm high. When worn in combination, each set of wings or wings and bars were set 0.5cm apart and sewn on a rectangle of backing material of an appropriate size. This backing material was in a tan cloth, similar to the light sandy-coloured materi-

Left: Oberstleutnant Werner Mölders presents the Iron Cross 1st Class to a senior NCO from his squadron. On his flight jerkin Mölders wears the flight clothing rank insignia that had white 'wings' and 'bars' on a light tan backing.

al of the Protective Flight Clothing Combination for summer wear, and was for wear on that particular garment.

Rank badges worn on the other two flight protective suits were backed with dark blue cloth. The two most senior ranks had designs embroidered on to an appropriately coloured oval backing. Badges that were worn on anti-gas, anti-acid or rubber protective garments were stuck to the material with a special adhesive.

Items 314 and 315 were embroidered in gold-coloured threads, item 314 having the addition of a pair of crossed silver batons at the base of the wreath of oakleaves.

Items 316 to 318 were produced from yellow cloth, and the remaining items, 319 to 329, were of white cloth. The rank star at the base of item 325 was embroidered in white threads.

The January 1936 instructions introducing these badges of rank also set out precise details regarding who was to wear these badges and on what garments. Items 316 to 324 and 326 to 329 were for wear on the three patterns of Flight Protective Clothing, the Protective Coat in grey material, the Anti-Gas and Anti-Acid clothing and the Sports Track Suit by all ranks from General der Flieger, etc., to Unteroffizier.

Luftwaffe Engineer Corps and Navigational Corps Flight Clothing Rank Insignia, circa 2 November 1940 to 1945.

330 Generalleutnant (Ing.).
331 Generalmajor (Ing.).
332 Oberst (Ing.).
333 Obersleutnant (Ing.).
334 Major (Ing.).
335 Hauptmann (Ing.).
336 Oberleutnant (Ing.).
337 Leutnant (Ing.).

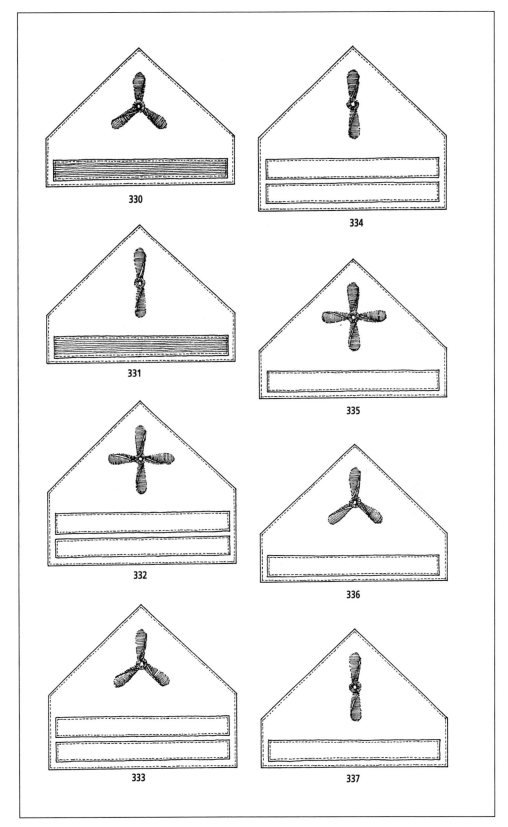

330

334

331

335

332

336

333

337

When worn on the Fatigue Clothing (Combination) in black drill material, both lined and unlined, and on the Motoring Protective coat in blue-grey rubberized material, only the officers' insignia was to be used (Items 314 to 324). This was because other forms of rank insignia had been authorised for the NCO ranks (see Volume 1933–40, page 240). Wartime economy measures made it necessary to reduce the two badges worn on the Motoring Protective Coat by officers to a single badge worn on the left upper arm only. On the rubber clothing only the insignia for NCOs was displayed (Items 326 to 329), presumably because officers were not expected to use this type of garment.

It was common practice, especially during the war years, for officers of the Luftwaffe to use the rank badges on other semi-official garments such as the variety of flight jerkins and animal-skin coats. The same system of badges was also used on the Parachute Jump Smock, the Luftwaffe Field Division camouflage jackets, and, to a limited degree, on the tropical shirt.

In December 1937 additional instructions were issued[16] setting out the regulations for the wearing of a new range of rank badges on all the various forms of protective garments, as previously listed, by members of the Luftwaffe Corps of Engineers.

In place of the double stylized wing badges, Engineer Corps members wore badges featuring four-, three- or two-bladed propellers worn above one or two narrow rectangular strips in the following manner:

A three-bladed propeller in yellow above a single yellow strip was worn by the rank of Leitender-Flieger-Chiefingenieur (Fig. 330).

A two-bladed propeller in yellow set above a single yellow strip was worn by the rank of Flieger-Chefingenieur (Fig. 331).

A white four-bladed propeller above two white strips denoted the rank of Flieger-Hauptstabsingenieur (Fig. 332).

A white three-bladed propeller set above double white strips was worn by a Flieger-Oberstabsingenieur (Fig. 333).

Luftwaffe Administrative Officials' Flight Clothing Rank Insignia.
The terms captioning these illustrations represent just a single type appointment per set of insignia. Rank terms shown in parentheses are the equivalent rank in the Luftwaffe proper. (For a complete list of Administrative Official types and terms of appointment see Volume 1933–40, page 124.)

338 Ministerialdirektor (Generalleutnant).
339 Ministerialdirigent (Generalmajor).
340 Ministerialrat (Oberst).
341 Oberregierungsrat (Oberstleutnant).
342 Regierungsrat (Major).
343 Oberregierungsinspektor (Hauptmann).
344 Regierungsinspektor (Oberleutnant).
345 Regierungssekretär (Leutnant).

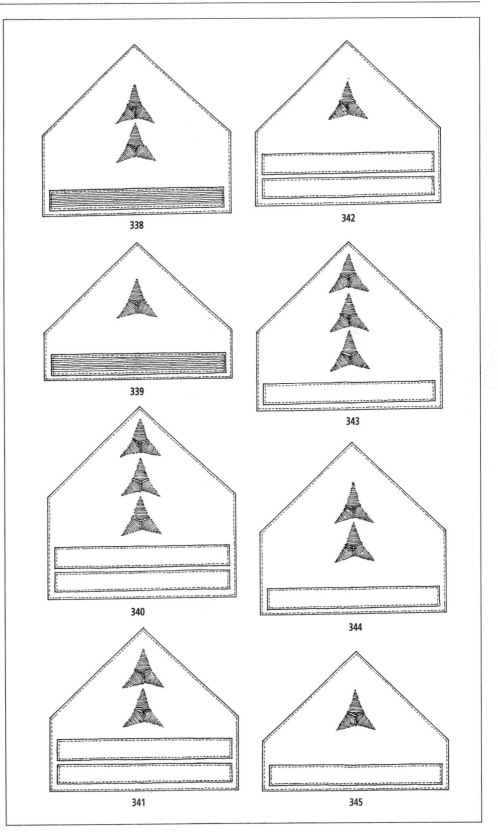

338

342

339

343

340

344

341

345

A two-bladed propeller in white above two white strips denoted the rank of Flieger-Stabsingenieur (Fig. 334).

A white four-bladed propeller above a single white strip was worn by a Flieger-Hauptingenieur (Fig. 335).

A white 3-bladed propeller above a white single white strip was worn by Flieger-Oberingenieur (Fig. 336).

The badge of the lowest Engineer Corps rank, Flieger-Ingenieur, was a white two-bladed propeller above a single white strip (Fig. 337).

The dimensions of the three types of propeller were given as 6cm high for the two-bladed type, 4.5cm high by 5.5cm wide for the three-bladed type, and 6cm high by 6cm wide for the four-blader. The horizontal strips were 10cm long by 1cm high. Each badge was set on a triangular-pointed patch of material of the same quality as previously described for the Flight Suit insignia worn by Luftwaffe personnel.

It should be remembered that these instructions were issued in 1937, when the above Engineer Corps ranks pertained. Early in 1940 these rank terms changed, and they changed again in November of the same year.

The rank terms used from 1935 to 1940 were:

Leitender Flieger-Chefingenieur
Flieger-Chefingenieur
Flieger-Hauptstabsingenieur

Flieger-Oberstabsingenieur
Flieger-Stabsingenieur
Flieger-Hauptingenieur
Flieger-Oberingenieur
Flieger-Ingenieur

In early 1940 the rank terms changed to the following:

Flieger-Generalstabsingenieur
Flieger-Generalingenieur
Flieger-Oberstingenieur
Flieger-Oberstabsingenieur
Flieger-Stabsingenieur
Flieger-Hauptingenieur
Flieger-Oberingenieur
Flieger-Ingenieur

On 2 November 1940 the ranks were changed for the third and final time, and for the duration of the war they were as follows:

Generalleutnant (Ing.)
Generalmajor (Ing.)
Oberst (Ing.)
Oberstleutnant (Ing.)
Major (Ing.)
Hauptmann (Ing.)
Oberleutnant (Ing.)
Leutnant (Ing.)

These changes in rank terms in no way altered the pattern of rank insignia worn on protective clothing. The badges were worn on both upper arms of the various garments until 4 August 1942 when, owing to economic measures, it was ordered that only one badge need be worn, on the left upper arm.

Regiment 'General Goring': Wartime Development.

Of all the units in existence from 1935 to 1945, the formation that bore the title Regiment 'General Göring' was arguably the fastest growing and probably the most complex of all Luftwaffe formations.

As is the case with the Regiment's pre-war development, to understand the changes of insignia and styles of dress brought into use during the war years, it is necessary to cover in broad outline the wartime development of the Regiment.

Established on 23 February 1933 as a Special Police Battalion, 'Polizeiabteilung Wecke' underwent various changes in its structure and a number of changes in its title. By 1 April 1935 it was known as Regiment 'General Göring' and on 1 October of that year it was officially incorporated into the Luftwaffe. The bulk of the Regiment spent the first months of the war in Germany, and not until the spring of 1940 were units engaged on active service, in the Norwegian Campaign. The main body of the Regiment took part in the assault on Belgium on 10 May 1940 and saw service during the invasion of the Netherlands. After the fall of France in June 1940 the Regiment was stationed on the Channel coast for a while, and later assigned to anti-aircraft duties around Paris. Later in 1940 the Regiment returned to Germany, where it took part in the air defence of Berlin until called upon to take part in the opening stages of the invasion of Russia in June 1941. By then it had been upgraded to a motorized regiment and was known as Regiment (mot) 'Hermann Göring'. The summer of 1942 saw the Regiment enlarged and on 15 July 1942 it was redesignated Brigade 'Hermann Göring'. The brigade consisted of one Rifle (Schützen) Regiment and one Anti-Aircraft Artillery (Flak) Regiment. The rank and file of these two regiments continued to wear their distinctive white collar patches edged in rifle-green and bright red respectively.

Personnel of this new unit continued to wear their former 'General Göring' formation cuff-title until late August 1942, this being the latest date for the change to the new cuff-title 'Hermann Göring', initially in Gothic lettering, later in block lettering.[17] (See p. 97 for further details.)

In October 1942 the Brigade was once more enlarged, this time to divisional strength. Again it was retitled as Division 'Hermann Göring'. The first pattern of 'Hermann Göring' formation cuff-title was replaced by a formation title with the Division's name in block letters.

Extensive changes in the arm-of-service colours worn within the Division were brought into effect by an Order dated 4 January 1943.[18]

While officers of the formation continued to wear their distinctive white collar patches edged in twisted silver cord, NCOs and other ranks were issued with new sets of collar patches. These were also of white cloth, but edged in a variety of colours according to their arm-of-service. Their blue-grey cloth shoulder-straps were without exception piped white. Officers had white underlay to their shoulder-straps (see p. 55). This range of insignia was shortlived, however, for in April 1943[19] a further complete change of insignia was undertaken. The coloured edging to the collar patches worn by the rank and file was done away with and all personnel wore white collar patches (officers' edged with silver twisted cording) and the shoulder-straps of all ranks displayed their various arm-of-service colours, underlay for officers and piping for NCOs and other ranks. Both the 4 January and 2 April 1943 insignia introductions are set out in full on pp.55 and 56.

This was the last change in distinctive insignia associated with this formation.

However, the Division was converted to an armoured division on 21 May 1943 with the title Panzer-Division 'Hermann Göring'. In February 1944 it was retitled Fallschirm-Panzer-Division 'Hermann Göring' and finally, on 1 October 1944, it was upgraded to a Parachute Armoured Corps (in all probability not a full-strength corps) and entitled Fallschirm-Panzer-Korps 'Hermann Göring'.

All personnel were issued with and wore regular Luftwaffe uniforms. When serving in hot climates they wore tropical uniforms. Crews of armoured fighting vehicles serving in temperate climates wore the distinctive black two-piece uniform normally associated with the crews of Army AFVs,

Below: Troops of the Regiment 'General Göring' parade along a street of an unidentified French town. Both the black panzer uniform and the blue-grey Luftwaffe uniform are in evidence.

Right: Field Post being passed out to the men of a 'General Göring' detachment. This shows an interesting mix of the black panzer uniform, blue-grey Luftwaffe garments and the Waffen-SS-pattern camouflage smocks.

with Luftwaffe insignia, breast eagle, collar patches, shoulder-straps and formation cuff-titles. Troops manning the 'Hermann Göring' tank destroyers and self-propelled assault guns wore the Army pattern of special field-grey uniform but with the addition of Luftwaffe and Hermann Göring Divisional insignia.

For full details of these items of insignia as well as the uniforms themselves see p.144 and below.

A limited number of Division 'Hermann Göring' personnel were issued with camouflage smocks and steel helmet covers of the same pattern as used within the Waffen-SS (see p. 228). They also wore heavy duty, padded and reversible winter uniforms, and camouflaged field smocks of the typed used extensively by troops of the Luftwaffe Field Divisions.

Details of all these items can be found elsewhere in this book under their appropriate headings.

The Special Black Panzer Uniform for Crew Members of Armoured Vehicles of the Luftwaffe

The uniform chosen as the Service Dress for Luftwaffe members of armoured fight-ing vehicles from the Regiment 'General Göring' and later Division 'Hermann Göring' was the special black Panzer Uniform as worn within the German Army. It consisted of a short black double-breasted jacket, worn with a mouse-grey collar-attached shirt and black neck tie and long black trousers (Fig. 346).

The jacket was normally worn open at the neck, with the two top buttons undone in order to fold back the wide lapels. When it was worn in this fashion, the mouse-grey shirt and black tie were visible. During cold weather the jacket's lapels could be folded across the wearer's chest and buttoned closed to afford a certain amount of additional frontal warmth.

The jacket was designed so that few buttons were worn on the outside of the coat and there were no external pockets. With the exception of the two small black horn buttons positioned one above the other on the far right side of the chest, which were intended to secure the left lapel when the jacket was worn closed up at the neck, and the two blue-grey metal buttons used to secure the shoulder straps, no other buttons were visible on the outside. This lack of external buttons, pockets and flaps, coupled with the tight fit of the jacket, facilitated the entering and leaving of the confined interiors of armoured vehicles. The large buttons used on the inside of the double-breasted, fly-fronted jacket were made of dark blue-grey or black horn.

The special black cloth trousers were of the same cut and design for all ranks. The full-length trousers had a built-in waist-belt fastened with a two-pronged buckle. The two side pockets, the single rear hip pocket and the small 'fob pocket' all had button-down pocket flaps. The ends of the legs were sharply tapered and were worn gathered and tied around the tops of the short black leather lace-up ankle boots or marching boots, giving the trousers a 'bagged' loose appearance over the ankles of the boots.

The insignia worn on the Jacket was a mixture of Luftwaffe and Army Panzer items, as follows.

1. The national emblem, worn over the right breast, was the standard-pattern Luftwaffe breast eagle and swastika. However, the design – in grey cotton threads for NCOs and men and silver-aluminium bullion for Officers – was initially worked on to a backing of blue-grey cloth, although later these emblems were produced with a black cloth backing.

2. The collar of the jacket was known to have been piped white, although contemporary photographs, some of which are reproduced here, show the majority of personnel wearing the Panzer jacket without piping to the collar.

3. Collar patches worn on this black uniform were of two types:

(a) Patches of the type, size and shape normally found on the Army Panzer Uniform. They were of black cloth piped white (as opposed to the Army's pink Waffenfarbe), and bore a white-metal Panzer skull (Fig. 347). These were worn by members of the Panzer Regiments.

(b) All-white patches, unpiped and of similar shape and size to normal Luftwaffe collar patches, bearing a white-metal Panzer skull (Fig. 348). These were worn by members of Panzerjäger abteilung (anti-tank detachments).

As with Army Panzer troops, the practice existed within the Luftwaffe Panzer regiment whereby, in place of normal collar

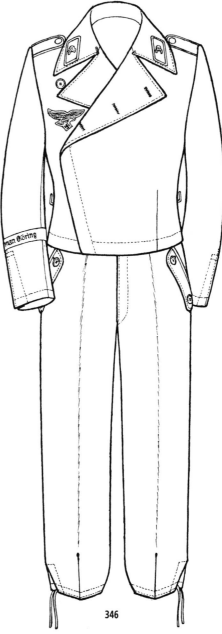

346

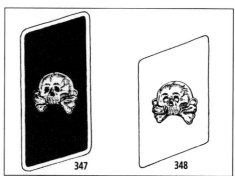

347 **348**

346 The Special Uniforms for crews of Armoured Fighting Vehicles and for Self-Propelled Assault Gun and Tank Destroyer Units. These garments were manufactured in black material for wear by troops of armoured vehicles of Division 'Hermann Göring' and in field-grey for the Divisions' artillery troops operating enclosed armoured self-propelled assault guns, tank-destroyer and armoured reconnaissance vehicles.

347 Collar patch for Panzer troops from Division' Hermann Göring'.
348 Collar patch for troops from the Anti-Tank Detachments of the Division' Hermann Göring'. The distinctive Death's Head collar patch associated with German Army Panzer Units was 'borrowed' by the Luftwaffe and adapted to their needs.

Right: RKT Karl Rossmann, Regiment 'General Göring'. Rossmann continued to wear the white piping to the collar of his Panzer uniform long after this distinction was abolished.

patches, only the white-metal Death's head was worn, mounted directly into each collar of the Jacket.

4. The shoulder-straps for men and NCOs were made from black cloth and, where appropriate, had NCO rank braiding of Luftwaffe patterning (see page 62). Officers insignia was of the standard pattern. Both the piping to the NCOs/Mens shoulder-straps and the underlay to the officers straps was white.

5. Those senior privates entitled to rank chevrons (see page 131) wore these on the left upper arm. The Luftwaffe patterned braiding was mounted on black material before being sewn to the sleeve.

6. Cuff titles of the appropriate type were worn on the right forearm. This subject is covered in the section devoted to Luftwaffe cuff titles (see page 97).

The head-dress worn with the special uniform varied. As early as April 1938, members of the Panzer-Späh-Zug from the Regiment 'General Göring' were issued with the black Panzer Beret (Schutzmütze) with Luftwaffe insignia. This type of head-dress was discontinued in January 1941. Crew members were issued with a black version of the Fliegermütze, and later still with the black version of the M43 Replacement Flight Cap, the Einheitsfliegermütze (for

further details see page 112, under 'Luftwaffe Head-dress').

It was permissible for the troops to wear the regulation pattern Luftwaffe Uniform Peaked Cap (Schirmmütze) with the Special Panzer Uniform, and steel helmets were frequently worn, both out of necessity and for parade purposes.

During periods of cold weather the crews of these armoured vehicles wore the reversible winter uniform (see page 229). The Luftwaffe blue-grey greatcoat was also worn with the black Panzer uniform (see opposite page).

The Special Field-Grey Uniform for Luftwaffe crews of Tank Destroyer and Self-Propelled Assault Gun Units of Division 'Hermann Göring'

This uniform, introduced in 1944, was of a similar design to the Special Black Panzer Uniform described above, but manufactured from field-grey material and later blue-grey cloth (actually the field-grey uniform was dyed blue-grey).

The insignia worn on the Jacket was the same as that used on the Panzer Jacket, except that the background material for the breast eagle and rank chevrons, where worn, was of field-grey or blue-grey cloth to match the fabric of the respective Jacket.

5. PROTECTIVE AND SPECIALIST CLOTHING

Fying Suits

Experience gained during the Great War enabled the Luftwaffe Clothing Authorities to design, manufacture and supply all German air crews with standardised protective flying suits for wear when undertaking military flights.

Pre-war there were three patterns of one-piece flying suits available, each designed to be worn for specific climatic conditions and for use over different terrain. These garments continued in service right up to the end of the war in Europe. During the war a two-piece flying suit, known as the 'Kanal Suit' was introduced and flight jerkins became popular.

All three of the protective flying suits were combination suits of the type that required the wearer to step into the legs of the garment before pulling on the upper part and then making fast the various zip fasteners, press studs and tabs.

It was essential that the flying suit was of a suitable fit for the individual airman. To achieve this the cut of the suit had to be

Below: After a seemingly successful flight, the crew of a Junkers Ju 88 remove their summer-weight flying uniforms.

such that when seated it was not constricting to the wearer and that the collar of the suit was not too tight. The suit had to be sufficiently loose fitting so as to be worn with comfort over any service uniform. The trouser legs of the flying suit had to be the same length as the trouser legs of the service uniform. This requirement was ascertained by the trousers part of the flying suit being pulled up moderately tight under the crotch and with the zip fasteners left undone the legs of the flying suit had to correspond in length to the service trousers.

The sleeves of the suit had to be wide enough at the armhole for the wearer to freely move his arms and clasp them together over his head without being restricted under his armpits. When standing at attention the length of the sleeves were required to reach down to the upper thumb joint. Finally the pockets of the flying suits were not to be covered by the straps of the parachute harness.

The Lightweight Tan-coloured Combination Flying Suit for flights during Summer over all types of terrain, Type K So/34. (Flieger - Schutzanzug für Sommer [Kombination], Baumuster K So/34).

This was manufactured from heavy-duty tan coloured cotton material, was raglan in style and had a built-in waist belt of brown leather. The garment weighed 1,700 grammes. It was normally worn with the unlined flying helmet of matching material. Rank insignia was worn on this suit, halfway between the shoulder seam and the elbow of both upper arms, the insignia usually stitched to a rectangle of material of the same quality and colour as the suit.

The Combination Flying Suit for use over Land in Winter, Type KW 1/33.(Flieger-Schutzanzug -Land-für Winter [Kombination], Baumuster KW 1/33).

Sometimes referred to as the 'Bulgarian Suit', this item was manufactured from blue-grey, impregnated heavy-weight material known as Velveton. It was a one-piece step-in garment, having a fleece lining and a black sheepskin covered collar. It was normally worn with the fleece-lined leather helmet and fleece-lined leather gauntlets. Fleece lined flying boots completed the outfit.

Rank insignia for all ranks from Unteroffizier to Generalfeldmarschall were stitched on a cloth base of coloured material matching the suit and worn in the same position as on the lightweight summer flying suit.

This garment weighed 5,000 grammes.

The Heavyweight Combination Flying Suit for Maritime Flying in Winter. (Flieger-Schutzanzug - See - für Winter [Kombination], Baumuster KW s/34).

This was a one-piece garment of dark brown calfskin leather lined with natural coloured sheep's fleece. The collar was faced with clipped sheepskin. It was worn with the fleece-lined leather flying helmet, gauntlets and heavy-duty flying boots. Rank insignia was stitched on to a base of thin, dark brown leather matching the suit

Below: The Lightweight Tan Summer Flying Suit for Flights over all types of terrain. Reichsmarschall Göring talks to aircrew members during a visit to an airfield somewhere on the Eastern Front, October 1942.

Above: The one-piece fleece-lined Flying Suit for Winter Flights over Water. The crew of a Heinkel He 111 after their safe return from a bombing raid on the Shetlands.

Right: A side view of the Winter Flying Suit.

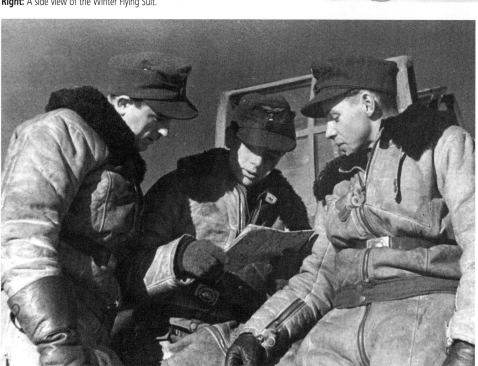

Left: The two-piece fur-lined flying suits introduced during the war, and worn by aircrews on both the Eastern and Western Fronts, are here being worn by fighter pilots operating from an airfield on the north-east front, February 1944.

Right: An interesting mixture of cold-weather garments. The airman on the left wears the one-piece fur-lined winter flying suit, while the man in the centre and the pilot on the right wear the fur-lined flight jerkin and the trousers of the 'Invasion Suit'. All are members of a Junkers Ju 87 dive-bomber squadron operating on the Eastern Front, February 1944.

Below: An NCO crew member of a Junkers Ju 52 removes his Winter Flying Suit. The thickness of the fleece lining is evident.

Below right: The Winter Flying Suit, showing the fur of the wide collar.

Left: The jacket of the two-piece fur-lined flying suit worn with the trousers from the so-called 'Invasion Suit'. A Stuka Unteroffizier pilot takes a hurried bowl of soup somewhere on the Eastern Front, January 1944.

and positioned on the arms as described for the lightweight summer suit. This item weight approximately 7,000 grammes.

The Electrically Heated Flying Suit.

This special suit was intended to be worn over the service uniform and beneath the flying suit. It was specifically designed to be worn for cold weather flying in order to supply additional warmth to the airman's hands, head and feet by means of electric-

ity drawn from the aircraft's own power supply passing through a series of insulated elements built into the fabric of the suit. A single, external lead from the back of the suit plugged into an electrical point inside the aircraft. The suit had drawbacks, not least of which being the restriction of movement caused by the plugged-in lead, and for this reason, despite the warmth it provided, it was not a popular garment to wear.

349 & 350 The Electrically Heated Flying Suit, front and rear views.

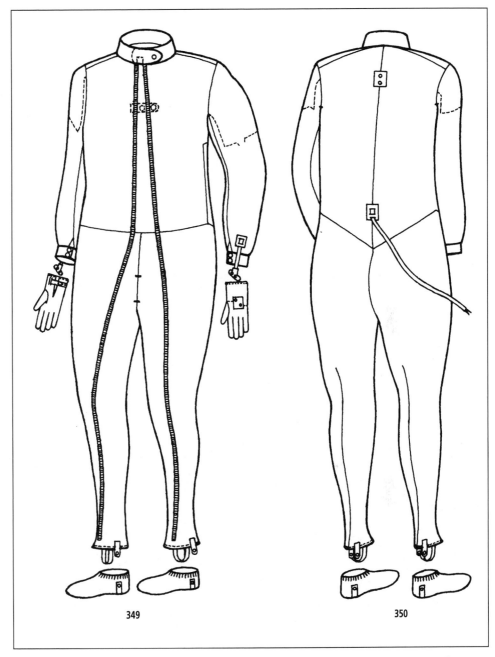

349

350

Flying Helmets

The use of flying helmets by aircrew dates back to the earliest days of flying. From the beginning of the First World War the open cockpits demanded some form of protection from the elements. Leather helmets that covered the head, from the upper brow to the nape of the neck covering the wearer's ears, were held in position on the head by an adjustable chin strap. These helmets gave the wearer a limited degree of protection from minor knocks and bumps, but were of little use for anything more severe.

The introduction of radio transmission for use in these early aircraft meant that the flying helmets were required to incorporate earphones and a microphone. However, advances in aircraft design brought about enclosed cockpits and cabins, so flying helmets were no longer needed to protect the occupants from wind and rain

151

and, to a lesser extent, cold weather. The Luftwaffe authorities and the manufacturers of flying helmets were aware that the helmet's principal purpose, therefore, was to support the earphones, microphone and, later still, the oxygen mask and flying goggles. It was realized that, to fulfil the requirements of a fully functional flying helmet, two important requirements had to be met:

1. The helmet had to guarantee a faultless fit without pressure on the ears, and must not hinder the free movement of the wearer.
2. It was imperative that the acoustic quality of the built-in microphone and earphones could provide a clearly audible and sufficiently loud transmission while at the same time suppressing most external sounds.

Left: A civilian test pilot at the controls of a Heinkel He 111 bomber. He wears the Luftwaffe-issue tan lightweight flying helmet.

The communication system incorporated in these helmets was used for radio transmission between aircraft, from air to ground and, in the case of aircraft with several crew members, for crew intercommunication. To use the system the pilot had to press a button on the control column or on the joystick grip.

During the decade from 1935 to 1945 the German Air Force made use of three basic types of flying helmet. These were:

a. Made of linen, for use during temperate summer. Most of these carried the designation 'S' for 'Sommer'.

b. Made of leather and lined with lambs wool fleece for winter weather, both with and without provision for radio communication. These were designated with a 'W' for 'Winter'.

c. A lightweight helmet formed from net panels for wear during hot weather or in tropical areas. These models carried the designation 'N' for 'Netz'.

There were a number of variations of these three types. All of these helmets, the

basic models and the variations, are described and illustrated below. Many of the features, regardless of the individual model, and many aspects of the wearing and use of these helmets, applied to all models. The first two helmets are therefore dealt with in some detail, and these details apply to the other helmets. All Luftwaffe flying helmets were issued with a machine-woven cloth label sewn to the inner lining, showing the name of the manufacturer, the supply number and the helmet model number. Additional information was sometimes provided.

Model FK 34 Flier's Helmet for Summer without Accommodation for Earphones (Flieger-Kopfhaube für Sommer ohne FT-Gerät, Baumuster FK 34)

This was manufactured from five sections of tan-coloured linen material lined with slate-grey synthetic satin, and was possibly the simplest of all of the Luftwaffe Flying Helmets. It was so designed that, when the helmet was correctly fitted, the edging to

Below: The right side of the summer flying helmet. Note the note pad fixed to the test pilot's right thigh.

Above left: A rear view of the lightweight flying helmet, showing the vertical leather straps that retained the elasticated strap of the flying goggles.

Above: The bomb aimer takes aim. A clear view of the crown to the lightweight summer flying helmet, showing the tunnel and the adjustable elasticated strap with its wire hook that supported the weight of the oxygen mask.

Left: The fleece-lined leather flying helmet – without earphones – worn by an aerial observer operating a camera from the rear cockpit of an early Luftwaffe biplane.

Right: Leutnant (later Major) Wick with a very young friend, photographed when he flew with 1/JG 53 in the summer of 1939; hence the net helmet. Helmut Wick was born on 5 August 1915 at Mannheim and, after Mölders and Galland, was the third most successful German fighter pilot until his presumed death in the autumn of 1940. On 28 November 1940, when he was Kommodore of JG 2 and had 56 aerial victories to his credit, his Bf 109 was severely damaged in aerial combat south of the Isle of Wight by Flying Officer John Charles Dundas of 609 Squadron. He was seen to parachute into the Channel, but his body was never recovered. Almost immediately after bringing down Wick, Dundas was attacked by Wick's No 2 and shot down after being chased out to sea. His body was never recovered.

the front part of the helmet was 1cm over the wearer's eyebrows, and it was tight enough to prevent air passing between the helmet and the wearer's head. Worn by air crews manning aircraft and gliders with no provision for radio, it weighed approximately 110g.

The FK 34 was secured by dual chin straps of calf leather. These crossed under the chin, and their respective lengths, which were passed through narrow retain-ing strips of leather, were fastened on either side of the helmet by a single-pronged metal buckle. The right-hand strap was 16cm long for helmets of 57cm headsize, and for helmets of 58cm head-size and over this strap was 2cm longer. On either side on the back of the helmet were two short leather straps. Each had a single snap fastener on its upper end which in effect provided two generous loops to accommodate the elasticated strap of the flying goggles. Positioned inside a tunnel on the crown and the front part of the helmet was a short strap of woven material fitted with a metal hook to support the weight of an oxygen mask.

Early-model Flier's Helmet for Summer with provision for earphones, the Model LKp S 53, and the Standard Flying Helmet for Summer with Provision for Earphones, Models LKp S 100 and LKp S 101 (Flieger-Kopfhaube für Sommer mit FT-Gerät)

The LKp S 53 was similar in appearance and manufacture to the FK 34, but incorporated a set of earphones and twin throat microphones. Unlike some other models, the external leather protections for the earphones on this helmet did not incorporate a notch or lip on the upper part of both coverings designed to stop the strap of the flying goggles from slipping off the leather mounds. It is believed that this helmet was renumbered as the Model LKp S 64.

The notches on the protective covering for the earphone housing were a feature of the next two models, the LKp S 100 and the LKp S 101.

The early model and the two variants of the summer-weight flying helmet were made from tan-coloured linen material with an inner lining of slate-grey synthetic satin. The LKp S 53/LKp S 64 and the LKp S 100 had bakelite protective housings for the earphones, while the housings on the LKp S 101 were of moulded dark brown leather. The housings on all three variants were lined internally with lambswool pads around the leather covered aperture ring. These pads helped to spread the pressure on the sides of the wearer's head, and left a central space between the ears and the earphones free from obstruction.

On the backs of the helmets were two short leather straps with snap fasteners, designed to hold the elasticated strap of the flying goggles. When the goggles were pushed up on to the head, these retaining straps stopped the strap from slipping off the helmet. Also on the rear of the helmets, in the centre of the base edge next to the nape of the neck, was the entry point for the short length of microphone cable complete with a four-pin male coupling jack plug. When in use, this cable was plugged into the female half of the

plug with its 1.3m length of corresponding flexible four-core cable, two cores feeding the microphone and the other two the earphones.

In the event of an emergency exit from an aircraft, there was no need for the wearer to disconnect the jack plug. The cable would separate from the helmet with just 3kg of pulling force. However, it was considered advisable, if possible, to remove the helmet and oxygen mask before abandoning the aircraft, and to leave the whole system hanging in the cockpit.

The helmets were secured on the head by the usual dual chin straps. Each left

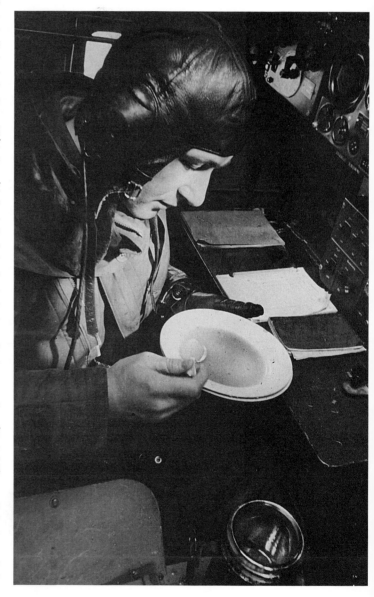

and right strap was adjusted and buckled to a single-pronged metal buckle on the opposite side of the helmet.

On the Model LKp S 64 the oxygen mask was simply attached by two hooks located on either side of the helmet. The throat microphone on the LKp 64 was of the built-in type, set inside the right-hand chin strap. The throat microphones on the LKp S 100 and LKp S 101 were mounted on two leather straps which were secured at the rear of the helmet. These straps, which contained the microphone cables, were adjustable on both sides of the neck by means of single-pronged metal buckles.

The straps met in the front of the neck and were fastened together by two snap fasteners.

The oxygen mask was secured to the flying helmet by having each end of its main supporting strap hooked on to a single hook on each side of the helmet, located just below the protective cover to the earphones. This ensured that the mask was pressed firmly over the nostrils and mouth, and it was further supported by suspension from a single, non-elasticated forehead strap attached to the strap and slide buckle fitted to the central crown of the helmet.

Left: The fleece-lined leather flying helmet – with earphones – worn by the wireless operator of a Focke-Wulf Condor long-range reconnaissance aircraft who is enjoying a mid-flight bowl of hot soup.

Right: The fleece-lined leather flying helmet with earphones.

Model LKp 54 Summer Flying Helmet with Accommodation for Earphones for use by Flight Commanders (Fliegerkopfhaube mit FT für Kommandanten — für Sommer)

This helmet was a variation of the Model LKp S 53 (above), its chief characteristic being that the two inputs of the earphones were connected to two different systems which allowed the wearer to receive two separate but different signals.

LKp W 54. The Luftwaffe Regulations, LDv 422, includes a description of the Flier's Helmet for Commanding Officers for Winter, given this designation.

Model K/33 Flier's Helmet for Winter without Accommodation for Earphones (Flieger-Kopfhaube für Winter ohne FT-Gerät)

Similar in construction to the FK 34, the summer-weight helmet without earphones, the Model K/33 helmet was made of dark brown goat's leather lined with lambswool. It was intended for wear during winter months and in cold climates by crew members who were not required to operate radio equipment, or by crews undergoing training. It had an average weight of 205g, and its official designation was 'K/33'.

Flier's Helmet for Winter with Accommodation for Earphones (Flieger-Kopfhaube für Winter mit FT-Gerät, Baumuster LKp W 53, LKp W 100 und LKp W 101)

Helmets with provision for both earphones and throat microphones were also provided for aircrew to wear during winter and in cold climates. A number of models existed, each with their own model number, but all were very similar in construction to the K/33 previously described.

The Model LKp W 100 was made of dark brown goat's leather with white lambswool lining. The earphone protective housings were of dark brown bakelite without the notch to prevent slippage of the goggles strap. Two snap-fastened leather straps located vertically at the rear of the helmet held the strap of the goggles in place. The helmet had twin leather chin straps attached left and right, the ends of which were fastened on either cheek of the helmet by a single-pronged metal buckle. The oxygen mask

was attached at three points on the helmet. A metal hook was located on each side just below the earphone housings, and a small triangular-shaped wire hook attached to a short length of adjustable woven strap was positioned on the brow of the helmet to support the weight of the mask. The openings for the earphones on the inside of the helmet were rimmed with a light-tan leather-covered metal plate, and were lined with lambswool to prevent undue pressure on the ears. The throat microphone was located on a single leather strap attached to an elasticated strap fastened to the left side of the helmet. In the corresponding position on the right side was an elastic strap with a single-pronged metal buckle. When buckled together on the right side of the neck, these two straps allowed an operationally correct and comfortable fit. The coupling for the microphone was the four-pole, break-type Model LKp W 100, which up to October 1937 bore the official Luftwaffe supply number Fl 31219.

The Model LKp W 101 was very similar in construction and appearance to the Model LKp W 100, but differed in having earphone housings covered externally in dark brown leather with a moulded notch for retaining the strap of the flying goggles. The oxygen mask was attached in the same manner as for the W 100. The forehead strap, which was anchored to the back of the crown of the helmet, was housed inside a flat 'tunnel' on the crown and was adjustable by means of a sliding metal buckle that ensured the correct support on the brow of the helmet for the non-elasticated, vertical supporting strap of the oxygen mask.

LKp N 101 Lightweight Netting Helmet (Netzkopfhaube LKp N 101).

This helmet was designed to be worn by pilots flying during summer months and in areas of hot tropical climate. Its purpose was to support the earphones, to accommodate the throat microphone and to accept the attachment of the oxygen mask. Because of its lightweight netting construction it afforded the wearer little or no head protection. It tended to be worn by pilots of fighter aircraft, since it was relatively easy to put on during a 'scramble'. The whole of the upper part, the crown of the helmet,

Right: In an effort to afford himself some form of head protection, the beam gunner of a Focke-Wulf FW 200 Condor long-range reconnaissance aircraft wears his Luftwaffe steel helmet.

and the neck at the rear were made from panels of dark brown cotton mesh netting. A band of dark brown leather traversed the brow, and was continued around the circumference by a cloth band. Dark-brown leather earphone housings were mounted on leather panels on either side of the helmet, and the protective covers to the earphones had moulded notches. A vertical leather strap, snap-fastened at its lower end, was positioned directly behind each earphone-housing mound on either side of the helmet to retain the strap of the flying goggles.

The throat microphones were located at the ends of two short leather straps. These were anchored at the nape of the neck and were adjustable for length around the throat by means of single-pronged metal buckles on either side of the neck straps. The two straps were fastened across the front of the throat by twin snap-fasteners (or sometimes a single fastener). A row of three small metal-rimmed holes on each side of the helmet, just in front of the lower portion of the earphone housing mounds, allowed a retaining stud to be screwed into one of three positions to serve as the anchor point for the two-point oxygen mask. Each end of the oxygen mask retaining strap had a shaped wire suspender hook which was hooked around these retaining studs. The left-hand wire hook had a short metal tab at right angles to the wire hook to enable the pilot easily to grip the hook at the end of the retaining strap and secure the mask across his face, or to undo the retaining strap before removing the mask.

Variants of the LKp N 101 model helmet had the addition of the usual third attachment point to support the oxygen mask and ensure a proper fit. Located on the crown of the netting helmet, this consisted of an adjustable strap and wire hook. The hook on the end of the vertical forehead strap attached to the upper edge of the rubber face mask was engaged in the wire hook on the helmet and, when correctly adjusted, supported the weight of the mask.

Protective Flying Helmet, Model SSK 90

On 8 May 1941 the Clothing Authorities announced[1] that flying personnel in active service units were to receive a special steel

Above: An aerial gunner wears his steel helmet back to front over his cloth flying helmet.

helmet as protection against small-calibre bullets and shell splinters. It would be worn over the normal flying helmet.

This oval-shaped helmet was constructed from overlapping armoured plates, 0.1cm-thick, of chrome nickel steel. It was covered in brown goats' leather on the outside, had foam rubber padding on the inside and was lined with brown cotton material.

The helmet had a distinctive shape, featuring a deep neckpiece and semi-circular cut-outs on each side to accommodate the earphones of whichever flying helmet was

351 A Model 1935 steel helmet specially adapted for wear by aircrew members requiring a measure of head protection. An example of this particular helmet is preserved at the Imperial War Museum, London. It is evident that the modification to the sides of the helmet were executed under local conditions. The sides have been heated and hammered out to form bulges large enough to accommodate the earphones of the flight helmet. The lining has been removed and extemporised neck and chin straps have been added.

being worn. For quick removal the upper front was fitted a grab pad (Anfasswulst, literally 'a grabbing hold of pad') which extended from just above the centre of the brow to the crown of the helmet. It was fitted with a snap-fastened chinstrap. The weight of the helmet was given as being about the same as the Model 1935 steel helmet.

It has been stated[A] that the helmet was unpopular because it was heavy and uncomfortable, and it saw only limited use. Being deemed 'unacceptable for service at the front' it was withdrawn from use on 26 May 1941. I have been unable to trace any order of that date, but evidently the helmet was not universally worn despite the claims for its protective qualities.

Development of Protective Helmets for Airmen

The medical authorities of the Sanitäts Versuchs -und Lehrabteilung der Luftwaffe (the Medical Experimental and Instruction Detachment of the Air Force) at Jüterbog concerned themselves with, among many other things, the problem of head injuries

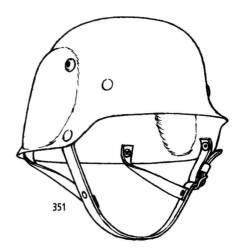

351

sustained by aircrews. The head was especially vulnerable to gunfire through cockpit windows, and in accidents was liable to strike the instrument panel or other hard surface, resulting in serious, if not fatal, injury.

The 'Fliegerstahlhelm'

A laminated steel helmet for airmen had been designed by the Von Diringshofen

Right: The special protective 'Fliegerstahlhelm' for Luftwaffe aircrews.

A. See page 321 of *'Headgear of Hitler's Germany' Vol. 1, Heer, Luftwaffe, Kriegsmarine.* by Jill Halcomb-Smith and Wilhelm P.B.R. Saris assisted by Otto Spronk.

Left and right: The special protective 'Fliegerstahlhelm' for Luftwaffe aircrews.

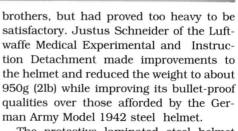

352 The special protective helmet for aircrew personnel, left side shown.

brothers, but had proved too heavy to be satisfactory. Justus Schneider of the Luftwaffe Medical Experimental and Instruction Detachment made improvements to the helmet and reduced the weight to about 950g (2lb) while improving its bullet-proof qualities over those afforded by the German Army Model 1942 steel helmet.

The protective laminated steel helmet was worn over the net-type flying helmet. It was fastened by a chinstrap fitted with a patent lock. Appropriate cut-outs were provided for earphones. The earpieces were of steel. The 'Fliegerstahlhelm' proved so satisfactory in service testing that in the winter of 1944/5 the medical authorities proposed its adoption. It was introduced in

352

several divisions towards the end of the war and satisfied all demands. With regard to accident protection it was superior to any non-rigid protective helmet, particularly the US Army Air Force crash helmet, by about 400 per cent. Further protection from shrapnel was afforded by splinter proof goggles.

Oxygen Masks

The oxygen mask was an essential item of flight equipment issued to all crew members who were required to operate in aircraft capable of high altitude flying. Its function was to provide an uninterrupted supply of oxygen to enable the wearer to

breath oxygen laden air when the ambient air supply was too rarefied to sustain life. It can be said that an oxygen mask consisted of a number of important, integrated parts: the oxygen which was provided from compressed bottles; the hose through which the oxygen was drawn; the valve within the hose which governed the flow in of oxygen and out of expelled air; the mask to which the hose was connected and which formed an air-tight fit to the wearers face; and finally the supporting straps which held the mask in place.

Considerable research was undertaken both before and during the war to perfect a satisfactory oxygen mask. The Luftwaffe introduced a number of different patterns of oxygen masks between 1934 and 1944, each one intended to be an improvement on the last or designed for specific aerial use.

The Model HM-5 and HM-15 Oxygen Masks

Pre-war Luftwaffe aircrews were equipped with either the Model HM-5 or HM-15 masks, the only difference between these two models being their size. Both types were produced in large quantities. The mask consisted essentially of the mask body, its T-shaped sealing frame and the attached soft chamois which made the mask warmer and softer to wear and, as it covered the chin and checks, also helped to protect the face from frost-bite. Each mask was provided with three straps; the head-strap which supported the weight of the mask and hose and the two side straps each with built-in steel wire spiral springs pressed the mask against the wearer's face. The harness supporting these straps was attached to the helmet. The connecting piece for the hose was attached to the mask body. At the back of this connection was the expiratory valve and in front was a re-inforcing rubber plate. Below the valve hung the hose, an elastic, flexible and cor-rugated tube (being corrugated prevented the tube from collapsing when bent). The hose had a total of 40 ridges with an exter-nal diameter of 30mm and an inner diam-eter of approximately 18mm. At the far end of this hose was attached the 'male' ele-ment of the quick-disconnect and the clothing clip.

The quick-disconnect, which had been in use before 1934, connected the hose from the oxygen system to the mask hose. It was designed and produced by the Drägerwerk of Lübeck and later by the Auergessellschaft, Berlin. The connection had to be fastened firmly enough to prevent unintentional disconnection, but loose enough to allow for quick manual or auto-matic disconnection in emergencies.

The greatest difficulty encountered with oxygen masks was the problem of icing with the consequent breathing of ambient air. The icing arose from condensation of the moisture contained in the expired air. During inspiration, the cold, dry oxygen passed from the system through the hose into the mask and then into the lungs of the airman. During expiration the warm, moist expired air flowed through the mask and the connecting piece and out through the expiratory valve. The expired air met the cold dry oxygen in the mask body and in the upper part of the hose with the result that the moisture in the expired air condensed and froze within the hose. Reg-ulations allowed for the quick-disconnect to be disengaged from time to time and the ice kneaded out of the hose. However, with this procedure it was possible for small pieces of ice to remain trapped in the expi-ratory valve during the expiratory phase, thereby freezing the valve in the open posi-tion. This resulted in the breathing in of ambient air and hypoxia. In order to detect such icing, it was necessary periodically for the wearer to occlude the mask hose and inspire deeply. He should have been unable to inhale either oxygen or air. Any entrance of air gave proof that the expira-

Below: The observer of a reconnaissance aircraft wears the type of oxygen mask worn with either the light-weight summer helmet or the fleece-lined leather winter helmet.

points. The airman could wear the mask hanging on one side of the head so that it was always ready for use, it taking only a matter of seconds to hook it on to the second clip on the other side of the flying helmet when required.

The problem of freezing in oxygen masks as described above led to experiments in electrically heating the most vulnerable part of the mask, namely the expiratory valve. It was found that heating the mask electrically did not protect it from freezing but only shifted the freezing zone. Preheating of the oxygen was often demanded but it was found to be very disagreeable since the preheated oxygen dried out the respiratory passages. In addition it was physiologically uncomfortable and unnatural to expose the body to sub-zero temperatures and at the same time to breathe warm air or warm oxygen. Several models of experimental oxygen preheaters were coupled to the quick-disconnect. In order to heat the oxygen in the mask to an agreeable temperature, the oxygen temperature had to be raised quite high when the ambient temperature was -60°C, since the preheated oxygen was cooled again in the numerous recesses of the mask hose before it reached the mask. Preheating directly at the mask was too disagreeable. On the basis of these results, preheating was rejected. The heating of the expiratory valve alone, aimed at protecting the models HM-5 and HM-15, masks was not satisfactory. Though the valve did not freeze, icing within the mask hose was not prevented. Furthermore, the valve body had to be made of metal instead of plastic, with the result that an unheated valve froze even more easily than did the standard plastic valve. Failure of the electric heating always had to be considered, produced by a loose contact, a blown fuse, a disengaged plug, etc.

Above: The type of oxygen mask worn with the net flying helmet.

tory valve had leaks caused by icing. In the event the valve was frozen, the only remedy was to change masks quickly or to descend to a lower altitude. Attempts to thaw the valve by hyperventilation were rarely successful.

The Fighter Mask Model 10-69

This mask was introduced early in 1937 and became very popular due to its handiness, although the mask was of the same basic design as the HM-5 and HM-15 Models and was also subject to freezing. This mask was produced in four sizes and in May 1937 instructions were published in *Luftwaffen-Verordnungsblatt* Nr.18 for 3 May 1937, Pages 226–7 Order Nr.545 giving details of the simplified retaining straps. The mask had two suspension

The Electrically Heated Oxygen Mask, Model HME 30

This was designed by the Drägerwerk of Lübeck and Noeckel of Berlin and represented the very latest type of electrically heated oxygen mask.

In this model the inspiratory duct was separated from the expiratory duct for the first time so that freezing in the mask hose was impossible. The inspired oxygen passed on both sides of the expiratory duct which was countersunk in the lower front part of the mask, and flowed through the oval openings on each side of the partition of the mask into the mask itself. The mask was shaped like the head of a snake. The mask body was constructed in two layers. The expiratory valve was heated electrically to 60°C. A thermostat installed in the expiratory valve switched off the current after this temperature had been reached. The current was carried by a cable vulcanised into the mask hose. This cable led to a special connection at the quick-disconnect. The measurements of this special disconnect were the same as those of a normal quick-disconnect, so the two were interchangeable. This disconnect was developed by the Drägerwerk of Lübeck, in collaboration with Noeckel of Berlin and with the Erprobungsstelle at Rechlin. Even though the expiratory valve would freeze after a few hours if used unheated, the mask was much better than earlier types. In 1938 the Erprobungsstelle, Rechlin recommended this mask to the German Air Ministry for adoption. It was not officially adopted because a non-freezing high altitude mask was invented which was not electrically heated. This model was adopted by the Luftwaffe and later by some foreign countries.

The Non-Freezing Oxygen Mask, Model HM 51 (10-67)

1939 saw the adoption by the Luftwaffe of the design for an oxygen mask that would not freeze even without electric heating. This mask, the Model HM 51(10-67), proved so satisfactory that foreign countries either copied the mask or adopted its principles.

It was so designed that the cold, dry oxygen flowed in through the hose entering the mask and the lungs through a soft rubber inspiratory flutter valve. The expired air, saturated with moisture, covered and heated the entire inner surface of the mask and flowed out through the expiratory valve which lay protected on the inside of the mask, into the expired air space and then into the ring chamber out into the open air. It was still possible for the actual condensation of the moisture of the expired air to occur within the mask but since the average temperature was between +14°C to +16°C within the mask whilst the outside

temperature was -60°C degrees centigrade ice was unable to form. However, ice did form on the outside of the hose where it was harmless and the slightest movement caused it to fall away. Cold air blowing against the mask was unable to reach the expiratory valve because the flowing air reaching the opening of the ring chamber and the expired-air space produced a dynamic pressure and could not enter the expired-air space. The opening tension of the expiratory valve was plus 13mm. This was sufficient to permit its use with the adjustable regulator. The double wall of the lower part of the mask gave it additional protection from the cold. However, it was later determined that this cold protection was unnecessary in cabin aircraft. There-

Above: An Unteroffizier poses by his aircraft. The flexible tube of the oxygen mask was corrugated to prevent it from collapsing when bent. When the mask was worn inside the aircraft, the end of this flexible tube was connected to the containers of pressurized oxygen carried on board. When the mask was worn outside the aircraft (which was very infrequently), as seen here, then it was a simple matter to tuck the loose end of the flexible tube inside the flying suit.

fore it was eliminated in the later Fighter and Fighter-Bomber Oxygen Mask, Model 10-6701.

The Fighter and Fighter-Bomber Oxygen Mask, Model 10-6701

This mask was identical to the non-freezing mask HM-51. However, the new model was provided with a two-point attachment similar to the old pattern of fighter mask Model 10-69. The anti-frostbite chamois and the double wall of the HM-51 mask were left out, which made the mask much lighter and handier. There were, however, complaints about the unsatisfactory fitting of the mask.

The Oxygen Mask '44

In 1944, the unsatisfactory fitting of the 10-6701 mask was corrected experimentally by adoption of the sealing frame as used in the non-freezing USAAF A-10 mask. The combination of the German 10-6701 and the American A-10 masks proved so satisfactory during testing that the Erprobungsstelle, Rechlin, proposed that it be adopted. However, as with a number of late war German experimental items they were devised too late to be put into production.

Fying Goggles

Airmen needed goggles to protect their eyes from wind, glare, dust, insects or flying fragments, but their use presented disadvantages. Inherent optical deficiencies, narrowing of field of vision, absorption of light, fogging and reflection made the wearing of goggles a necessary evil.

Fogging of the goggles was annoying. Moisture was deposited on the lens when it was in contact with air whose saturation point for water vapour was higher than the temperature of the glass itself. In winter weather, goggles were normally warmed up before use, by such means as keeping them in a pocket of a flying suit. Contact with the goggles by air saturated with moisture, escaping through leaks in the upper rim of the oxygen mask, had to be avoided. In combat, pilots whose missions required very rapid changes in altitude, especially fighter and dive-bomber pilots in the Mediterranean theatre, complained of their goggles fogging over. During steep dives, marked sweating occurred on both the inner and outer surfaces of the goggles because they had been cooled at the higher altitude.

Flying Goggles (Fliegerbrille)

A number of different companies produced flying goggles (Fliegerbrille) for the Luftwaffe, but in general the goggles appear to have been of two basic designs. The most common type were those that had a pair of large curved lenses held in metal frames mounted on rubber eye pieces. The second type had much smaller, oval-shaped glasses, and were frequently worn with shatterproof dark-tinted lenses.

The first type of goggles were produced under the trade names of German manufacturers such as Auer, O.C. Wagener GmbH of Rathenow, Uvex, Leitz, Philipp M. Winter of Fürth, and Cellowaro. The second type were universally known as 'Nitsche und Günther', after the two optical scientists who designed the goggles in collaboration with Professor Knothe, head of the Medical Experimental and Instruction Detachment of the Luftwaffe.

First Type of Flying Goggles

Although the goggles produced by individual firms had slight differences, the overall appearance and function of all models was very similar. They all had large, elliptical, curved lenses, each lens set into a light metal frame which in turn was stitched

Below: An Oberleutnant navigator of a Dornier Do 18 flying boat wearing Auer Model 306 flying goggles of the two-piece large-lens type. The small metal linking bar across the bridge of the goggles, joining the two separate eyepieces, can be seen.

Above: The Auer 305, model 295 flying goggles. The one-piece moulded rubber face mask is well illustrated.

Left: The dorsal turret gunner of a Focke-Wulfe Fw 189 looks down the sights of his twin MG 18Z 7.9mm machine-guns. He is wearing the dark, oval shaped Nitsche and Günther shatterproof goggles on his lightweight summer flying helmet.

Above: A Hauptgefreiter wearing what appear to be Auer Neophan motorcyclist's goggles on his steel helmet.

Right: The Leitz anti-dust and anti-glare goggles issued and worn in great numbers by German troops serving in North Africa. They were small, inexpensive, lightweight, protected the eyes from dust, and, being fitted with lenses of dark brown glass, were well suited for the strong sunlight of desert regions. They were not suitable as flying goggles.

either to a moulded rubber eye piece in two-piece goggles, or to a moulded rubber face mask in the one-piece variety. The colour of the metal frames varied from blue-grey to dark green. The lenses were removable and interchangeable between clear glass and tinted green or brown glass. On most two-piece goggles of this type the two lenses were joined across the bridge of the goggles by a small metal linking bar that housed an adjustable screw which held the two eye pieces together. This screw allowed a limited amount of adjustment to the fit of the lenses against the wearer's face. Each pair of goggles had a wide, adjustable elasticated head strap.

The goggles were usually issued in a purpose-made cardboard box with a removable lid. This contained one complete set of goggles, a spare head strap and two extra sets of lenses, one set in clear glass, the other of tinted (Umbral) glass. Each lens was wrapped individually in thin brown paper, and they were placed as pairs inside a specially shaped cloth cover. Other types of container were also used, as many as five sets of replacement lenses being provided in some instances.

Goggles similar to those described above were also produced as a one-piece item, the metal frames holding the lenses being stitched to a single, moulded rubber face mask.

Nitsche and Günther Shatterproof Flying Goggles

The Luftwaffe medical authorities knew that perforation of the eye, even by minute metal, glass or plastic fragments, could destroy a person's vision, so flying goggles had to be shatterproof, with lenses of plastic or of splinterproof glass of Triplex quality. The advantages of this glass were that it could be produced with ground-in refraction, it was not easily scratched, and it was impervious to harmful ultraviolet rays. These requirements led to the development of the German Nitsche and Günther splinterproof flying goggles (Nitsche und Günther Flieger-Splitterschutzbrillen). The lenses had a minimum thickness of 2mm, and their great curvature made them highly resistant to impact.

The first pattern of these goggles was of rigid construction, but later models had a folding nose-piece across the bridge of the nose and elastic head straps for ease of fit. They were supplied in an elongated oval metal storage case clearly marked with the specification of the contents.

While these goggles brought a marked reduction in the number of perforation injuries in the Luftwaffe, they offered no protection against very large fragments capable of causing cerebral injury. On the other hand, many cases were recorded in which there were many small fragment wounds scattered over the exposed part of the face whilst the eyes behind the goggles were unharmed.

Flying Boots

Aircrew were issued with fur-lined boots that were normally intended to be worn for flights that exceeded a height of 10,000ft.

Left: Oberstleutnant Galland and his squadron pet. Galland is wearing what appears to be an Irvin suit – jacket and trousers – plus his issue Luftwaffe flying boots.

Right: Wearing a combination flying suit and an inflatable life jacket, and with flare pistol cartridges strapped around the tops of his flying boots, an NCO pilot on standby checks details over a field telephone, 25 June 1942.

353 Luftwaffe-issue flying boots, right boot shown.

353

Flying boots were an intergral part of the issue flight clothing and, being fur-lined, were particularly well suited for cold weather. However, these boots had disadvantages: after they had been worn for any undue length of time the nap of the inner fur sole flattened down and this reduced the boots insulating properties; they afforded no protection against fractures and joint injuries; they were unsuitable for walking any distance, for instance, after a forced landing.

The authorities were aware of these drawbacks and considered that airmen at risk of being brought down or having to make a forced landing on difficult terrain would have a better chance of surviving if they were to wear adequately sized climbing or skiing boots. Galoshes of windproof canvas, which could be worn in snow and which afforded good insulation because of the enclosed air layer, were also consid-

Left: A precious moment of relaxation is interrupted. Lux, an Alsatian, takes an interest in the black rabbit comfortably nestling in the lap of a pilot officer on standby on a German airfield somewhere in the West.

Right: Part of the winter flying suit were the fleece-lined gloves, worn here by the observer of a Heinkel He 111 bomber.

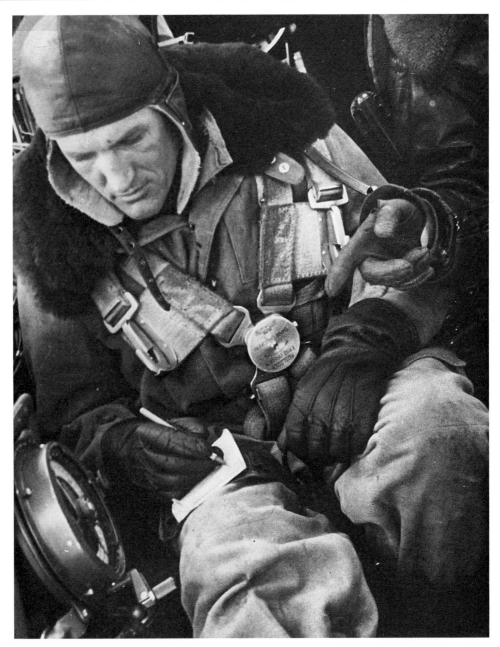

ered, but, like many late-war innovations, were never put into effect. The problem of whether or not to replace the issue flying boots with some other more suitable form of footwear was never resolved.

Flying Gloves:

Gloves were an integral part of the flying suit. Their purpose was to both protect and to warm the hands of the wearer. Made from either black or dark brown calf leather and lined with fleece they had the normal complement of four fingers and one thumb and had either a shortened wrist or were of the gauntlet type.

Flight Jerkins

The flight jerkin was a convenient, semi-official garment very much favoured by aircrews, particularly those flying single-seat aircraft. There seems to have been a wide

Flight Jerkins were produced in a variety of materials and in many designs.

Above: A photograph taken on 22 May 1942 of four fighter aces from Jagdgeschwader Mölders, I/JG 51. All are holders of the Knight's Cross, and when the photo was taken had between them over 250 air victories to their credit. From left to right: Oberfeldwebel (later Hauptmann) Heinrich Höfemeier (51 kills), Leutnant Erwin Fleig (65 kills), Hauptmann Heinz Bär (105 kills), and Hauptmann Josef Krafft (48 kills).

Left: An unidentified Hauptmann wearing an animal skin fleece-lined jerkin.

Opposite page, top left: Obersleutnant Walter Oesau wearing a white linen jerkin. 'Gulle' Oesau was a fighter ace who ranked alongside Mölders, Galland and Wick in

1940–41. He flew approximately 300 missions and scored 123 air victories, eight in Spain and 44 in the East, including ten four-engined bombers. He was killed in action on 11 May 1944 during aerial combat with Lightnings over the Eifel mountains.

Above right: An unidentified Major wearing a natural leather fleece-lined jerkin.

Right: Major Anton Hackl wearing leathers. 'Toni' Hackle was among the leading fighter pilots of the Luftwaffe, with over 1,000 missions to his credit. He scored 192 victories, of which 87 were in the West, including 32 four-engined aircraft, plus a further 24 unconfirmed kills. During his five years of flying he was operational on all fronts. He was severely wounded a number of times, and was shot down on eight occasions.

range of jerkins, presumably made to suit the individual requirements and using a variety of fabrics. Contemporary photographs show that these garments were manufactured from linen, leather and suede in different colourings. Two features of these various jerkins were particularly notable: pockets came in various shapes and numbers, and the jerkins themselves were tailored to waist level.

The Two-piece 'Kanal' Flying Suit

Details of this outfit, which saw widespread use, have proved difficult to establish. The two items that comprised the flying suit were a flight jerkin and a very distinctive pair of trousers, made from matching blue-grey material. The precise date for its introduction has not been established, but it seems that it began to be used during 1943. The reason for its introduction was its undoubted convenience as a two-piece form of flight clothing when compared with existing single-garment suits. The suit was obviously cheaper to produce in terms of both material and labour costs, and damaged jackets or trousers were easier and cheaper to replace or repair than in the case of a one-piece suit.

This had a concealed, zippered front opening and a dark blue-grey woollen knitted waist band. There was a single external pocket with a simple slit-opening high on the left side of the chest, and an internal pocket on the left side. The Luftwaffe national emblem was sewn to the right chest, shoulder-straps were worn, but there were no collar patches.

These were colloquially known as 'Kanalhose', or 'Channel Trousers', which is thought to be a reference to their use by pilots engaged in air activity over the English Channel. They were very distinctive,

their most noticeable feature being the large bellows pockets on the front of each leg, with broad pocket flaps each secured by two press studs. The trousers were front-opening, with a prominent metal zip running from the waist to the crotch. The legs were tapered, allowing flying boots to be worn with ease, although the trousers could be worn over the boots. For this purpose each leg had a metal zip fastening on the inside leg, reaching from the knee to the ankle. When unzipped, these permitted the trousers to be pulled on over the feet or flying boots. On the lower part of the right outer thigh was a specially shaped pocket designed to take a pistol and provided with

Left: The two-piece flying suit referred to as the 'Invasion Suit' had a very distinctive feature in the bellows pockets on the front of each leg. NCO fighter pilots are seen here reporting to their superior at a front-line airfield believed to be on the Normandy front.

Right: Two German fighter aces pose in front of a Messerschmitt Bf 109G. Both wear the two-piece 'Invasion Suit'.

a flap secured by two press studs. The trousers had built-in cloth braces which were stitched into the waistband at the rear and were adjustable at the front; these were very similar to the cloth braces used on the reversible camouflaged winter uniform (page 323).

The Immersion 'Foam-Suit' (Schaumgerat) Developed for Aviators

The losses of aircrew at sea, especially during cold seasons and in Arctic waters, were particularly high, since death occurred not only from drowning but also from hypothermia. The use of special lifeboats in which attempts were made to revive rescued personnel with warm water and then wrapping them in warm blankets proved only partly successful. In many cases death occurred from heart attack soon after rescue from the water. It was established that life could not be saved if the body temperature had fallen to a low of 31°C.

Both the Royal Air Force and the United States Army Air Force were aware of the need to protect their aircrews from immer-

Above Luftwaffe aircrews and ground mechanics believed to be operating in the Normandy area. All of the fliers wear either the complete flying suit or just the trousers. There is a noticeable difference in the colouring of the individual garments.

Left: A close-up of the bellows pocket on the left leg of the suit.

sion in cold or freezing water. Research directed towards producing some form of protective garment had been instigated by the Shirley Institute and the RAF Physiological Laboratory at Farnborough, Hampshire, and in the USA, the effort being focused on the production of extremely tightly woven fabrics with a sufficiently water-repellent finish or coating to keep water away from the skin of an immersed person. Clothing made from leather with a waterproof coating had been developed, but had proved unsatisfactory. The Royal Canadian Air Force had produced a rubberized protective suit that was sealed at the neck, wrists and ankles and worn under the regular flying suit. This, too, proved unsatisfactory, because aircrew began to suffer from stiffness in their joints caused by a build-up of body heat and perspiration.

German interest in, and development of, specialist protective clothing was somewhat limited, not only for protection against military hazards, but also against industrial ones. However, in one respect Germany was in the vanguard of experimentation in their development of a special immersion protective 'foam' suit. This embodied a revolutionary concept of 'protection created when needed'.

The German solution was to produce a suit of clothing that was permeable when dry, so as not to impede body movements or make the wearer uncomfortably hot, but would enable a person immersed in cold water to survive for many hours, rather than for only a few minutes. The importance of this is evident when it is realised that, even in the North Sea, the average water temperature is 5°C or less for a considerable time during the winter months.

The first of these immersion foam suits were made at the Technikum für Textile Industrie in München-Gladbach under the supervision of its inventor, Professor Dr Ing Mecheels. Their protective properties lay in the materials used, their construction and the special foaming powder used.

Each garment was manufactured from three layers of fabricated cloth and a special foaming powder, combined as follows:

a. an outer layer of cellulose acetate silk poplin;
b. a middle layer of white viscose silk plush called Wollinplush;
c. an inner lining of white, heavy viscose artificial silk material;
d. a powder produced from a combination of sodium bicarbonate, citric acid and a foaming agent called Mersolat H-30 that was non-irritant to skin.

The outer acetate fabric had no special properties other than being dyed. The reverse side of the middle layer of Wollinplush was spot-treated with a liquid soap called Preukutan. Once this application had dried, the foam-producing powder was sprinkled into the pile of the plush and worked in by hand on the front surface of the fabric, and this pile face was then applied to the back surface of the outer layer. The inner layer of viscose silk faced the Preukutan-prepared reverse side of the Wollinplush. To retain an even distribution of powder within the fabric, the three layers were quilted together, stitched overall with a pattern of diamonds between 2in and 3in in size. Each suit contained approximately 2kg of foaming powder.

When the wearer was immersed, the cold seawater would rush in through the flying suit and through the outer acetate silk poplin layer of the protective suit. However, when the water combined with the powder it would immediately produce the protective foam, generating a large quantity of foam bubbles which effectively prevented any further water penetration. The wearer's body heat was sufficient to warm any small amount of water that might have seeped in, and this kept the man from freezing.

A complete suit consisted of a pair of trousers, a jacket with a tight sponge-rubber neck band, which was normally worn open but could be closed quickly by pulling on a drawstring, inner shoe soles, and gloves. These individual items were considered more practicable than a one-piece suit, as the separate garments could be put on and taken off more easily and were more comfortable.

The neck lacked protection, and had to be rubbed with grease. In the water the airman's head was held above water by the neck chamber of the life jacket. This was essential for survival because the neck is the most cold-sensitive part of the body, and had to be kept above water level all the time. There was a 'cap', but this proved unsatisfactory because the foam ran into the eyes and down the face. The suit was worn on top of undergarments designed to absorb perspiration and beneath the regular flying suit.

Although it was designed especially for aircrews operating over Norwegian waters, the suit was later issued for general use. It was claimed that a person equipped with a complete outfit could survive in water of about 0°C for three hours or more, and that the insulating mass was effective for as long as 60 hours. Used suits were washed out, opened and refilled with powder before being sewn together and reissued. Between 10,000 and 15,000 suits were produced in three sizes and delivered to the Luftwaffe Bekleidungsamt between early 1944 and March 1945, when production ceased owing to the Allied occupation.

Life Jackets

Aircrew forced down into the sea relied on the life jacket in order to remain afloat. A dependable life jacket had, and still has, to fulfil the following criteria:

1. To have sufficient buoyancy, even when the wearer was unconsious.
2. To be capable of keeping the wearer afloat long enough for rescue to be effected.
3. To have maximum resistance to damage.
4. To be so designed that the wearer's head was held in a position that would keep the mouth and nose of an uncon scious man out of the water.
5. To be sufficiently tight-fitting so as not to slip off an unconscious man.

Below: Fighter pilots from the JG 53 'Pik As' or Ace of Spades squadron. All wear the inflatable life jacket.

354 Luftwaffe pneumatic inflatable life jacket, front view.

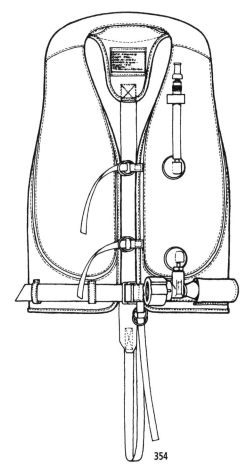

354

Below right: The crew of a Dornier.

6. It had not to restrict the wearer's movements.
7. To be clearly visible in the water, an aid to air-sea rescue.
8. To be so designed that mass production was feasible.

Two types of life jacket were adopted. One, used by fighter pilots, consisted of a single-chamber pneumatic vest that could be filled with compressed air (Fig. 354). The other was a kapok-filled jacket and was used by crews of bombers, transport and air-sea rescue aircraft (Fig. 355).

Inflatable Life Jackets

The pneumatic life jacket was normally worn deflated. It was inflated by opening a compressed-air cylinder attached to the lower left side of the jacket. The jacket could also be filled orally, a tube with a one-way valve being fitted vertically towards the wearer's neck on the front left side of the jacket. Although this type of jacket had practically indefinite flotation time, its single inflatable chamber was vulnerable to damage. If worn correctly the wearer's head was generally kept out of the water because the jacket enclosed the neck like a collar. The large bladder space in front of the chest would automatically right an unconscious man who had tilted forward. The criteria listed above were ade-

Left: A happy group of night-fighter pilots, all wearing inflatable life jackets.

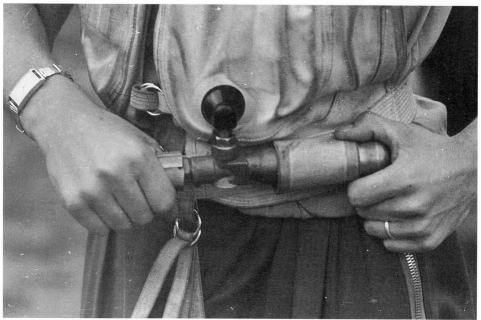

Left: A close-up of the cylinder of compressed air used to inflate the life jacket.

quately fulfilled with this type of jacket, but if the wearer was already unconscious when he hit the water he inevitably drowned because the jacket did not inflate automatically.

Kapok-filled Life Jacket

The kapok filled Luftwaffe life jackets, as long as they were new to fairly new, had good floatation qualities, sufficient to keep

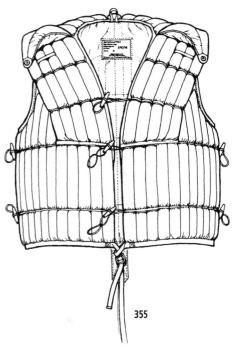

355

Above: The oral method of inflating the life jacket.

Right: A correct fit of the life jacket was essential.

Above right:
355 Luftwaffe kapok-filled life jacket, front view.

Left: Members of a Luftwaffe Flak unit prepare for a flight to Sicily aboard a Junkers Ju 52/3M. As they are to fly over water, they are required to wear kapok-filled life jackets.

Below left: German airmen enjoy an impromptu boat race. As a safety precaution the men wear kapok-filled life jackets, the man on the far left wearing a variant of the standard pattern of jacket.

Below: An excellent study of the kapok-filled life jacket.

a person afloat for at least 24 hours. The floatation qualities of older jackets was considerably reduced. Since the kapok filled jacket consisted of tubular shaped bladder spaces of 3cm to 4cm each in diameter, it was less susceptible to the damage that could affect its floatation qualities. This style of jacket was of no use in the narrow confines of fighter and dive bomber aircraft. It was too cumbersome for use by these crew members. Numerous complaints were lodged concerning the danger of the kapok filled tubes being caught up on protruding aircraft parts, especially so since the tubes were not directly attached to each other. Although this type of life jacket had a special deep

collar that could be buttoned in front and which supported the head upright, the wearer was turned forward and was forced face down in the water since the buoyancy in the back was higher than that in the front. This deficiency was relieved but not completely eliminated in 1943 when some of the kapok tubes on the back of the jacket were left off and thus the buoyancy was reduced. This modification did not entirely prevent the airman from turning over. All the other requirements were adequately fulfilled.

Both types of jacket had leg straps to stop them slipping upwards, but the straps were uncomfortable when correctly adjusted because they chafed the legs. Many men were drowned because they failed too fasten the straps or fastened them too loosely, with the result that they were immersed so deeply that their heads were not kept out of the water. Even aircrew of air-sea rescue aeroplanes were recorded as having died in this way despite repeated warnings about the danger of inadequately fastened life jackets.

Aircrew Parachute Harness

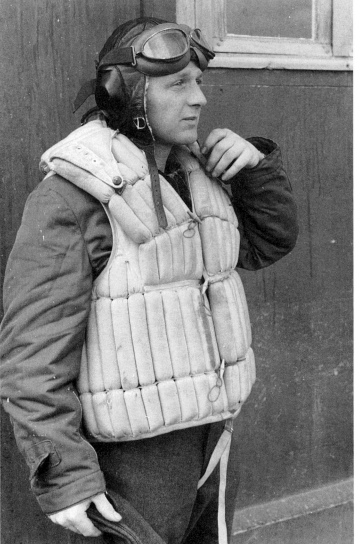

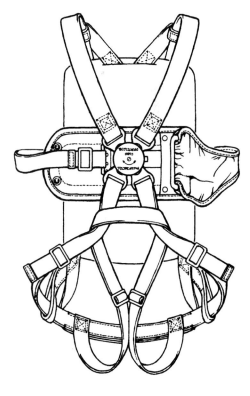

356 Luftwaffe aircrew parachute harness, front view.

Left: The parachute harness worn by aircrews. The crew of a Junkers Ju 88 prepare for their next flight.

Right: The harness worn by a test pilot.

Left: The rear view of the harness worn without the parachute pack. Men of a Luftwaffe Kriegsberichter film unit board a Junkers Ju 52/3M.

Body Armour

The German Air Force made no attempt whatsoever to design and produce body armour for use by aircrew until the end of 1943, when a set of US Army Air Force body armour was captured and sent to the Sanitäts-Versuchs und Lehrabteilung der Luftwaffe at Jüterbog. The captured armour consisted of a strong and intricately-sewn fabric containing small 4cm square plates made from a very tough steel which was austentic, non-magnetic and non-magnetizable. The plates overlapped each other and proved very successful in resist-

ing gunfire. The Germans found that, when it was fired at by a test rifle with a muzzle velocity of 298–305m/sec, the captured vest could not be pierced by a 13g lead-antimony bullet. This resistance corresponded to the protective value of the issue German steel helmet. However, because of its weight, about 8.75kg, this otherwise perfect armour could only be used in transport aircraft and bombers, in which the wearer was not subjected to high accelerations. It was removed simply by pulling on a loop, allowing it to fall off the wearer's shoulders. So impressed were the Luftwaffe scientists that they recommended that a similar set of body armour be developed for German aircrews. Unfortunately for the Luftwaffe this project failed owing to a lack of raw materials.

As an alternative to body armour manufactured from steel plates, it was suggested by Professor Knothe, head of the Sanitäts-Versuchs und Lehrabteilung der Luftwaffe, that body armour manufactured from fabric woven from the synthetic fibre Perlon should be developed. The German experiments, which had begun tentatively shortly before the end of the Great War in Europe, were based on the observations that projectiles penetrated cotton wool only with difficulty. In tests with cotton wool, the strength of the material was not, as in sheet iron, utilized in the sense of armour, but virtually as a breaking path which consumed the energy of the projectile. In the process the fibres were found to be deformed, lengthened or torn. Fabric and cotton wool from high-molecular synthetic materials were found to be far superior to ordinary wool.

Orientation experiments showed that fabrics and cotton wool of Perlon in an uncompressed layer of about 3cm resisted the bullet of a 6.35mm Mauser pistol from a distance of 5m, and a slightly thicker layer even resisted a 7.65mm-calibre bullet.

These tests did not progress beyond these rough qualitative results, but at the time the question was raised whether such a protection, which in effectiveness was comparable to that of small armour plates, could have been worn as a complete protective suit or simply attached to the pilot's cockpit seat or used to line the aircraft's cabin walls.

Paratroop Specialist Clothing

The two patterns of pre-war Paratroop Jump Smocks have been dealt with in Volume 1933–40, pp.70-2.

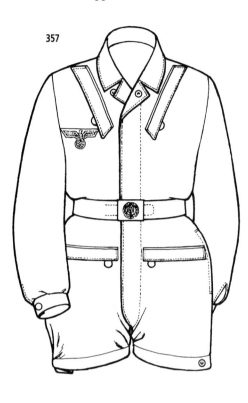

357

Jump Smock, Second Model (Fallschirm-schützenbluse)

This was the pre-war pattern issued to the Luftwaffe's own Fallschirmjäger troops. It was a step-in blouse with a central front opening from neck to crutch secured by a fly-fronted heavy-duty brass zipper (early examples used buttons). It was produced in olive-green, water-repellent gabardine. The stand and fall collar could be worn open or closed. The legs of the blouse reached to approximately mid-thigh and each had a single press-stud with which the ends of the legs could be gathered and secured.

The blouse had four pockets, two diagonal pocket openings on each side of the chest and two horizontal pocket openings on the front of each thigh. All the pockets were closed by metal zips concealed by fly-fronted flaps. The national emblem was

sewn on the upper right breast. Rank insignia of the type used on flight clothing was worn on both upper arms of the Smock.

Jump Smock, Third Model

This final pattern of Fallschirmjäger smock was manufactured from 'splinter' pattern camouflage material. It was similar to the previous model in many ways, but, most noticeably, it did not have step-in legs, and so appeared to be longer in the body. The lower edge of the smock had press stud fasteners which enabled the skirt to be gathered in around the thighs and secured to form short 'legs'.

Like the second-pattern smock, it had two diagonal pocket openings on each side of the chest and two horizontal pocket

357 The second-model parachute blouse in olive green.

Above: An early variant of the second-pattern Fallschirmjäger jump smock, worn by former world heavyweight boxing champion Max Schmeling (centre) and other paratroopers. Note the absence of external pockets on these smocks. Schmeling was an early volunteer in the German paratroop arm. It was falsely reported that he had been killed during the fighting on Crete, but he survived the war.

openings at the front just below waist level. All were closed by zip fasteners and all were concealed by a fly-fronted flap. Two more openings, one on each hip, gave access to the trouser pockets. At the back on the right buttock was a built-in holster to accommodate a flare pistol. The holster was in two parts: a short tubular pouch to take the end of the barrel and a shaped flap which covered the grip and trigger area. This arrangement supported the weight of the pistol, and when the flap was buttoned the weapon was secure. On the opposite rear side of the skirt was a single loop of cloth, set diagonally, to accommodate the end of an entrenching tool handle. Both these innovations reflected the state of the Parachute arm since the Crete campaign. After the severe mauling inflicted on the Fallschirmjäger on Crete, almost all the fighting in which they were involved was of an infantry nature, and there was a change

Left: Certain improvisations were frequently carried out on the jump smocks. Flare pistol cartridge loops were a popular addition to the upper arms. German paratroops are seen here operating on the Nettuno front in Italy.

Below: Somebody is not in step! Fallschirmjäger undergo anti-invasion infantry exercises somewhere in France. All of the troops wear the third pattern of jump smock, and some wear normal patterns of the Luftwaffe steel helmet.

358 The third-model parachute smock, front view. The camouflage patterning covered all of the garment, but, for clarity, only a small portion of the smock has been shown with this patterning. The same applies to all other camouflage garments illustrated in this book.
359 The third-model parachute smock, rear view.
360 Detail of the built-in holster for the flare pistol worn on the rear of the third-model parachute smock.

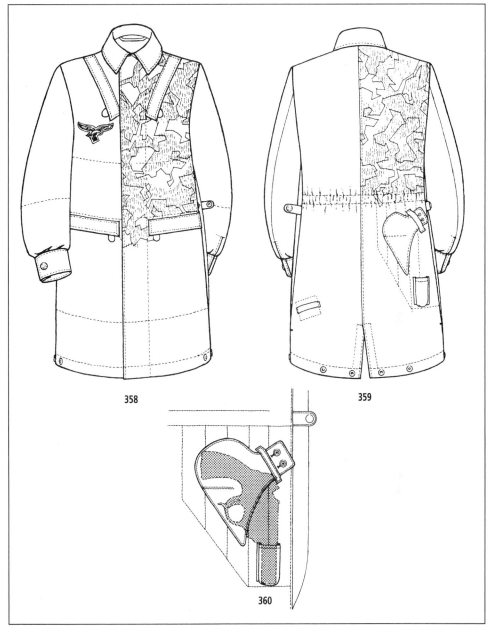

358

359

360

of emphasis with more consideration being given to improvements in the clothing for these paratroops, who would no longer be required to jump from aircraft but to fight in the role of ground-holding infantry.

On either side of the smock at waist level was a short cloth tab with a press stud by which the waistband, elasticated at the back, could be tightened or loosened.

The eagle was worn on the right breast. Rank insignia of the type used on flight clothing was meant to be worn on the

upper arms of the smock, but contemporary photographs reveal that this practice was not widespread.

Parachutists' Trousers, Second Model
The second-model trousers worn as part of the Fallschirmjäger field dress were manufactured from field-grey woollen cloth. They were full length and had two side pockets, two hip pockets, two leg openings set into the outer seams just above knee level and a single fob-pocket. The waistband was cut

Left: A rear view of the third-pattern jump smock, showing the special pocket for a flare pistol.

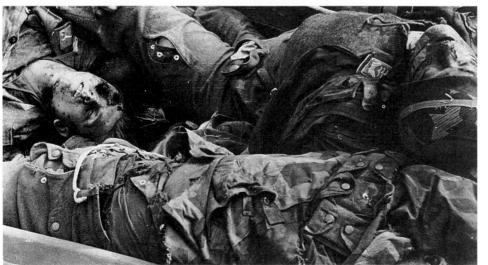

Left: German paratroopers, killed in the fierce fighting in Normandy, lie at the bottom of a farm cart ready for transport to a nearby cemetery and burial. The names of the dead were recorded and communicated to the German OKW through the International Red Cross. Gruesome though this photograph is, it does show clearly the paratroop trousers with the side pockets in the leg.

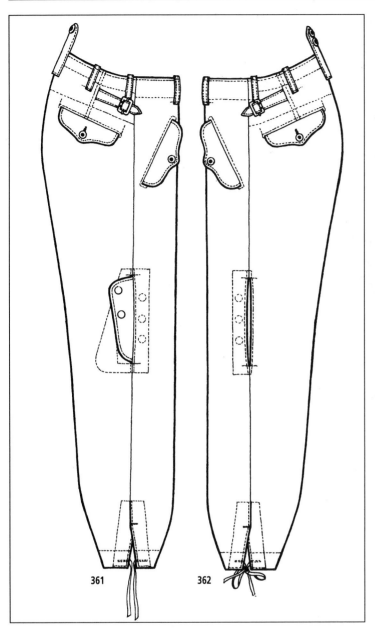

**Fallschirmjäger
field-grey trousers.**
361 Right side.
362 Left side.

press-stud fastener and a single horn button respectively. The small patch pocket just below the waistband on the right of the trousers had a flap and a single button. This was intended to accommodate a pocket watch.

The opening let into the outer seam of the right trouser leg had three concealed internal press-stud fasteners, and the leg pocket had an external wedge-shaped flap sewn into the leg seam and secured by two further press studs. The paratrooper's utility knife, also known as the 'gravity knife', was housed in this narrow pocket on the inside of the leg, access to which was by the right-hand leg opening.

An opening in the outer seam of the left leg, identical to that on the other leg, permitted easy removal of the internal knee protectors when these were worn.

Fallschirmjäger Jump Boots
In addition to being issued with normal items of Luftwaffe footwear, German paratroopers were also equipped with special 'Jump Boots'. These high-sided boots were intended to give additional support to the ankles, particularly important when landing by parachute.

First Model, side lacing. These, the first pattern of boots to be issued, laced up along the outside of the foot and ankle with eleven or twelve lace holes depending upon the height of the boot (Fig. 363). They were

high at the back and had eight belt loops. Short strap-and-buckle arrangements at each side of the waist allowed adjustment. The ends of the legs had a short 'V' section cut into the outer portion of the cuff, and two short lengths of tape sewn into each side of these sections enabled the cuff to be gathered in and tied around the ankle of the boot. When adjusted correctly this arrangement gave the trousers a loose, 'bagged' appearance.

The two side and two hip pockets had shaped flaps secured by a single metal

363 The first-model side-lacing Fallschirmjäger jump boot.

manufactured in black leather. The soles and heels were of moulded rubber with a large chevron patterning. The top of the boots reached to just below mid-calf. They had no toecap seams, but had a broad reinforcing seam running along the front and back.

Second Model, front lacing. This new pattern was introduced shortly after the outbreak of war, and was worn concurrently with the side-lacing pattern until some time after the battle for Crete, when stocks of the original boot became exhausted. Of a more conventional design, this front-lacing black leather boot was soled and heeled in leather and was usually studded. It was shorter in the ankle than the side-lacing boot

Right: The patterning of the sole and heel of the side-laced parachute jump boots.

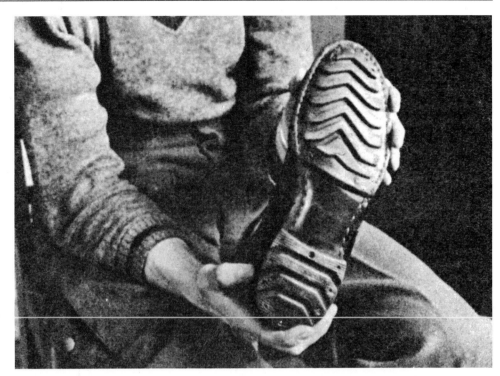

Right: The front-laced second model parachute jump boot.

Fallschirmjäger Gloves

These were of black leather and had an extended gauntlet-type wrist, elasticated on the back to give a tight fit to the wrist and lower forearm. They were unlined for summer wear and fur-lined for cold weather wear.

Fallschirmjäger Steel Helmet

Prior to the Army Parachute Battalion being absorbed into the Luftwaffe, the Army paratroops were issued with the second-model parachute helmet. This became standard issue to all paratroops, and was worn by them not just for combat

Left: Fallschirmjäger climb aboard a Junkers Ju 52 transport aircraft. This photograph clearly shows the black leather gloves.

364 Second-model Fallschirmjäger steel helmet, left side.

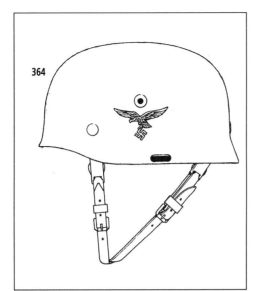

364

Right: The similarity between the protective clothing (smocks and helmets) of the German Fallschirmjäger and that of the British paratrooper is very striking. This was because the British based the design of their items on smocks and helmets captured from the Germans.

but as part of their normal Luftwaffe uniform.

Its introduction marked a revolutionary development in military protective headwear. Its shape and construction was designed with the paratrooper's unique needs in mind. It provided the wearer with a certain amount of protection from gunfire and shrapnel; was manufactured to resist the hard knocks encountered on a difficult air drop; and was so shaped as to reduce the risk of any part of the helmet fouling harness lines.

Not only was its shape different from that of the M35 and M42 helmets (as used by other troops including Luftwaffe personnel), but the inner liner was completely different, consisting of a dome-shaped piece of leather pierced with circular ventilation holes. This

Left: Two official cloth covers existed for the Fallschirmjäger steel helmet, and both are shown here. The soldier on the left wears the cover made from camouflage material, while his companion wears the plain olive-green cloth cover. Improvised coverings for the Fallschirmjäger steel helmet came in a variety of materials and 'styles'.

Lower left: Parachute Field Police operating in Normandy, August 1944. The man in the centre wears a covering of chicken wire on his steel helmet, while the other two helmeted soldiers wear loose cord netting.

Right: A covering designed to break up the hard outline of the steel helmet, produced from a loose piece of cloth held in place on the helmet by a section of chicken wire, bent and shaped to the contours of the helmet and held on by a series of hooks set around the rim.

was held in position inside the steel shell by a band of strong but flexible aluminium, backed with resilient rubber padding, and fixed to the shell by four screws. These screws also served to anchor neck and chin straps at the rear and at both sides.

Early versions were painted on the inside and outside with a rust-preventative matt blue-grey paint. Helmets issued and worn later in the war, when the Parachute arm was being used in an infantry role, were frequently painted dark grey-green, a more practical colour than the original blue-grey. Fallschirmjäger helmets used in North Africa, Sicily and Italy and other countries with a hot, dry climate were usually overpainted in a sandy-buff colour, sometimes sand was

sprinkled on the wet paint that when dried gave a non-reflecting surface. In snow-covered terrain a matt-white finish was achieved by a thick coat of whitewash – preferable to white paint because when spring arrived the whitewash could be scrubbed off with water and the helmet restored to its original colour.

Fallschirmjäger helmets bore the same pattern of insignia as used on the steel helmet worn within the Luftwaffe, the national emblem on the left side, the tricolour shield on the right. In the summer of 1940 orders were published[2] abolishing the black, white and red shield for the duration.

Helmet coverings were commonly extemporised: chicken wire, sacking or cloth netting were used to disrupt the solid outline of the helmet.

Fallschirmjäger Knee Protectors

To protect their kneecaps from the heavy abrasions or serious injury easily caused by a difficult parachute landing, German paratroopers were initially issued with knee protectors. These consisted of a pair of flat, kapok-filled rectangular canvas-covered pads worn directly over the kneecaps inside the trouser legs, and tied in position

Above: German paratroops in Italy. The Unteroffizier in the foreground has used a Fallschirmjäger helmet cover as a cover for his Model 1943 steel helmet.

Left: A helmet covering produced from what appears to be a British Airborne face veil.

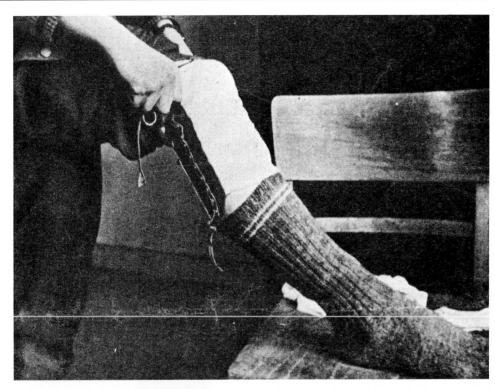

Right: A contemporary photograph of the first-type knee protectors being put on.

Right: The first type of knee protectors were normally worn under the cloth trousers.

with tapes or laces. Although they provided sufficient protection for air drops, they proved a hindrance if worn on the march, tending to restrict the movement of the knees and rapidly causing chaffing to the skin. The pads were removed as soon as possible after a parachute descent, the two slit side openings in the paratroopers' combat trousers allowing this to be done.

Fallschirmjäger Knee Pads

Knee pads were issued to German paratroops to replace the earlier knee protectors, and were worn by paratroopers undertaking parachute jumps. They consisted of six tubular horizontal pads formed from sorbo rubber and covered with either black or dark brown leather, or later by olive green cloth. Each pad was held in position by a set of two strong elasticated and adjustable straps which crossed behind the knee and clipped on to small button-hooks on the opposite side of the pad.

Unlike the earlier knee protectors, these pads were worn over the trouser legs. It was normal practice to take them off, but not to discard them, once a descent had been effected, since they tended to become uncomfortable if worn for any length of time whilst marching.

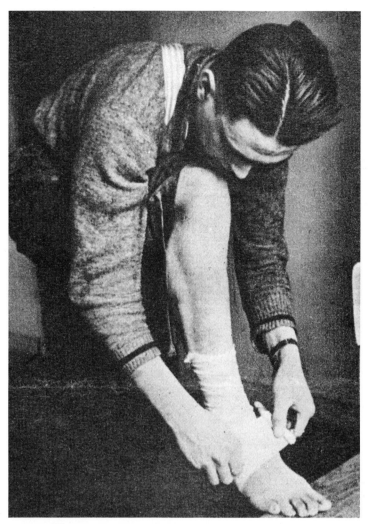

Left: Bandages were worn to give support to the ankles. Any paratrooper who had sustained a foot or ankle injury and felt that he required additional support for his ankles, although he was passed as medically fit to jump, could wear linen ankle bandages. Worn under the woollen socks and bound fairly tightly around the instep and ankle, they extended about a third of the way up the paratrooper's lower leg.

Below: The knee pads in use.

Right: Paratroopers load a drop canister into a Junkers Ju 52/3M. For the sake of convenience the man in the centre has hung his knee pads on his waist-belt.

Parachute Harness for Parade Purposes

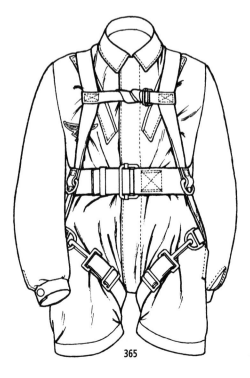

365

Above: A massive and impressive military parade was staged in Berlin on 20 April 1939 to mark the fiftieth birthday of the Führer. Here, German paratroops march past the saluting dais. The troops wear their distinctive Fallschirmjäger Parade Uniform with the early pattern of parachute harness, less the actual parachute.

Left: Max Schmeling poses in the doorway of a Junkers transport to demonstrate the correct jump-off position. He wears the early pattern of parachute harness.

Far left:
365 Parachute harness for parade purposes.

Right: The correct method of wear and the locking mechanism of the late-pattern parachute harness is demonstrated to members of the Reichsarbeitsdienst by an officer of the Fallschirmjäger, 6 October 1943.

Left, upper and lower: The late-pattern parachute harness as worn for parade purposes, front and rear views. Fallschirmjäger officers, all of whom had fought with distinction at Monte Cassino ('grünen Teufeln von Monte Cassino') in conversation with Reichsmarschall Göring after he had presented them with awards for valour at a special ceremony in Berlin on 4 May 1944.

Right: A young Obergefreiter paratrooper on guard duty somewhere on the Eastern Front.

Left: A Fallschirmjäger wearing the cloth container for the gas mask. German paratroopers were issued with these special non-rigid canvas carrying bags instead of the normal cylindrical metal gas-mask containers carried by other members of the German armed forces. These soft containers eliminated the possibility of injury by the metal case during a parachute landing.

Right: The paratroop containers consisted of a short tubular bag of grey-green or blue-grey canvas with a heavy-duty metal zip fastener running its entire length and a flap secured by two press-stud buttons at one end. The case was normally hung around the neck on an adjustable strap.

Top, far right: The container opened to show the gas-mask. The mask was initially of the standard-issue type, but by 1940 a new model (Gasmaske 40), produced from a very strong high-grade rubber, had been issued to the paratroops.

Right: Fallschirmjäger wait to board transport aircraft. While the troops relax and talk in groups, the positions for the order in which they were to emplane are marked by the numerous clothing bags.

Left: The carrying sack, or clothing bag (Bekleidungs-sack) issued to paratroops. Manufactured from olive-green canvas, with twin sewn-on webbing handles, it had a top opening with a flap that was secured on three sides by a series of five press-stud fasteners.

Left: The issue fur-covered pack being worn by a Para-troop medical orderly captured in Italy.

Luftwaffe and Fallschirmjäger Tropical Clothing

Extensive tropical clothing was issued to personnel of all ranks of both the Luftwaffe and the Fallschirmjäger operating in hot countries. A full complement initially consisted of the items listed below.[3] With the obvious exception of items 5 and 18 and the Tropical Helmet, a number of the khaki-brown garments were tropical versions of temperate-climate clothing. Most of these tropical items were manufactured in what the Luftwaffe authorities termed

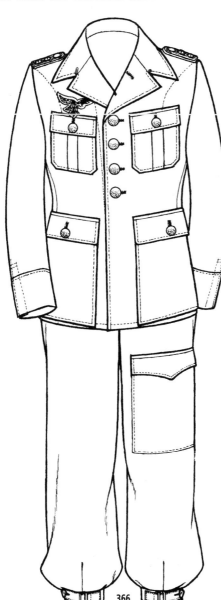

366 The Luftwaffe Fallschirmjäger tropical uniform.

A. These overtrousers ('Uberfallhose') were the very distinctive tropical, tan-coloured trousers much favoured by German paratroops. They were readily identifiable by the large map pocket on the outside of the left leg and the bagged appearance of the trouser around the ankles.

B. For further information on sports clothing, running shoes and swimming trunks of the colour and pattern worn within the Luftwaffe see Volume 1933–40, pp. 249 to 252.

'khakibraun' coloured material, but which is better described as light tan. Other garments in white or grey were normally worn or used in temperate climates.

1. Two khaki-brown Flight Caps
2. Two khaki-brown Jackets
3. One grey drill material blouse
4. One pair long khaki-brown trousers
5. One pair long khaki-brown over trousers A
6. One pair khaki-brown shorts
7. One pair drill material trousers, normal colour
8. One greatcoat of normal blue-grey colour and pattern
9. One khaki-brown raincoat
10. Three khaki-brown shirts with long sleeves and attached collars
11. Three khaki-brown shirts with short sleeves and attached collars
12. Six white vests (undershirts)
13. Three pairs long underpants (long johns) of normal pattern
14. Three pairs white undershorts
15. Three khaki-brown neck ties
16. Six pairs white woollen socks
17. Three pairs khaki-brown sports socks
18. Two pairs khaki-brown canvas boots
19. Two pairs khaki-brown canvas shoes
20. One blue-grey blanket, as per other ranks pattern
21. One sports shirt in normal colour B
22. One pair sports shorts in normal colour B
23. One pair training shoes B
24. One pair swimming trunks B
25. One woollen khaki brown sweater
26. Two neck sweat bands of normal pattern and colour
27. Three hand towels of normal colour
28. Four pocket handkerchiefs of normal pattern and colour
29. One pair trouser braces of naval pattern
30. One protective coat, only for motorcyclists

Interestingly, listed amongst the items of tropical equipment rather than the items of clothing was one khaki-brown tropical helmet. ·

Two years later another listing of tropical clothing was published[4]. This amended the previous allocations of tropical clothing that had been published in *Luftwaffen-Verordnungblatt* 2 March

Above: Luftwaffe troops arrive at a port somewhere in Italy. Preceded by their unit colour, the tropical-uniformed troops march away from the dockside.

Left: Vehicle maintenance carried out under the Egyptian sun.

1942, page 273, Order Nr.492, issued 14 February 1942, which had laid down what was then to be worn by Luftwaffe and Fallschirjäger troops serving in Italy south of the line Naples-Foggia, on Sicily and Sardinia, in Greece and on Crete.

1. One tropical peaked cap with neck protector (flap)
2. One tropical tunic
3. One pair long tropical trousers
4. One pair tropical shorts
5. Two tropical shirts with long sleeves
6. Two tropical shirts with short sleeves
7. Three tropical vests
8. Three pairs tropical underpants
9. Two tropical ties
10. Two 'body binders'
11. One pair lace-up boots/shoes.

It is evident that the number of garments available for issue as a full complement of tropical clothing was being decreased as the war progressed.

Right: Feldwebel Herbert König, a pilot NCO with a transport squadron, wearing correct Luftwaffe tropical uniform.

Above: Luftwaffe troops of the Afrikakorps drive themselves into captivity after the defeat of all Axis forces in North Africa. A mixture of temperate and tropical uniforms are worn by the troops, and some wear the tropical version of the Replacement Flight Cap, bleached white by washing and strong sunlight.

Tropenfliegermütze (Tropical Flight Cap)
This tropical cap was similar in design to the normal blue-grey Fliegermütze, and with only the distinction of the colour of the cap piping and the insignia worn on the cap, it was worn by all ranks serving in hot climate countries.

The tropical version was manufactured from tan coloured (khakibraun) cotton material and was usually lined in either bright red or tan coloured cloth. On the upper part of the front of the cap was dis-played the tropical quality of the Luftwaffe national emblem, machine-embroidered in white threads on to a tan background. Worn directly below the emblem but in the centre of the lower part of the cap was the national cockade. This was either the padded ('bumped') version or the flat, machine-woven pattern produced on a small square of tan backing material.

As was normal Luftwaffe practice, those Tropical Flight Caps worn by officers below

the rank of General, Administrative officials with equivalent officer rank and Senior Officer Candidates (Oberfähnrich) were distinguished by silver-aluminium 0.3cm-thick piping around the upper edge to the curtain of the cap. General officers had gilt piping and insignia.

Lightweight Blue-Grey Tropical Flight Cap

A blue-grey, lightweight cotton version of the tropical Fliegermütze existed. This item matched, both in colour and quality of material, the blue-grey tropical uniform that was occasionally worn in hot areas together with the blue-grey cloth-covered tropical helmet.

The Model 1943 Tropical Replacement Flight Cap (Tropeneinheitsfliegermütze)

This was the tropical version of the blue-grey Luftwaffe Einheitsfliegermütze. It was produced in tan-coloured cotton material, had a bright red or tan lining [A] and the insignia, including piping, was the same

A. I have seen an example of this tropical Replacement Flight Cap that had a bright yellow cloth lining.

Above: An unusual, privately purchased tropical tunic, believed to be of Italian origin, worn by Oberleutnant (later Hauptmann) Heinrich Eppen, holder of the Knight's Cross (awarded 5 July 1941) and a crew member in a Junkers Ju 87 dive-bomber squadron. On 4 June 1942 he was shot down by fighters of the 4th and 5th Squadrons of the South African Air Force over Fort Bir Hacheim, and was reported missing in action.

quality and colour as that used on the tropical Fliegermütze.

The Tropical Field Peaked Cap (Tropenschirmmütze)

This distinctive item of tropical head-dress was introduced in 1941, to be worn by all ranks of the Luftwaffe. It had features similar to those found in other forms of peaked caps, namely that it had a crown, a body, a band and a peak.

The cap was produced in tan-coloured cotton material, and the band was stiffened to impart the correct shape to the cap. The large crown and body overhung the band around three sides, with the front of the cap raised. On each side of the body, on the underside portion that over-

hung the sides, there were two ventilation holes with metal rims and fine metal gauze screens. Some caps had smaller metal-rimmed holes without the screen. The large, stiffened peak was covered in tan material.

On the front of the body was displayed the tropical woven version of the Luftwaffe national emblem, and on the front of the cap band there appeared the tropical, flat-woven version of the metal or embroidered bullion insignia normally found on the Luftwaffe blue-grey Uniform Peaked Cap (Schirmmütze) (see page 106). The cap had a flat leather chin strap. This was stained black on the outer surface, while the underside was of untreated, unpolished light brown leather. It was secured to each

Above: Four young paratroopers, believed to be from the Division 'Hermann Göring', taken prisoner somewhere in Italy.

Right: German officers taken prisoner in Sicily are handed food packages on arrival at a port in England for consumption during the next stage of their journey to a PoW camp, 25 July 1943. The Hauptmann reaching out to take his food parcel wears the Luftwaffe tropical peaked cap.

The Luftwaffe-Fallschir-mjäger tropical field cap.
367 Three-quarter front left view showing the neck protector tucked up inside the cap.
368 Three-quarter rear right view showing the neck protector buttoned in position.

A. According to Wim Saris in his excellent book *Headgear of Hitler's Germany*, Volume 1, *Heer, Luftwaffe, Kriegsmarine*, there were purpose-made tropical peaked caps for wear by Air Force officers, including Generals, that had bullion piping built into the seam around the crown of the cap and cap insignia produced from flat, machine-woven metallic threads in either silver or gold appropriate to the wearer's rank.

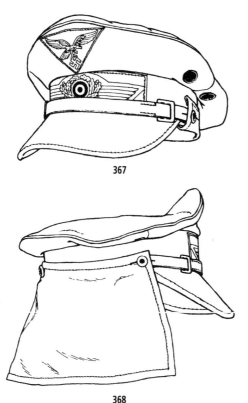

367

368

side of the cap band by a small plastic or metal button.

The cap also had a single plastic (or metal) button sewn to the lower edge at the rear of the cap band. This button and the two side buttons that secured the chin strap were used to attach a tan-coloured neck flap designed to protect the neck from exposure to sunlight. However, these 'Neck Protectors' (Nackenschutz) proved unpopular and were frequently tucked up inside the cap or discarded altogether.

Although the cap was intended to be worn by all ranks of the Luftwaffe, including Paratroops, instances were frequently recorded where officers replaced the leather chin strap with the silver-aluminium cap cords normally worn on their Uniform Peaked Caps.[A]

This item of tropical head-dress was known affectionately within the Luftwaffe as the 'Hermann Meyer' cap, a reference to the Reichsmarschall's misplaced boast made at the start of the war that 'The Ruhr will not be subjected to a single bomb. If an enemy bomber reaches the Ruhr, my name is not Hermann Göring; you can call me Meyer'.

Left: Arnold Hübner in Tunisia (see also the photo on page 119). He wears the short-sleeved tropical shirt and the tropical version of the Fliegermütze.

Right: A young paratrooper from Fallschirmjäger Regiment 3 on guard duty.

Left: A clear view of the strap and buckle arrangement on the ankle cuffs of the Luftwaffe tropical trousers. This is a Fallschirmjäger machine-gun crew operating in Italy.

The Luftwaffe Tropical Helmet (Tropenhelm)

Luftwaffe and Fallschirmjäger troops taking up station in North Africa were provided with Tropical Sun Helmets. As will be seen from the 1941 listing of Luftwaffe tropical clothing, the Sun Helmet was considered an item of equipment rather than an item of clothing.

The standard-issue Luftwaffe item was the tan-coloured (khakibraun) canvas-covered tropical helmet lined with red cloth. It was very similar in construction and shape to the olive-green felt-covered version initially worn by Army troops of the Deutsches Afrika Korps. The edge to the helmet rim was trimmed with light brown leather, and the leather chin strap was of the same colour.

Insignia worn on the helmet consisted of a white metal version of the Luftwaffe national emblem and a metal shield bearing the German national colours.[A] The eagle and swastika was mounted on the right side of the helmet, facing towards the front, and the black, white and red shield on the left side. To allow the eagle to face forward, the design of the emblem was the reverse of that normally used, the eagle facing left instead of right. The shield was divided diagonally, and the central 'white' portion was in fact the unpainted aluminium of the shield.

Although this was an official form of tropical head-dress, its use was not universal. Nor was it a practical item of wear, many men preferring to wear other forms of tropical cloth headwear.

Other official-pattern Sun Helmets covered in light olive green or blue-grey canvas, all of which carried Luftwaffe insignia, are also known to have been used.

Shirts and Ties

The subject of the type and colour of shirts and ties was touched on in Volume 1933–40 (see page 247). Wartime economy measures brought about an issue of a new style of shirt that combined a number of features not previously found on pre-war-issue shirts, and which at the same time improved the manufacturing process. The new shirt was itself more suitable for use under combat conditions, especially by Luftwaffe ground forces.

The Trikot Shirt with Attached Collar

September 1943 saw the introduction of a new style of Luftwaffe shirt,[5] brought in to replace the former collarless Trikot shirt worn with the issue, single-button neck band. The new shirt had an attached collar, breast pockets with button-down pocket flaps, long sleeves, and was buttoned at the cuffs and at the neck as well as down the front by a series of five small composite shirt buttons. The shirts were manufactured in blue-grey material for universal use within the Luftwaffe and in grey-green for members of the Hermann Göring Division, the Luftwaffe Field Corps and those serving in Luftwaffe Mountain Units.

The new shirt eliminated the need to wear the single-button neck band when the Fliegerbluse or the Waffenrock or was worn. This in turn meant that the earlier collarless Trikot shirt and the neck-band were phased out, and only continued to be worn until stocks were exhausted.

Specific instructions were laid down regarding the wearing of these new shirts with the Fliegerbluse. When the blouse was worn closed at the neck, the amount of shirt allowed to be visible above the upper edge of the collar to the Fliegerbluse was set at 0.5cm, and where it was fastened at the front of the throat a height of 2cm was permitted. When the collar of the Flight Blouse was worn open at the neck, the collar of the shirt had either to be left open or the collar button and the first top button were to be undone and the collar turned back in on itself and tucked under in such a way as to correspond to the size of the 'V' neck opening of the Fliegerbluse collar.

During periods of warm weather the new shirt could be worn without the Flight Blouse. It could also be worn with the new reed-green uniform by those persons on active service undertaking any type of duty or when off duty. When worn in the confines of a barracks within the area of the German homeland, or when the wearer was undertaking service outside the barracks, the shirt was to be worn with the Fliegerbluse, the Denim tunic or the reed-green suit. For the purpose of walking-out, a black tie was required.

NCOs and Men wore detachable shoulder-straps on the shirt of either reed-green denim or blue-grey material. Each shirt

A. The insignia first used on the Luftwaffe Tropical Sun Helmet was stamped out of sheet brass. Later it was produced in silver-white aluminium alloy. The national tricolour carried on the right side of the helmet was painted black and red. The so-called 'white' central portion was in fact the un-painted aluminium alloy. It is of interest to speculate why it was that, whilst the national tricolour was removed from the steel helmet by an order dated 12 June 1940, this same order did not extend to the shield carried on the tropical sun helmet.

was issued with a single pair of shoulder-straps. Officers made use of their normal pattern of shoulder-straps. Collar patches, rank chevrons and trade badges were not worn on these shirts. The Luftwaffe national emblem worn on the shirt had either a reed-green or a blue-grey backing and was worn on the right breast at the same height as on the Fliegerbluse.

Although the September 1943 instructions made no mention of the light tan tropical shirts, shirts were produced in this colour that were identical in style to the new collar-attached shirts. They were intended to be worn with the Luftwaffe light tan tropical uniform (described on page 211), and were manufactured with long sleeves which, when worn without the jacket, were allowed to be rolled up. How-

ever, contemporary photographs frequently show this type of shirt with short sleeves.

The Breast Eagle insignia worn on these tropical shirts conformed to that worn on the blue-grey Trikot shirt, except that the backing material was light tan cloth. Shoulder-straps for NCOs and Men were of the normal Luftwaffe blue-grey type, or, if they had been issued, the tropical version. These tropical shoulder-straps had a light tan base with appropriately-coloured piping. If rank braiding was used, it was produced in a copper-brown shade of 'Litzen' whilst retaining the patterning peculiar to the Luftwaffe. While the small shirt buttons were normally of a light brown shade, the buttons used on the shoulder-straps were of the type normally used on straps, made

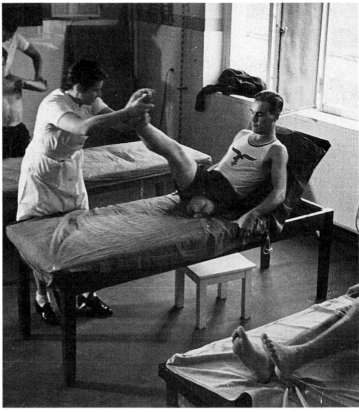

of light metal, domed with a pebbled sur-face and with a light brown painted finish. Officers wore their own normal pattern of shoulder-straps. As before, no collar patches, rank chevrons or trade badges were to be worn on these tropical shirts.

Sports Clothing

The regulation issue sports clothing, which consisted of vests, shorts, running shoes, bathing trunks, shirts, football and hand-ball shirts and training and tracksuits, together with their related insignia, was dealt with in detail in Volume 1933–40, pp.249–52.

So far as I am aware there was no wartime development in this sports clothing.

The Luftwaffe Field Divisions

The autumn of 1942 saw the deployment of the first of the new Luftwaffe Field Divi-sions, albeit only a few in number at first, on the southern flank of the Eastern Front.

These divisions, ten at first, followed by a further ten, had begun to be raised with

Above left: In one of the loveliest hospitals in Germany, wounded and crippled mem-bers of the German armed forces were brought back to health by sport and gymnastics. Modern apparatus and equip-ment were at their disposal to help the 'honorary members of the nation' regain their fitness. An amputee member of the Luftwaffe takes part in a sports event for convalescents.

Above: Wounded soldiers receive physiotherapy. The amputee member of the Luft-waffe wears a sports vest with a single, 1cm-wide black band around the neck to indicate that he is a non-commissioned officer (see also Volume 1933–40, p.249).

Left: A Luftwaffe physical train-ing instructor, wearing sports clothing, helps a wounded soldier, wearing regulation military hospital clothing, to exercise his injured arm.

astounding rapidity in the summer of 1942. They were formed from surplus air force personnel drawn from Anti-Aircraft formations, Air Signals troops, Ground Crew personnel, administration units and certain numbers of recruits and foreign Luftwaffe personnel. This 'combing out' process was necessitated by the desperate shortages in manpower inflicted on the German Army fighting in the East. The original plan to make up these shortages had been for the German Navy to provide 10,000 or 20,000 personnel and the German Air Force to give 50,000 men to the Army. However, Göring raised strong objections to what he saw as his 'good, young National Socialists being dressed up in grey', meaning the reactionary field-grey uniform of the Army. Instead, Göring agreed to raise Luftwaffe ground divisions on condition that, from the Divisional Commander down to the last man, they consisted solely of Luftwaffe personnel. Agreement was reached, but twice the number of Air Force personnel were required in order to match the numbers that the Navy was no longer supplying.

Despite the rapid formation of these Luftwaffe Field Divisions, the intake of high-class recruits would have served the Army better had they been used to fill the yawning gaps in the seasoned Army formations. The Luftwaffe Divisions were eager to get to grips with the enemy, but from the very beginning they suffered from their innate deficiencies, inexperienced leadership, insufficient formation training and, to some extent, unsuitable equipment.

Their organisation and initial combat training took place at Mielau, East Prussia (Wehrkreis I), and other training areas. Originally 22 Luftwaffe Field Divisions were raised, but two of these were disbanded. Of the remaining 20 divisions, most were sent to the Russian Front in the winter of 1942–43 and some were also engaged on the Italian Front and in France.

A typical Luftwaffe Field Division consisted of 2 Jäger-Regimenter, each of three Abteilungen, plus normal divisional supporting troops and an additional anti-aircraft battery. The strength was originally intended to have been 10,000 all ranks. The Jäger-Regimenter were numbered in numerical sequence beginning with the first Division, e.g.: Luftwaffe Feld-Division 11 had Jäger-Regimenter 21 and 22. In other words, the number of the second Jäger-Regimenter equalled the divisional number multiplied by two, and that of the first Jäger-Regimenter equalled the divisional number multiplied by two, minus one.

Despite receiving from Hitler the title of 'Assault Divisions' the Luftwaffe Field Divisions, for reasons already stated, suffered badly and many of the units failed in heavy fighting. In the autumn of 1943 the OKW finally succeeded in getting them incorporated into the Army, but those that had suffered heavy losses were disbanded in 1943 and 1944 and the remaining Divisions were reorganized along the lines of the Army's Infantry Division, 1944 type.

Field Divisions Camouflage Jacket

When the first of the Luftwaffe Field-Divisions was raised in 1942 it was considered necessary that the troops be issued with a camouflage jacket of a design suited to their infantry role.

The Fallschirmjäger smock was of too high a quality and too expensive in terms of

369 The camouflage field jacket worn by personnel of the Luftwaffe Field Divisions.

369

production costs and materials, so a much simplified Jacket was designed and manufactured, and became a 'trademark' of these Luftwaffe infantry. Using the Wehrmacht's ubiquitous green 'splinter' pattern camouflage material, the jacket was simple in design and easy to manufacture.

It was single-breasted, front-fastening with a single row of five large blue-grey plastic buttons. The skirt reached to the thigh. The sleeves had gathered-in cuffs fastened by a single button. On each side was a large pocket with a letter-box flap fastened by a single plastic button.

Loops were provided for the attachment of shoulder-straps. When first issued, the jackets were supplied with simple cloth shoulder-straps of the same camouflage material as that used for the jacket, but both officers and other ranks frequently replaced them with their own straps.

The Luftwaffe eagle and swastika was worn on the right breast. This item was normally in situ when the jackets were issued, machine-embroidered on a backing of green, but sometimes camouflaged, material.

Left: Somewhere on the Normandy front, men of a Luftwaffe Field Division riding astride a heavily camouflaged Citroen anxiously scan the sky for Allied aircraft. Both men wear the splinter-pattern-camouflage field jacket.

Opposite page, bottom: A loader rams home another round into an 88mm. Dug into the Normandy bocage and well camouflaged, these cannon proved deadly in the anti-tank role.

Below left: Men of a Luftwaffe Field Division on the alert in a well constructed trench and bunker complex somewhere on the Russian front. Both men wear the Luftwaffe field jacket and both have mosquito netting draped over their steel helmets.

Below right: A pause for food during the battle for Caen, 24 July 1944.

Decorations such as cuff-titles, cloth or metal badges and awards could be worn on this garment, as photographic evidence occasionally shows, but in general the jacket was worn unadorned.

Red Cross Identification 'Vests'
The wearing of a Red Cross arm band not only fulfilled one of the prime conditions for the safety of a non-combatant as laid down in the Geneva Convention, but also served as a means of identification both for friendly troops in need of medical aid and those of the enemy.

The fighting on all fronts in the European theatres, however, seemed to have brought about a need for front-line medical personnel to be far more clearly identified than could be achieved by just wearing an arm band. To this end, these troops took to wearing identification vests made from white material, on which was

Left: German medical personnel surrender to the Americans at Aachen on 19 October 1944. The man in front wears a purpose-made Red Cross identification vest, while the Army prisoner bringing up the rear wears the type of Red Cross identification panel used to mark vehicles carrying wounded or sick troops.

Below: A parachute medical orderly tends the injuries of German prisoners in February 1945. In addition to wearing the Red Cross arm band required under the terms of the Geneva Convention, he also wears the purpose-made Red Cross identification vest.

Right: As with the German Army, the Luftwaffe utilised stocks of Italian Army camouflage material to produce garments for their own troops. Here, an Army General-leutnant talks with a Fallschirmjäger Hauptmann wearing a field jacket produced from Italian material.

stitched a large red cross. These were of very simple manufacture, being nothing more than two panels of material joined by tapes at the shoulders and tied around the waist by more tapes. No precise specifications have been found regarding their size.

Luftwaffe Garments made from Italian Camouflage Material
As with the German Army, the Luftwaffe produced various combat garments from stocks of surplus Italian Army camouflage material. It is not known how widespread this practice was. Occasionally these garments can be identified in contemporary photographs, but examples are few and far between.

The Waffen-SS Pattern Camouflage Clothing worn by Troops of Brigade, later Division, 'Hermann Göring'
The question as to what type of camouflage field clothing was to be issued to troops of

Right: Troops of the Regiment 'General Göring', later Division 'Hermann Göring', training with an 8cm mortar. They all wear Waffen-SS-style and camouflage-patterned smocks and helmet covers.

the Brigade 'Hermann Göring' was resolved by a memorandum dated 21 July 1942, which stated that certain troops were to be issued with camouflaged smocks and helmet covers of the type worn by troops of the Waffen-SS, and that these items were to be worn only for combat purposes and not during training exercises. The issue was restricted to certain units, and the numbers of garments available was limited.

The Waffen-SS-style camouflage of the ragged-spot design (sometimes referred to as 'oakleaf pattern') and the leaf design (referred to as 'palm leaf clump' pattern) was worn extensively in North Africa, Sicily and Italy. It was superseded a year later by standard Wehrmacht 'splinter' and later 'splotched' pattern garments.

The Camouflage Jacket

The jacket was a smock-like, reversible pullover garment, collarless and elasticated around the waist and wrists. A central vertical neck opening was closed by being laced up. There were two vertical pocket openings with letterbox flaps, each secured

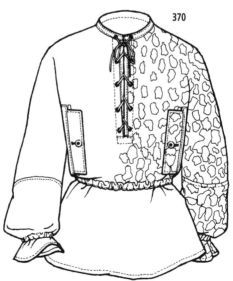

370

by a single horn button on either side of the chest front. No insignia was worn on this jacket.

The Camouflage Steel Helmet Cover

This was a reversible cloth cover made from the same camouflage-patterned material

Above and right: Troops of the Regiment 'General Göring', later Division 'Hermann Göring', operating various weapons. They all wear Waffen-SS-style and camouflage-patterned smocks and helmet covers.

370 The Waffen-SS Smock in 'ragged spot' camouflage patterning.

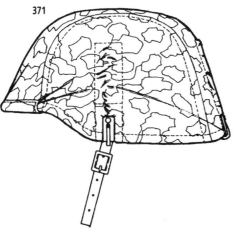

371 The Waffen-SS-pattern steel helmet cover, the left side shown.

371

used for the Jacket, and designed to be worn over the Model 1935 Steel Helmet. It was secured to the helmet at three points around the neck rim by three aluminium, spring-loaded, double-sided metal clips. The curved front edge of the cover had a shallow reinforced 'pocket' that was pushed on to the helmet's visor rim. When this was correctly positioned and the three spring-loaded clips were anchored to the

helmet rim, the cover was securely attached to the helmet.

Reversible Winter Garments

Luftwaffe troops fighting as infantry on the Eastern Front during the winter of 1942/3 were issued with reversible winter clothing of the same pattern as was issued to Army personnel. This clothing was extremely comfortable compared to the issue great-coat, allowing freedom of movement and easy use of equipment while at the same time affording protection both against severe cold and overheating during periods of exertion.

The garments consisted of a heavy-duty, double-breasted over jacket (Fig. 372) and matching over trousers (Fig. 373) and were worn together with a removable hood (Fig. 374) and mittens (Fig. 375).

The jacket and trousers were made large enough to be worn over the normal service uniform, including basic field equipment, but, like their Army counterparts, Luftwaffe personnel preferred to wear their leather equipment over the outside of the winter jacket.

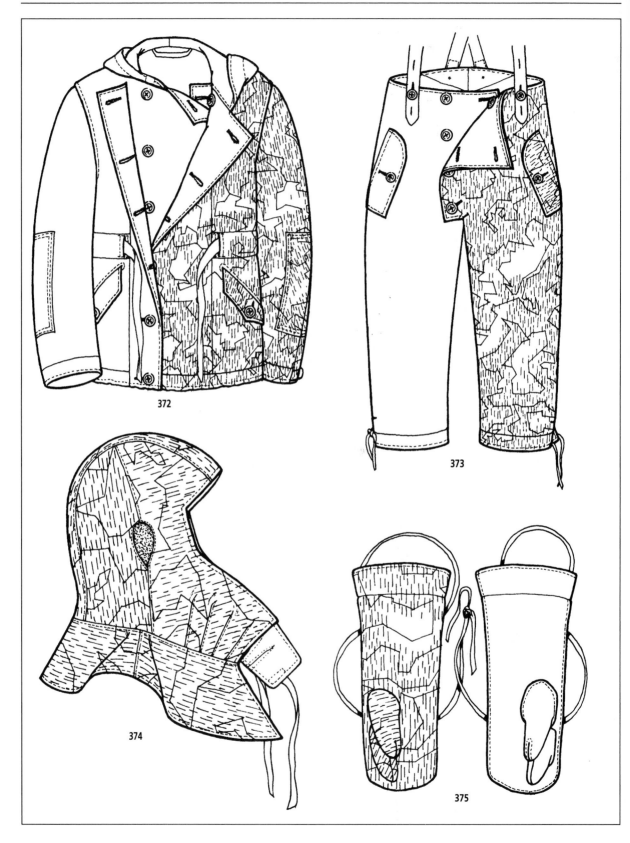

372

373

374

375

The Reversible Padded Winter Uniform.
372 The jacket.
373 The trousers.
374 The hood.
375 The mittens.

Right: Troops of the German Air Force receive supplies of the double sided reversible winter clothing.

Because all the garments were completely reversible, features such as pockets, draw-strings and buttons were duplicated on the camouflage and white sides.

The jacket was double-breasted for extra frontal warmth, with double-buttoned overlaps to the flaps at the front which when securely fastened provided a windproof closure. There was a concealed waistbelt which could be gathered in from the outside irrespective of which side was being worn outermost. The bottom edge of the jacket had a drawstring, and the ends of the cuffs were adjustable. The jacket had long sleeves and an attached drawstring-adjustable reversible hood. Six buttons were visible down the front of the jacket and there was one button on the pocket flap on each side of the skirt.

These metal buttons were painted field-grey on the camouflaged side and white on the white side. Two small fibre buttons were located on the front and rear seams of both arms of the jacket approximately 20cm from the point of the shoulder. These were intended to be used to button on the bands of coloured cloth, used by front line German forces to help identify friendly troops. Like passwords, these bands of cloth were changed every day and a new colour was used for this purpose. This arrangement could be used on either or both sleeves, the small fibre buttons being sewn on to the white as well as the coloured side of the reversible jacket.

The trousers were of the same quality, colouring and manufacture as the jacket. They were also completely reversible,

Left: The crew of a heavy artillery piece. All wear the reversible winter uniform. The officer on the left wears the splinter-pattern camouflage side outermost, while the other two crew members wear the mouse grey to white reversible garments. Each of the 25 visible tank silhouettes painted on the face of the gun shield represents a Soviet tank destroyed, and white rings painted around the gun barrel (not visible) represented Soviet aircraft shot down. 11 January 1944.

Below: A Luftwaffe motor-cyclist wearing the reversible winter uniform, white side outermost. Whilst not wearing a steel helmet, he does wear the reversible hood.

including the pockets. They were shorter in the leg than normal trousers and could be tucked inside the marching boots or tied by the drawstrings around the calf of the boot.

Braces of white webbing, sewn into the waist of the trousers at the back which supported the weight of the garment, were buttoned on each side of the front opening at one of three height positions. The large black buttons were of smooth plastic with four holes.

The trousers had two pockets with large reversible buttoned flaps. There were four buttons down the fly front. Two tapes were sewn into the rear of the waist to allow the waistband to be drawn in tight. There were tapes at the bottom of each leg.

The camouflage pattern of this clothing was either the Army's 'green splinter' pattern or the 'mouse grey' shade. Personnel of the Division 'Hermann Göring' would have worn Waffen-SS camouflage patterned reversible winter clothing (see also p. 227).

It is not known if Luftwaffe personnel wore any rank insignia on their winter clothing. The pattern of rank insignia introduced for wear on camouflage and special combat clothing that did not use shoulder-straps to display rank was first introduced into the Army on 22 August 1942, and was

Right: Continuous wearing of the reversible winter uniform with the white side outermost rapidly defeated the purpose of the snow camouflage. These paratroopers operating on the Eastern Front look decidedly soiled. It must be said, however, that these grubby uniforms were probably better for blending with the slush and thawing mud of the terrain during the period between the winter snow and the coming of spring.

Below: The reversible winter uniform, splinter pattern outermost, worn by a Luftwaffe motorcyclist..

also used by the Waffen-SS, but these would have been inappropriate for Luftwaffe troops. It is possible that they used flight clothing insignia to indicate rank (for illustrations of this insignia see p. 134).

The tight-fitting reversible hood, which was a separate item and not to be confused with the built-in hood attached to the collar of the winter jacket, had a thick blanket lining and a large 'collar' which spread out over the neck and shoulders to provide excellent protection against the cold. The hood was shaped to fit the head and the neck and could be closed over and tied with one long and one short length of tape, the long tape being wound around the neck and tied in front. There was a small area on each side of the hood that had no outer layer of material and the blanket lining showed through. This was designed deliberately for easier hearing when the hood was worn.

The fourth item of the winter clothing were the reversible mittens. Each had a separate compartment for thumb and forefinger, the remaining three fingers being contained in the body of the mitten. The mittens were joined together by a length of white tape which passed around the inside of the jacket and down each sleeve to prevent them being mislaid or lost.

Left: Having arrived at a rail-head somewhere on the Eastern Front, troops of a Luftwaffe Field Division load their equipment on to hand carts in readiness for their move to a front-line position, 23 April 1943. Most of the men are wearing the reversible winter uniform, which from the brightness of the white side appears to be newly issued.

Cold Weather Over-boots

The harsh Russian winter of 1941/42 brought home to the military the fact that the troops needed warmer clothing than they customarily wore in the comparatively temperate winter weather of Germany.

The universally issued leather marching boots proved inadequate, particularly for guards, sentries and personnel manning static emplacements. The sub-zero temperatures of the ground very quickly penetrat-ed the leather soles of the boots. To counter this problem, 'guard boots' with wooden soles were designed to be worn over the leather marching boots.

There were several types of cold-weather boots, including straw over-boots and boots made from moulded felt, but the pattern illustrated here was probably the most elaborate of all.

They were much larger than normal footwear (32cm high) because they were

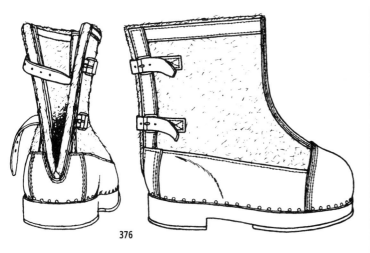

376 Cold-weather overboot, rear and side views.

Far right:: The purpose-made cold-weather snow boots. These should not be confused with either the guard boots illustrated and described below or the straw overboots.

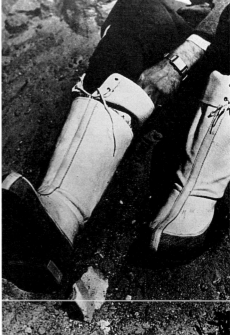

required to be worn over the marching boot. They were constructed from 1.5cm-thick block-felt, covered with brown leather on the upper welts and toecaps, with solid wooden soles at least 4cm-thick at the heel tapering to 2cm at the toe, and these in turn had rubber soles and heels stuck to their surface. The boots were trimmed with brown leather and were fastened down their split-back seam by two 16cm-long leather straps and metal buckles.

The boots could be worn on either foot. Because of their size and unyielding thickness, they were not pulled on over the normal boots, but the wearer stepped into them before fastening the twin straps. They were not suited to rapid movement.

Snow Camouflage

Luftwaffe and Fallschirmjäger troops serving on the Eastern Front during the winter months from 1942–43 onwards were confronted with the same problem as their Army compatriots. The reversible winter clothing proved so popular with these Air Force troops that they, too, tended to wear the garments day and night for weeks on end. As the uniform was a warm

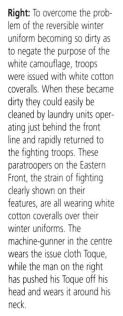

Right: To overcome the problem of the reversible winter uniform becoming so dirty as to negate the purpose of the white camouflage, troops were issued with white cotton coveralls. When these became dirty they could easily be cleaned by laundry units operating just behind the front line and rapidly returned to the fighting troops. These paratroopers on the Eastern Front, the strain of fighting clearly shown on their features, are all wearing white cotton coveralls over their winter uniforms. The machine-gunner in the centre wears the issue cloth Toque, while the man on the right has pushed his Toque off his head and wears it around his neck.

Left: Medical troops, two of whom are wearing white cotton coveralls, prepare a purpose-made paper insulating cover. These white covers were wrapped around the bodies of wounded or sick soldiers before they were placed on stretchers prior to being removed to a field hospital by motor transport, rail or aircraft. Note the use of the special winter boots.

garment designed to keep out the severe cold and, when worn with the white side outermost, to provide camouflage in snow-covered terrain, the white side to the jacket and trousers soon became filthy, defeating the purpose of the white camouflage.

To overcome this problem, those troops operating in the front line were issued with thin white cotton covers, capes or

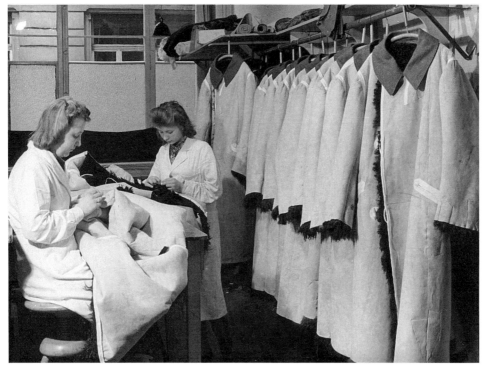

Left: The normal cloth greatcoat was found to be inadequate to protect the troops fighting on the Eastern Front from the ravages of the Russian winters. Consequently those troops that were required to operate in exposed positions began to be issued with heavy-duty guard coats purpose-made from animal skins. Here women working in a German factory produce animal-skin fur guard coats.

Above right: The crew of a heavy Flak gun wearing the purpose-made animal skin fur coats.

Right: Other forms of improvised cold-weather clothing were frequently encountered. This photograph shows an 88mm gun crew wearing animal-skin jerkins.

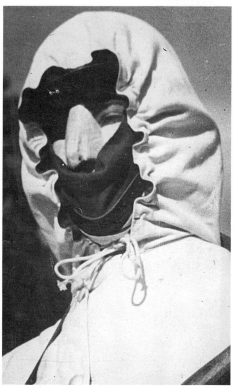

Opposite page and above:
Fur caps, a mode of dress copied from the Russians, were a popular form of head-dress for German troops operating on the Eastern Front during winter. They were produced in a variety of styles and colours.

Above right: Adolf Galland wearing an animal-skin fur-lined coat whilst rabbit hunting in January 1941.

Right: A cold-weather face mask.

suits, similar to those used in the German Army, which could be worn over all uniforms and equipment and could be easily washed and cleaned. For further details of these snow garments see *German Army Uniforms and Insignia, 1933–45*, pp. 181–182.

Facemasks

The extreme cold of the Russian winters, with temperatures that fall below freezing for long periods frequently combining with wind chill to become dangerous, was such that it was not uncommon for a soldier to have the tips of his ears frozen to the rim of his steel helmet with the result that the wearer frequently lost parts of his ears. It was necessary to wear gloves or use sacking when grasping metal, such as rifles, vehicle jacks, etc., for bare hands would freeze to the metal.

Facemasks were issued to those men whose duties exposed them more than ordinarily to the elements: guards, sentries, and men in open lorries or railway trucks.

One side of the mask was white, and this completed the snow camouflage afforded by the winter clothing.

The Gas Mask Model M1938

As part of the precautions taken to protect their troops from the possible dangers of gas attack, all Luftwaffe personnel were issued with a gas mask carried in a purpose made case. An early model gas mask and case – the Model M1924 – left over from the Reichwehr, was in use with the Luftwaffe in the mid 1930s (see Volume 1933–40, pages 201–202) but by 1939 the

majority of the Air Force troops were equipped with the standard Model M1938 gas mask housed in its distinctive cylindrical, fluted metal, canister.

Paratroops, as has been explained, used a special gas mask and cloth carrying case (see page 208) and those Luftwaffe personnel engaged on flying duties were not required to carry, or had reason to wear, gas masks.

Zeltbahn, Model 1931 (Waterproof Shelter Triangle)

This item, issued to Luftwaffe troops, was identical with that used throughout the Army.

It could be used for a variety of purposes, but was primarily designed to be worn as a waterproof cape. It was manufactured from tightly woven, water-repellent, cotton drill, printed on both sides with the standard pattern of Army and Luftwaffe camouflage patterning, dark on one side, lighter on the other. The triangle measured 203cm x 203cm x 240cm, the last dimension being the base edge.

Thirty dish-shaped, rustproof gunmetal buttons were sewn on each side, and there were twelve buttonholes along each of the shorter edges and six along the base edge.

Two zinc grommets were set into the fabric at the two base corners and in the centre of the base edge, through each of which was threaded a 28cm length of thin rope with knotted ends. These were used to tie the cape to three others to form a tent. There was another, larger zinc grommet at each corner of the shelter triangle.

In the centre of the Zeltbahn was a double-flapped opening which enabled the item to be pulled on over the head when worn as a cape. The buttons and buttonholes, all of which corresponded exactly on both sides, were so disposed that the cape could be fastened around the body in different ways, each offering maximum protection yet freedom of movement. When not in use the Zeltbahn was folded or rolled and strapped to the field equipment or pack.

Right: Troops of a Luftwaffe Field Division parade wearing the Zeltbahn as a garment.

6. LUFTWAFFE WOMEN'S SERVICE

Germany took longer to employ women to assist their armed services than was the case with Britain. This was probably due to a combination of the official Nazi Party attitude towards their women citizens and the fact that, for the first months of the European war, Germany was victorious and it was probably felt that it was unnecessary for women to assist in the war effort. However, by early 1940 the need for servicemen to be released from office administration work for combat duty resulted in women being recruited for the German Army Female Signals Service (Nachrichtenhelferinnen des Heeres) and as Air Force Female Assistants (Luftwaffenhelferinnen).

Women between the ages of 17 and 45 were recruited and trained by the Air Signals Troops (Luftnachrichtentruppe) as clerical staff, telephonists, teletype printer operators, radio operators and assistants in the Intelligence Service. They had a choice of serving with units based within the borders of the Reich or joining those units operating on foreign soil.

By 1943 the increase in the scale of the Allied bombing offensive against the German Reich, and the growing decrease in those areas under German occupation, resulted in many Luftwaffenhelferinnen being transferred from office duties to assist in the air protection services. Many women were drafted into the Luftwaffe to fill the depleted ranks of the Reich air defence system.

Volunteers drawn from the Luftwaffen-Helferinnenkorps were employed to act as auxiliary crews operating searchlight units, serving on anti-aircraft fixed battery sites and operating sound-locating and radar apparatus. They were formed into Flakwaffen-Helferinnen units stationed within the borders of Germany, and although they were not members of armed forces, they were governed by military regulations and

discipline. They were distinguished by a special arm badge worn on the right upper arm of their uniform (Fig. 423). By 1944 women were also acting as medical staff attached to Flak units.

In 1944 the 'Ostkampfhelferinnen der Luftwaffe' was formed. In the main this consisted of female refugees from eastern Europe, but by November 1944 it contained so many refugees from all the countries of Europe that its title was changed to 'Luftwaffen-Kampfhelferinnen'.

Early in 1945 another female organisation, the 'Wehrmachthelferinnenkorps', was formed from the wives and girlfriends of German Army, Navy and Air Force personnel. The authorities felt it expedient that these females should at least have the protection of the articles of war as set out in the Geneva Convention, although Soviet Russia was not a signatory to this agreement. Significant additional help was afforded by these women.

This tri-service organisation was divided into three main groups: a. Stabshelferinnen; b. Nachrichtenhelferinnen; and c. Truppenhelferinnen. Personnel from the third group were assigned to transport and anti-aircraft duties, etc.

As late as 8 March 1945 the formation of the 'Helferinnenkorps der Luftwaffe' took place, although its organisation had been announced on 1 February that year. Their uniforms were of the same pattern as worn previously by earlier female formations. Their rank insignia was different, as is illustrated as Figs. 413 to 422.

Kriegshilfsdienstmädchen

Mention must be made of the female personnel of the Reichsarbeitsdienst. Known as Kriegshilfsdienstmädchen, they too were actively employed in the defence of the Reich. Originally in 1943 they formed part of the Flugmeldedienst, and were later

Right: A Luftnachrichten-Führerin acting as Duty Officer. This officer wears the blue-grey 'kostume' (suit) consisting of a jacket and skirt together with the 'Schiff-schenform' (little boat) cap. Note that no cockade was worn on this item, and that, to distinguish this person as an officer of the Ln-Helf-erinnenschaft, her cap was trimmed with gold-brown cording. She wears a light blue service blouse (shirt) with attached collar and black tie, on to which is pinned the small white-metal eagle and swastika stick-pin insignia. The matt gold-yellow duty cord worn around her right shoulder was the same pattern of cord as worn by male Duty Officers and NCOs. and is described and illustrated on page 87.

assigned to radar sites. In the spring of 1944 their tasks were enlarged to help crew Flak batteries and in January 1945 they took over the operation of all searchlight batteries. These women wore the female version of the RAD uniform.

Luftnachrichten-Helferinnen

The Luftnachrichten-Helferinnen, abbreviated to Ln-Helferinnen, was part of the Luftwaffenhelferinnen. The Female Air Signals Assistance service was made up of the Flugmeldedienst (literally, Flight Reporting

Service and not to be confused with the Air Protection Warning Service, better known as the Air Raid Warning Service) and the Fernsprech -und Fernschribbetriebsdienst der Luftwaffe (Telephone and Teletype service of the Luftwaffe).

The duties of the Flugmeldedienst were very similar to those of the Luftschutzwahrndienst (Air Raid Warning Service). Although these two organisations worked in close unison, the Flugmeldedienst, however, was considered the first line of air defence, operating as it did with binoculars, searchlights and sound locating equipment, identifying enemy aircraft, observing their flight path and reporting their findings to the Flak units, fighter defence and the Air Raid Warning Service.

Females working with the Flight Reporting Service up to June 1940 wore standard-pattern male Luftwaffe rank insignia. From June 1940 to July 1941 the insignia illustrated here applied (see Figs. 388 to 392).[1] The insignia was worn on the left forearm of the blue-grey jacket.

On 28 July 1941 lengthy instructions were published[2] that changed the rank insignia yet again, but this time the new insignia continued to be worn for the duration of the war (see Figs. 398 to 404).

The uniforms worn by the women of the LN-Helferinnenschaft and the LS-Warndienst-Helferinnenschaft were given as:
1 blue-grey cloth cap of fore and aft pattern (Schiffchenform, literally 'little boat shape').
1 double breasted blue-grey wintercoat with two rows each of four buttons.
1 rain cape of a new pattern.
1 suit (Köstum) which comprised:
  1 blue-grey single breasted jacket fastened by a single row of three buttons, a half belt at the back with two securing buttons, two side pockets with flaps and an inner pocket on the left side.
  1 straight blue-grey skirt with pleat.
  1 service blouse of a new pattern but not for use by officer grades.
  3 light blue service blouses with collars attached.
  1 white service blouse of artificial silk of new pattern.
  1 blue-grey work smock.
2 service frocks with 3 white collars, all of new patterns.
1 woollen jacket.
3 pairs of blue-grey artificial silk stockings.
2 black neck ties of new pattern in place of the dark-blue clip-on ties.
1 service handbag.
2 pairs black shoes.

Included in this list was 1 large Luftwaffe national emblem for the suit, 1 small emblem for the side cap, badges of appropriate rank and 1 service brooch worn on the tie both for the Ln-Helferinnen and the LSW Helferinnen.

Left: Telephone operators of the Luftnachrichten-Helferinnenschaft. All wear rank insignia on the upper left sleeve of their blue-grey jacket, above which they display their trade badge.

377 The blue-grey Jacket and Skirt (Köstume) of the type worn by women of the various female Luftwaffe and Air Defence Formations (with certain modification of insignia). The uniform shown was for an Oberführerin of the Luftnachrichten-Helferinnen, as a qualified Flight Reporting Service operator in charge of a Flugmeldedienst-Helferinnen Kameradschaft.

Trade and Proficiency Badges for Service Women.
378 Air raid warning service personnel.
379 Air Signals personnel with qualification as a 'B' Class telephone operator.
380 Air Signals personnel with qualification as a 'B' Class teleprinter operator.
381 Air Signals personnel with qualification as a 'B' Class radio operator.
382 Air Signals equipment administrator.
383 Signals personnel in flight and anti-aircraft units (non-air signals units).
384 Searchlight equipment administrator.
385 Direction-finder operator.
386 Sound-locator operator.
387 Qualified radio instructor.

377

Other items of clothing were also listed, such as winter garments and sports clothing.

Details of the Blue-Grey Uniform, Flight Cap and Specialist Insignia worn by Females of the various Luftwaffe and Air Defence Formations

The standard-pattern Luftwaffe eagle and swastika emblem was worn on the right breast of the blue-grey jacket, and in a smaller version on the front of the Fliegermütze (side cap) by personnel of the Luftnachrichten-Helferinnenschaft. These emblems were machine-embroidered in matt-grey cotton for ranks from Helferin to Haupthelferin, and in silver-aluminium thread for all ranks from Führerin and above. A small, white-metal stick-pin in the form of the Luftwaffe national emblem was worn below the knot of the black tie by all personnei.

Female Leaders of the rank of Führerin and above in the Ln-Helferinnenschaft wore 0.3cm-wide gold-brown piping around the upper edge to the side flaps of their blue-grey Fliegermütze. They were further distinguished as Leaders by wearing silver-aluminium piping, 0.3cm wide, around the edge of the collar of both their Jacket and their Winter Coat. They also bore a 1cm square silver-aluminium star embroidered into each collar point of both garments.

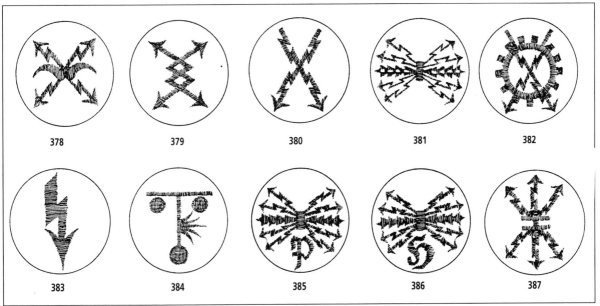

| 378 | 379 | 380 | 381 | 382 |

| 383 | 384 | 385 | 386 | 387 |

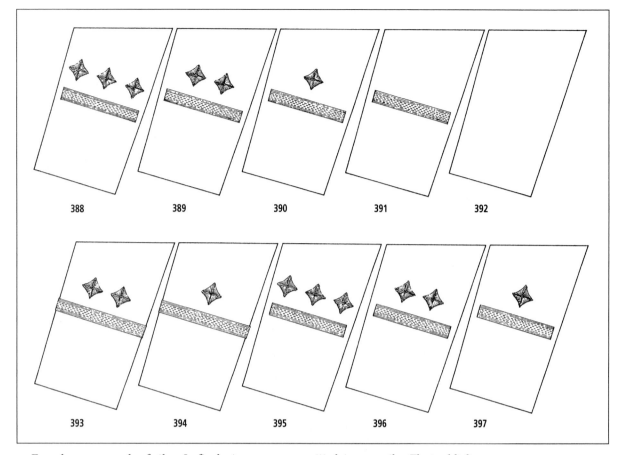

388   389   390   391   392

393   394   395   396   397

Female personnel of the Luftschutz-warndienst, regardless of rank, wore the machine-woven Luftschutz emblem (see Fig. 69) on the right breast of their Jacket and also on the front of their blue-grey Flight Caps. All LSW-Helferinnen female personnel were distinguished by 0.3cm-wide green piping along the upper edge to the side flaps of the Fliegermütze. This same Luftschutze emblem in white metal was worn as a small stick-pin on the black neck tie. They also wore the Luft-schutzwarndienst emblem on their left upper arm, halfway between the point of the shoulder and the elbow.

Speciality badges (Tätigkeitsabzeichen), where these were worn, were worn on the left upper arm of both the Jacket and the Winter Coat, positioned 12cm below the point of the shoulder. Where rank insignia was also worn, the uppermost chevron was positioned 1cm below the lower edge of any speciality badge.

Qualified Ln-Flugmeldehelferinnen personnel, both Leader grades and rank and file,

were permitted to wear the Flugmeldedien-stabzeichen, the Luftwaffe speciality badge for the Flight Reporting Service (see Fig. 378).

Qualified Ln-Betriebshelferinnen personnel, both Leader grades and rank and file, were allowed to wear Luftwaffe special-ity badges of the type worn by Luftwaffe Signals Troops. Although the instructions published in the *Luftwaffen-Verordnungs-blatt* for 11 August 1941[3] did not specify which signals badges these were, it is safe to assume that they were those shown here as Fig. 379–Fig. 387.

Female Leaders in charge of a Flug-meldedienst-Helferinnen-Einsatzgruppe or a Luftnachrichten-Helferinnen-Betriebszug were distinguished by a single strip of sil-ver-aluminium flat braiding, 0.5cm wide, on both sleeves of the Jacket, the Working Smock and the Winter Coat, 12cm from the bottom of each cuff.

Female Leaders in charge of a Flug-meldedienst-Helferinnen-Kameradschaft or a Luftnachrichten-Helferinnen-Betriebs-kammeradschaft wore two 0.5cm-wide

Insignia of rank for the Luftnachrichten-Helferinnen, August 1940 to July 1941.[4]

388 Betriebs-Gruppenführerin und Heimleiterin.

389 Betriebs-Gruppenunterführerin.

390 Aufsichtshelferin.

391 Flugmeldehelferin.

392 Anwärterin (no insignia worn).

Both the pre-August and post-August 1940 insignia were of the same dimensions and colouring. Only the rank titles were altered. The insignia was worn on the left forearm, 10cm above the lower edge of the sleeve. The stripes were 1cm wide by 7cm long, in silver-aluminium flat braiding. The stars were 3cm square, hand-embroidered in silver-aluminium threads.

Insignia of rank for female personnel of the Luftschutz-Warndienst.[5]

393 LS-Warndienstoberführerin.

394 LS-Warndienstführerin.

395 LS-Warndiensthaupthelferin.

396 LS-Warndienstoberhelferin.

397 LS-Warndiensthelferin.

The insignia was worn on the left forearm, 10cm above the lower edge of the sleeve, on both the blue-grey jacket and the top-coat. For the two most senior ranks of LS-Warndienstoberführerinnen and LS-Warndienstführerinnen the 1cm-wide silver-aluminium braid was worn around the cuff. The remaining three ranks had stripes of 1cm-wide silver-aluminium braid that was 7cm long. All the stars were 3cm square, hand-embroidered in silver-aluminium threads.

Right: This officer is shown here operating a telephone switchboard. This clearly shows her rank insignia, trade qualification badge and the single sleeve stripe worn on both cuffs.

stripes of silver-aluminium braiding around both cuffs of the blue-grey Jacket, the Working Smock and the Winter Coat. The stripes were set 0.5cm apart, with the lower stripe positioned 12cm from the bottom of each cuff.

Women who held the rank of either Oberhelferinnen or Haupthelferinnen and who were appointed to the positions of responsibility as given above were also distinguished accordingly by the single or double sleeve stripes.

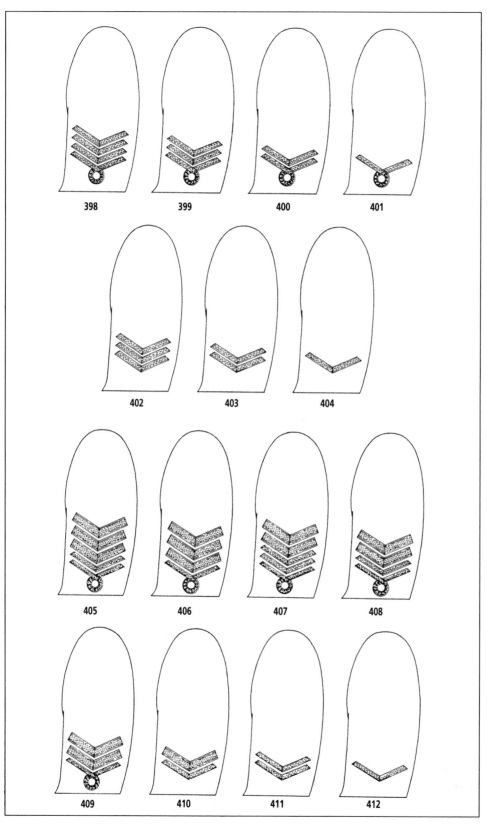

398

399

400

401

402

403

404

405

406

407

408

409

410

411

412

Insignia of rank for Luft-nachricten-Helferinnen-schaft, introduced 28 July 1941.[6]

398 Stabsführerin.
399 Hauptführerin.
400 Oberführerin.
401 Führerin.
402 Haupthelferin.
403 Oberhelferin.
404 Helferin.
Anwärterin (no insignia worn). Similar insignia of the same pattern was also introduced at the same time to be worn by females of the Flugmeldehilferinnen and the Betriebshilferinnen. All the chevrons were of flat, 0.5cm-wide silver-aluminium braiding fashioned to give a shallow 130°-angled chevron. The inner length of each arm of the chevrons was given as 3.3cm, but examination of actual items shows that this was not the case; there was a tendency for these arms to be 4cm long. The curl at the base of the lower chevron worn by the four senior ranks had an inner diameter of 1cm. The insignia was worn on the left upper arm, halfway between the shoulder and the elbow.

Insignia of rank for female members of the Flugmelde-dienst[7]

398 Ln. Flum. Stabsführerin.
399 Ln. Flum. Hauptführerin.
400 Ln. Flum. Oberführerin.
401 Ln. Flum. Führerin.
402 Ln. Flum. Haupthelferin.
403 Ln. Flum. Oberhelferin.
404 Ln. Flum. Helferin.
Ln.flum. Anwärterin (no insignia worn).

Insignia of rank for female members of the Fern-sprech-, Fernschreib-und Funkbetriebsdienst.[7]

400 Ln-Betriebs-Oberführerin.
401 Ln-Betriebs-Führerin.
402 Ln-Betriebs-Haupthelferin.
403 Ln-Betriebs-Oberhelferin.
404 Ln-Betriebs-Helferin.
Ln-Betriebs-Anwärterin (no insignia worn).
The rank of Ln-Betriebs-Oberführerin was the most senior rank in this organization.

Rank insignia for Luftwaffen-Helferinnen personnel independent of other female Luftwaffe units, as of 17 March 1944.

405 LW-Oberstabsführerin.
406 LW-Stabsführerin.
407 LW-Hauptführerin.
408 LW-Oberführerin.
409 LW-Führerin.
410 LW-Haupthelferin.
411 LW-Oberhelferin.
412 LW-Helferin.

The insignia was similar to the chevrons used by the Ln-Helferinen, previously described. The narrow silver-aluminium braid was 0.5cm wide, the thicker braiding 1cm wide. The inner diameter of the curl was 1cm. All insignia was worn on the upper left arm of the blue-grey jacket and top coat, halfway between the shoulder and the elbow.

Insignia of rank for females of the Flakwaffenhelferinnenschaft.

405 Flakw.-Oberstabsführerin.
406 Flakw.-Stabsführerin.
407 Flakw.-Hauptführerin.
408 Flakw.-Oberführerin.
409 Flakw.-Führerin.
Flakw.-Obertruppführerin (as 410, but with two narrow-width chevrons).
410 Flakw.-Truppführerin.
411 Flakw.-Oberhelferin.
412 Flakw.-Helferin.

The insignia was of silver-aluminium flat braiding, 0.5cm wide for the narrow-width chevrons and 1cm wide for the thicker-width chevrons. The curls had an inner diameter of 1cm. All were worn on the upper left sleeve of the blue-grey jacket and top coat, halfway between the point of the shoulder and elbow. Women who held leader ranks from Führerin to Oberstabsfüherin were further distinguished by wearing an aluminium star on both collar points and having the collar of their Jackets piped in 0.3cm-wide silver-aluminium twisted cording.

Above: An Oberst, Commandant of a Flak Battery, talking with a Flakwaffen-Truppführerin in charge of one of his searchlight units. On her left upper sleeve is the arm badge for personnel of the Flakwaffenhelferinnen-Korps.

Below: Women of the Flakwaffenhelferinnen-Korps operating a high powered optical rangefinder.

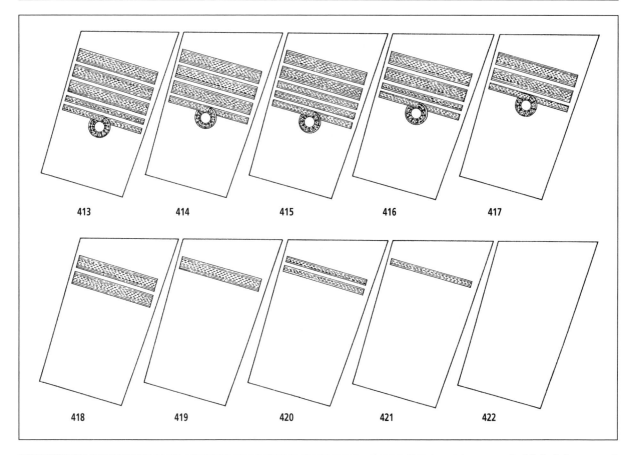

Rank insignia for personnel of the 'Helferinnenkorps der Luftwaffe' and their equivalent Luftwaffe male ranks.

413 Oberstabsführerin, equivalent to an Obersleutnant.
414 Stabsführerin (Major).
415 Hauptdienstführerin (Hauptmann).
416 Oberdienstführerin (Oberleutnant).
417 Dienstführerin (Leutnant).
418 Obertruppführerin (Feldwebel).
419 Truppführerin (Unteroffizier).
420 Haupthelferin (Obergefreiter).

Female Personnel of the Luftschutz-Warndienst.
The females serving in the LS-Warndienst wore uniforms and clothing of the same colouring and pattern as that issued to the LN-Helferinnen and described above. Their ranks and rank insignia however differed and is shown here as Figs. 393–397.

Female Personnel of Independent Luftwaffen-Herlferinnen Units
On 17 March 1944 those Luftwaffen-helferinnen personnel not attached to either the LN-Helferinnen or LS-Warndienst units underwent a change in their rank insignia. This new system is shown here in Figs. 405–412.

Left: The arm badge for personnel of the Flakwaffen-helferinnen-Korps.

Opposite page and below: Photographs taken in June 1944, somewhere in the Belgium-Northern France Air District. Women operating a high powered searchlight. These photographs vividly show the scale of the searchlight in relation to the operators. Note also the use of headscarves, worn instead of the Replacement Flight Cap.

421 Oberhelferin (Gefreiter).
422 Helferin (no insignia worn) (Flieger/Grenadier). The insignia, worn on the left forearm of the blue-grey jacket and top-coat, was made from both 0.5cm- and 1cm-wide silver-aluminium flat braiding. The curl had an inner diameter of 1cm. An order dated 8 March 1945 called for the creation of two new ranks, that of General-führerin and Vertreterin (Deputy) der Generalführerin. The insignia of rank for these two appointments is not known.

423 The blue-grey Service Uniform worn by members of the Flakwaffen-Helferin-nenkorps. This was worn with a single-buttoned blue-grey M43 field cap complete with Luftwaffe eagle and swastika (not illustrated).

424 The blue-grey top-coat worn by members of the Flakwaffen-Helferin-nenkorps.

425 The special arm badge for members of the Flakwaffen-Helferinnenkorps. This was worn on the right upper arm of the blue-grey jacket and top-coat. The design was machine-embroidered in white cotton threads on to a shield of blue-grey uniform cloth.

Right: Women, of the same unit as on the previous spread, operating a high powered searchlight. Note the Replacement Flight Cap.

7. LUFTWAFFE HEIMAT FLAK UNITS

Left: Three women, described as being employed as radio operators with an anti-aircraft battery, captured near Blosein by troops of the 2nd US Infantry Division, 1st US Army, in April 1945. The woman in the centre is wearing a rain cape of the pattern issued to members of the Hitlerjugend. The woman on the right wears the two-button version of the Replacement Flight Cap and the top coat with correct insignia.

426 The blue-grey Fliegerbluse, complete with arm band and collar stick-pin as worn by a civilian member of a Heimatflak battery.
427 The stick-pin worn by factory personnel of the Heimatflak units.

The increased intensity of the Allied bombing campaign against the industrial areas of the German Reich, and the growing shortages in manpower, forced the German authorities to create Home Defence Anti-Aircraft Artillery Units from among the employees of the factories and offices that the Allies were trying so hard to destroy.

These Heimat flak units, as they were termed, were usually staffed by males under or over military service age and specialist workers who were in reserved occupations and therefore exempt from military service. Their defence responsibility was to crew the light anti-aircraft batteries that defended their own areas of employment.

Each member of a battery was issued with a Luftwaffe blue-grey Fliegerbluse (devoid of insignia) and trousers, or black or grey one-piece work overalls. They all received a blue-grey Fliegermütze complete with insignia, and a steel helmet. Their distinguishing insignia was a white arm band worn on the upper left sleeve and bearing a blue Luftwaffe eagle and swastika above the words 'Deutsche Luftwaffe'.

These 'Flakwehrmänner' were divided into two areas of community responsibility: factory workers, who wore a white-metal stick pin bearing a swastika contained inside a cogged wheel, and civilians in the service of the Luftwaffe, who wore a small

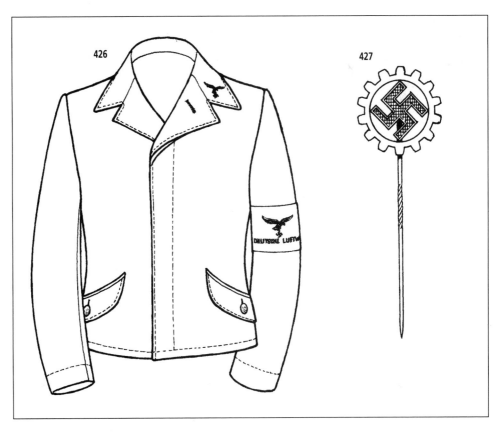

426

427

DEUTSCHE LUFTW

white-metal Luftwaffe eagle and swastika stick pin. These insignia were pinned either to the left lapel of the civilian jacket or to the left collar of the Flight Blouse or overalls.

The Flak crews were trained outside their working hours by qualified Luftwaffe instructors. Upon the successful completion of their basic training period, the battery commander awarded each civilian crew member an appropriate stick pin. These pins were required to be surrendered if a recipient left the service.[1]

Above: Men of a Heimat-Flak unit man a light anti-aircraft gun guarding an armament plant somewhere in Germany, 26 December 1942. The Flakwehrmanner wear black working overalls, Luftwaffe steel helmets and, contrary to normal practice, the 'Deutsche Wehrmacht' black on yellow arm band.

8: HITLER YOUTH FLAK UNITS

The Hitler Youth proved to be a valuable source of potential manpower, at least from among those older members who were too young to be conscripted for military service but old enough to carry out many important and essential functions for the defence of the German home front.

Members of the Hitler Youth designated as 'Luftwaffen-Hitler Jugend', abbreviated to 'LwH-HJ' but more commonly referred to as 'Flakhelfer' (literally Assistants to Anti-Aircraft Artillery Units, or 'Flak Helpers') were called upon to supplement the many Luftwaffe Flak crews defending the Reich. Initially they served as messengers, weather observers, signallers and ammunition carriers, but after January 1943 they began to be increasingly involved in the active air defence of the Reich.

By early 1943, with the United States Army Air Force bombing by day and the Royal Air Force by night, the situation within the borders of Germany was such that on 7 January previously-formulated regulations were published[1] that made provision for all Hitler Youth boys (and later BDM girls) of 15 years or older to act as auxiliaries in any branch of the Luftwaffe that might require them. These youths were initially employed part-time, but later served regular periods of duty, operating search lights and sound locat-

Below: Flakhelferen being issued with travel warrants before going on leave. They wear the special blue-grey greatcoat and Luftwaffe Fliegermütze.

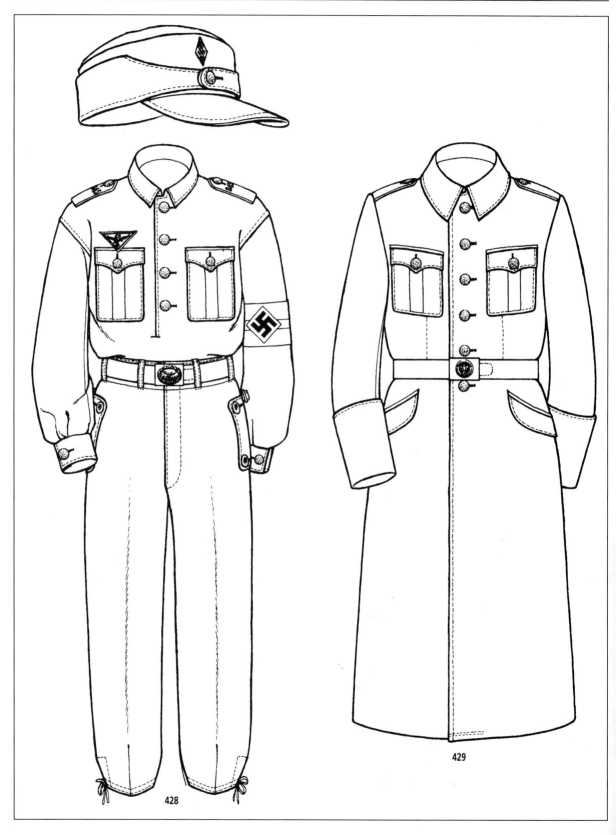

428

429

428 the special blouse, trousers and cap as worn by Hitler Youth members of HJ-Flakhelfer units.
429 The special greatcoat for Hitler Youth members of HJ-Flakhelfer units.

Below: Hitler Youth Flakhelfer members being presented with the Luftwaffe Anti-Aircraft War Badge on the occasion of the Führer's birthday, 20 April 1944. The youths wear the distinctive two-piece blouse and trouser uniform described and illustrated here.

ing equipment and acting as gun crew members manning guns both on Flak towers and in anti-aircraft-battery emplacements. By the summer of 1943 the Flak Helper organization had some 100,000 German youths serving within its ranks.

Initially, these HJ Flakhelfers wore their normal summer or winter Hitler Youth uniform (depending on the seasons), but by 1943 they began to receive their own distinctive uniform. This comprised a blue-grey waist-level blouse, matching long trousers gathered at the ankles and a blue-grey version of the Hitler Youth winter cap. In the winter of 1943/44 these youths were also issued with a distinctive blue-grey greatcoat which was not unlike the Luftwaffe Greatcoat, but had the addition of

two pleated breast patch pockets. Interestingly, it was worn with the Luftwaffe Fliegermütze complete with its Luftwaffe eagle and swastika and the national cockade, and not with the previous pattern of cap.

Their insignia consisted of the Hitler Youth arm band worn on the upper left arm of the blouse, Flieger-HJ shoulder straps (black straps with light blue piping) and a special triangular badge worn above the left breast pocket of the blouse. This black cloth badge had a narrow light blue inverted triangular frame surrounding a Luftwaffe eagle and swastika machine-embroidered in light blue, above which were the light blue gothic letters 'LH'. A small HJ diamond badge was worn on the upper part of the front of the cap.

9: HERMANN GORING: THE MAN AND HIS UNIFORMS

Hermann Wilhelm Göring was the most powerful and influential personality in the National Socialist Movement, second only to Adolf Hitler. Göring held many appointments of great importance within the Party, the State and the Armed Forces, all of which required him to be attired in a particular uniform. As an introduction to the range of uniforms he wore, a brief summary of Göring's life and rise to power is given, to show the organizations and formations that he created and headed and the appointments he took up, together with the relevant dates.

Born in the Marienbad Sanatorium at Rosenheim, Bavaria, on 12 January 1893, Hermann was the fourth of five children and the second son of Dr Heinrich Ernst Göring. Dr Göring had been the former, and first, Reich Commissar (Colonial Governor) for German South-West Africa, known today as Namibia, and Hermann's mother, Franziska 'Fanny' Tiefenbrunn, was Heinrich's second wife.

Göring was trained for service in the German Army, first as a Cadet at the Officer-Cadet School at Karlsruhe, and later at the Military Academy at Gross Lichterfelde, Berlin.

In March 1912, a month after the death of his father, he was gazetted as a Leutnant in the Prinz Wilhelm Infantry Regiment Nr.112, headquartered at Muelhausen in German Alsace. He fought throughout the First World War, initially in the infantry and later in the German Air Arm. When serving with his Baden Regiment he was awarded the Imperial Iron Cross, Second Class, and five weeks into the war he was hospitalized with arthritis. While convalescing at Freiburg he met Bruno Lörzer, and subsequently transferred into the German Air Arm, where he flew initially as an observer and later as a pilot.

Göring proved to be a competent fighter pilot, and his war record was exceptionally fine. He stood 46th on the list of First World War German fighter aces, accredited with 22 victories. He received the First Class Iron Cross from the hands of the Crown Prince, then commanding the German Fifth Army, and on 2 June 1918 the Kaiser bestowed upon him the highest Prussian military decoration it was possible to receive, the coveted Order Pour le Mérite, the famous 'Blue Max'.

On 14 July 1918 Leutnant Göring was appointed to command Jagdeschwader Freiherr von Richthofen Nr.1, the famous 'Flying Circus' previously led, until his death on 21 April 1918, by the 'Red Baron', Manfred von Richthofen.

When the Armistice finally brought the war to an end, Göring would not accept defeat, refusing to hand over his aircraft to his superior officers until forced to do so. In 1920, at his own request, he was discharged from the German Army with the rank of Hauptmann and with the right to wear the uniform of the German Air Arm.

Much embittered by the terms of the Versailles Treaty, Göring left Germany to live in Sweden, where he became a civilian pilot. It was in Sweden where he met, fell in love with and married his first wife, the Swedish Baroness Karin von Fock-Kantzow.

In 1921 Göring and his wife returned to Germany, where he enrolled as a student of history at Munich University. Whilst in Munich, in November 1922, Göring first heard of and met Adolf Hitler, and with almost immediate effect he enrolled as a member of Hitler's National Socialist German Workers' Party.

Göring: The Party Man
On 28 January 1923 Göring was at the mass meeting of the Nazi Party held at

Above: Leutnant Göring photographed as the commander of Jagdgeschwader Freiherr von Richthofen Nr.1.

Göring energetically set about building up this body of men.

Göring took a prominent part in the Munich Putsch of 9 November 1923. Marching alongside Hitler, he sustained a dangerous wound which almost cost him his life. He was extricated from the melée that ensued after the German Police opened fire on the Nazi demonstrators. His life was undoubtedly saved by Frau Ilse Ballin, the wife of a Jewish merchant, assisted by her middle-aged sister. They tended his wound and hid him from the authorities. His groin wound was operated on by Professor von Asch and, under the threat of a warrant issued for his arrest and gravely ill, he managed with the help of his wife and friends to escape the authorities. He first went to Garmisch, then to Innsbruck in the Austrian Tyrol, where he received proper hospital treatment, and later to Italy.

Addicted to morphine, administered to him to overcome the pain of his wound, and living on charity from friends, supporters and admirers, Göring and his wife, still under the threat of arrest, made their way to Stockholm via Czechoslovakia, Poland and the Free City of Danzig. It was not until 1927, when an amnesty was declared for the National Socialists who had taken part in the 9 November 1923 March, that Göring and his wife were able to return to Germany. Hitler had been released from Landesberg prison and had revived the Nazi Party, and Göring immediately rejoined him and the Party.

In May 1928 Göring became one of the first of twelve National Socialist Deputies to enter the Reichstag (the German parliament), serving as Hitler's political representative. He displayed an ability for a rather summary kind of leadership, and displaced the more moderate parliamentarians. With the sweeping Nazi election victories of 31 July 1932 he was appointed President of the Reichstag on 30 August 1932.

After the Nazi 'Seizure of Power' on 30 January 1933, when Adolf Hitler became Chancellor of Germany, Göring was appointed Minister-President of Prussia. He was also appointed Commander-in-Chief of the Prussian Police, and was both the founder and head of the Geheime Staats Polizei, the Secret State Police universally known by its initials GESTAPO, an appointment he relinquished to Heinrich

Marsfeld, during which the Sturmabteilung (SA), made its first official appearance in formation and received the first four SA standards. It was at this meeting that Göring was publicly made Commander-in-Chief of the SA, with the rank of SA-Obergruppenführer, replacing his predecessor, the first SA leader Johann Ulrich Klintzsch. Charged with the task of organizing the SA,

Himmler on 1 April 1934, together with control over concentration camps.

Göring founded the Deutsches Luftsports Verband (DLV), the German Air Sports Association, forerunner of the Luftwaffe, in March 1933. On 28 April he founded and was head of the Reichluftschutzbund (RLB), the Reich Air Defence League, the German air raid protection service, and five days later, on 5 May, he took on the appointment of Reich Minister for Aviation when the Reichskommissariat for Air, which he had headed since January 1933, was upgraded to a ministry.

On 31 August 1933, Göring, who held the First World War Air Arm rank of Captain (Hauptmann), was created a General of Infantry in the German Army by the Supreme Chief of the Reichswehr, President Field Marshal von Hindenburg. Göring also held the SS Honorary rank of SS-Obergruppenführer, bestowed on him by Reichsführer-SS Himmler.

On 26 February 1935 Hermann Göring became Commander-in-Chief of the newly constituted German Air Force, with the rank of Luftwaffe General. Two months later, in April, Göring, now a widower, married Emmy Sonnermann, his first wife Karin having died in Stockholm on 17 October 1931.

Hitler promoted Göring to Luftwaffe Generaloberst on 20 April 1936, and that same year Göring became Chief Forester and Hunting Master of the German Reich. In September 1936 he was appointed Plenipotentiary for the Four-Year Plan. He was also Chairman of the Council of Ministers for the Defence of the Reich and head of the 'Reichswerke Hermann Göring'.

To celebrate Göring's 44th birthday on 12 January 1937, SA Chief of Staff Viktor Lutze appointed him honorary Commander-in-Chief of the élite SA Standarte 'Felderrnhalle'. He already held the rank of SA-Obergruppenführer.

On 4 February 1938 Göring was once again promoted by Hitler, this time from Generaloberst to Generalfeldmarschall, being the first Luftwaffe officer so honoured (see Volume 1933–40, page 79).

On the day the Germans attacked Poland, 1 September 1939, Hitler named Göring as his successor, an appointment which he was to hold for the next five-and-a-half years. (This decree was revised on 29 June 1941, after the flight of Rudolf Hess to Scotland.)

Göring: The Reichsmarschall

After the Fall of France Göring was yet again promoted, this time being elevated to the newly-created and extraordinary rank of 'Reichsmarschall des Grossdeutschen Reichs' (Reich Marshall of the Greater German Empire). This appointment was publicly announced during the evening of Friday 19 July 1940. In a speech to the German people delivered before a special meeting of the Reichstag held in the Kroll Opera House, Hitler celebrated the victory in the West with an appreciation of the role played by his loyal Party comrades and with a succession of dazzling military promotions.

In reference to Göring the Führer said:

'I have resolved, as Führer and Supreme Commander of the Armed Forces, to honour my officers before this forum which represents the German nation. I name first the man whose merits in the service of the Movement, the State and the Luftwaffe are such as to make any expression of gratitude difficult. Since the time when the SA was founded, Party comrade Göring has been inexorably bound up with the development and rise of our Movement. Since the Seizure of Power his capacity for work and his initiative have achieved results for the Reich and the nation in various fields all of which are an intrinsic part of the history of our nation and our Movement.

He became the creator of the German Luftwaffe when the task of building up the German Armed Forces began. Few mortals are granted the opportunity in the course of a single lifetime to create a military instrument from nothing and to forge that instrument into the strongest weapon of its kind. Above all he has installed his spirit into the Luftwaffe. Generalfeldmarschall Göring has, in creating the German Air Force, as a single individual rendered the highest contribution towards the reconstruction of the German Armed Forces. In the course of this war, as Commander of the Luftwaffe he helped to create the conditions necessary for Victory. His merits are unique.

I appoint him Reich Marshall of the Greater German Reich and decorate him with the Grand Cross of the Iron Cross'.

Left: Göring in the uniform of an SA-Obergruppenführer. He wears six Imperial medals on a full medal bar, an Imperial Breast star and the Imperial Iron Cross 1st class, the Commemorative (Army) Pilots badge, a 1914–18 wound badge in black and, around his neck, the coveted Order Pour le Mérite.

Right: Hermann Göring as President of the German Reichstag, wearing SA uniform, presides over the new government in 1932. Seated in the front row, from right to left, are Vice Chancellor von Papen, Foreign Minister von Neurath, and Minister of the Interior Dr Frick. In the second row, from right to left, is Minister for Food Geheimrat Higenberg and the Reichs Labour Minister Seldte. The remaining persons are unidentified.

Right: Prussian Minister President Hermann Göring, wearing his uniform as SA-Obergruppenführer, collects donations in the Unter den Linden, Berlin, on the Day of National Solidarity. Although Göring is known to have worn the early verison of the SA kepi, his preference was for a peaked cap.

Left: On 31 August 1933 President Field Marshal von Hindenburg, the Supreme Chief of the Reichswehr, conferred on Hermann Göring the rank of General of Infantry of the German Army. Göring is seen here in the uniform of a General der Infanterie at a ceremony held at the Ehrenmal in the Unter den Linden, Berlin, on the occasion of Heroes' Memorial Day. In February 1938 Göring was promoted to the Army rank of Generaloberst when, at the same time, Generalfeldmarschall von Blomberg was removed from his post as Reichskriegsminister and Oberbefehlshaber der Wehrmacht (Minister of War and Commander-in-Chief of the Armed Forces).

Right, upper and lower: German Forestry and Game Administration, controlled and administered before 1936 by the Länder or individual German states, was united by the Nazis into the Office of the Forest Master (Reichsforstamt) under the control of Hermann Göring as Chief Forester and Hunting Master of the German Reich. Göring was an accomplished huntsman and a good shot, enjoyed most forms of Germanic blood sports, and took an active interest in the Deutsche Jägerschaft.

Above: Minister President Hermann Göring takes the salute of his State Police at the conclusion of a special parade held to mark his 41st birthday in the garden of his Berlin palace in the Leipzigerstrasse, 12 January 1934. Göring, who wears the uniform of Reichsminister der Luftfahrt (Reichs Minister of Air Travel), is accompanied by Oberst Jakoby, his LPG 'General Göring' Adjutant (see also Volume 1933–40, p.37).

Above right: On his next birthday, Göring received a handsome gift of a hunter's carriage drawn by two magnificent black horses. He is seen here on 12 January 1935, wearing the DLV kleiner Rock.

Opposite page, top: After the surprise birthday gift, Göring reviewed troops of the State Police Group 'General Göring' drawn up in the garden of his Berlin residence on 12 January 1935. Göring, seen here wearing the greatcoat for general officers of the DLV, is accompanied by (left to right) Staatssekretär Körner, Adjutant and SS-Sturmhauptführer Grützbach and, on Göring's left, Oberleutnant Bodenbach, his DLV Adjutant.

Opposite page, bottom: General Göring speaking at the official completion of the additional doorway built into the frontage of what the Nazis called the 'Horst Wessel Haus', Berlin, 16 November 1935. On the left of the speakers' stand is Dr Popitz, the Prussian Finance Minister, and on the right is the mother of Horst Wessel. This building had originally been the Communist Party headquarters, and was known as the Karl Liebknecht Haus. It stood on Weydinger Strasse, in front of the Bülowplatz, and was only 200m or so from the cemetery where Horst Wessel lay buried. On 8 March 1933, five weeks after the Nazis came to power, SA Troop 6/6 occupied the Communist Party building and seized it for the National Socialists (the Sturmfahnen for SA Troop 6/6 is shown in the photo on the right). As well as adding an extra entrance and changing the name of the building, the Nazis renamed the street Horst Wessel Strasse and the Bülowplatz the Horst Wessel Platz.

Left: Accompanied by Reichs-leiter Robert Ley (right) and NPEA officers, Göring inspects the newly constructed Ordensburg training establish-ment at Vogelsang on the Urftausse Lake, Germany. Göring, in casual attire, is wearing one of his favourite edged weapons. So fond was he of this hunting dagger, presented to him by the Swedish Count Eric von Rosen, his brother-in-law by his first wife, that he wore it when he surrendered to the American forces at the end of the war (see page 303).

Below: Göring, as President of the Reichsluftschutzbund, speaks before 18,000 office holders of the organization in the Berlin Sportpalast on 14 November 1935.

Below: On 10 April 1935 the wedding of General der Flieger Hermann Göring and Emmy Sonnemann took place at the Berlin Dom, the Evangelical Cathedral. This church ceremony was a State occasion that followed the civil wedding per-formed earlier that same morning. Adolf Hitler was best man and he, together with 300 other invited guests, attended the wedding breakfast at the Hotel Kaiserhof.

Left: The final day of Benito Mussolini's five-day state visit to Germany. On 29 September 1937 a massive military parade was held along the Charlottenburger Chausee in honour of the Italian Dictator, during which 14,000 troops of the three services marched past the saluting dais, an event that lasted 1hr 20min. The photograph shows the Führer, Generalfeldmarschall von Blomberg, Il Duce and Generaloberst Göring waiting for the parade to begin. Mussolini is wearing the Golden Pilot-Observer badge with Diamonds bestowed on him by Göring the previous day. This was the highest pre-war Luftwaffe decoration that could be awarded.

Lower left: In celebration of Göring's 44th birthday, Viktor Lutze, the SA Chief of Staff, appointed Göring honorary Commander-in-Chief of the élite SA-Standarte 'Feldherrnhalle', 12 January 1937. Göring, surrounded by members of the Luftwaffe, Allgemeine-SS (including a Reserve-SS officer in the background), SA and HJ, is collecting voluntary contributions for the Winterhilfwerk from Berlin shoppers on the Day of National Solidarity, 4 December 1937. He wears his version of a senior SA officer's uniform in his capacity as honorary Commander-in-Chief of the SA-Standarte 'Feldherrnhalle'. For some inexplicable reason he is wearing his 'Feldherrnhalle' formation cuff-title on his right cuff.

Right: The Commander of
the SA-Standarte 'Feldherrnhalle', accompanied by other
senior Regimental officers,
greeting their honorary Commander-in-Chief, Gener-
aloberst Hermann Göring. On
this occasion Göring was presented with the SA Feldherrnhalle dagger, seen here in its
presentation box being carried
by the SA-Gruppenführer
standing in front of the officers.

Below: A studio portrait of
Generalfeldmarschall Göring.
Interestingly, the four decorations he is wearing are being
worn incorrectly. The 'Blood
Order' medal (more correctly
the 'Decoration of 9th November 1923') lacks the arc of
ribbon around the button of
the right breast pocket flap.
Normally the three decorations
pinned to his left breast were
worn in the reverse order to
that shown here. The Golden
Party badge should have been
worn above his Imperial Iron

Cross, 1st Class, and, in turn,
the Iron Cross should have
been worn above his Golden
Pilot-Observer badge with
Diamonds.

Below right: Adolf Hitler,
Leader, Reichs Chancellor and
Supreme Commander of the
German Armed Forces, is
greeted by Generalfeld-

marschall Hermann Göring on
the Führer's arrival in the Lust-
garten before the start of the
parade held to mark the
National Holiday of the

German People, 1 May 1938.
In this photograph Göring is
wearing his decorations in the
correct manner.

Left: Despite its quality, this photograph is of particular interest. It is claimed to have been taken in March 1939, when Generalfeldmarschall Göring was visiting German troops garrisoned on the Western Front. On the collar of his cloth greatcoat Göring appears to be wearing the insignia of his rank on collar patches of black material. The reason for this is not known. It may have been that, for a very limited period, black Waffenfarbe collar patches were worn not just by those persons on the permanent staff of the German Air Ministry, as instructed in the 1935 listing (revised to April 1938) published in *Dress Regulations for the Air Force* (see Volume 1933–40, p.114), but by all Air Ministry personnel, Göring included.

430 White Summer Tunic. This was a double-breasted, open-neck tunic manufactured in white material. It had two rows each of three gilt buttons. There were two side pockets set at an angle with squared-off pocket flaps. The tunic was worn with a white shirt, a black or light brown tie, white trousers, white buckskin shoes and a white-topped summer peaked cap. Göring wore his General Field Marshal's collar patches and shoulder-straps on this tunic, together with a pin-on Luftwaffe national emblem in gold-coloured metal and those of his medals and decorations that he felt proper.

430

Opposite page, bottom left: An official portrait photograph taken in 1938 of Generalfeldmarschall Göring wearing the Luftwaffe kliener Rock and various decorations and awards.

Opposite page, bottom right: Göring greets guests at an official but unidentified pre-war reception presumed to have been held in his Air Ministry. Göring wears the Luftwaffe general officer's 'kliener Rock'.

Below left: Göring, accompanied by his wife Emmy (holding flowers), looks with obvious pleasure at the gifts presented to him by the people of Danzig to mark his 45th birthday, on 12 January 1938. Compared with the previous photograph, it can be seen that Göring wears his 'little coat' without collar patches.

Below: Generalfeldmarschall Göring with Paul, Prince Regent of Yugoslavia, at the entrance of the guesthouse in the grounds of Karinhall, Göring's private residence. Göring is wearing the white summer uniform for an officer of the Luftwaffe. The guest house is guarded by men of the Regiment 'General Göring'. The officer wearing a peaked cap is Generalmajor Bodenbach, and standing behind Göring, also wearing a Luftwaffe white summer uniform, is former SS officer and Staatsekretär, now Luftwaffe Major, Körner (see also upper photograph on page 269).

Left: Generalmajor Hans Jeschonnek, Chief of the Luftwaffe General Staff, studying a map with his Commander, Generalfieldmarschall Göring. Göring is wearing a white summer version of the officers' Fliegerbluse, a style of tunic that he continued to wear with appropriate change of rank insignia after he was promoted to Reichsmarschall.

Below: During cold or inclement weather Göring frequently favoured wearing the blue-grey Luftwaffe officers' cloak for those occasions that did not require the cloth greatcoat. Here he is wearing his officers' cloak to take the salute of a drive-past of a detachment of motorcycles from the Berlin Schutzpolizei on 12 January 1938. To the right of Göring stands Heinrich Himmler, and on Göring's left is Kurt Daluege and Reinhard Heydrich. For details of the Luftwaffe officers' cloak see Volume 1933–40, pp.244–247.

Right The Field Marshal wore other forms of wet weather coat, such as this waterproof raincoat.

Left: Göring often wore the standard pattern of the officers' leather greatcoat during cold weather. He is seen here talking with pilots at an unidentified airfield. The occasion must have been of importance, as at least five of the officers accompanying Göring are General officers.

Right: Generalfeldmarschall Göring, Oberbefehlshaber der Luftwaffe, receives the award of the Knight's Cross of the Iron Cross from the hands of the Führer on 30 September 1939.

59

Left: Generalfeldmarschall Göring visiting what is believed to be an air force squadron somewhere in the east, probably Poland. He is wearing his Knight's Cross, so this dates the photo as post 30 September 1939.

Shoulder-straps and collar patches

Above: Reichsmarschall des Grossdeutschen Reiches, first pattern.

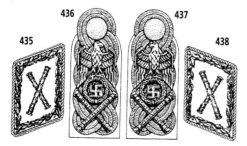

Above: Reichsmarschall des Grossdeutschen Reiches, second pattern.

439

439 Officer's Leather Greatcoat This was a privately purchased garment, made to measure from fine-grain quality leather dyed to a blue-grey shade. It conformed in general appearance to the design of the cloth greatcoat for officers of the Luftwaffe. On appropriate occasions throughout his Third Reich Air Force career Göring wore a leather greatcoat. He displayed his rank by means of the shoulder-straps. The coat had pebble-finished gilt metal buttons worn down the front in two rows each of five buttons. No collar patches or other items of insignia were worn on this coat.

Opposite page, left: Göring, newly promoted to Reichsmarschall, wears the Luftwaffe officers' version of the Fliegerbluse. It could be claimed that this was something of a 'transitional uniform'. Points of interest are the first pattern of Reichsmarschall collar patches (see opposite page), the lack of the breast eagle, the addition of the 1939 bar to his 1914–18 Imperial Iron Cross, 1st Class, and his Grand Cross to the Iron Cross worn at his neck. He is also still wearing his normal Luftwaffe officer's white-topped summer peaked cap.

Left: Even after his promotion to Reichsmarschall, Göring continued to wear his officer's leather greatcoat, but with the addition of his new shoulder-straps. This photograph seems to suggest that all was not well with the course of the German air war over Great Britain. Adolf Galland (looking down), the Reichsmarschall and the troops in the background all look decidedly grim.

Right: Göring takes his leave of Mölders (left) and another pilot. This shows the rear of his leather greatcoat.

Left: Another distinctive, and unique, coat was worn by Göring. During the early part of the war he favoured a three-quarter-length double-breasted top coat made from dark blue-grey material. It had deep side pockets and an extra pocket on the front. A somewhat worried-looking Reichsmarschall is seen here on his 48th birthday during a visit to a squadron engaged in the attack on the United Kingdom. Others with him are, from left to right: Staatssekretär Körner, General der Flieger Loerzer and Generalfeldmarschall Sperrle. The officer in the foreground is un-identified.

Lower left: A rear view of Göring's special three-quarter-length top coat.

440 Three-quarter-length Greatcoat. During his first six months or so as Reichsmarschall of the Greater German Reich, Göring favoured a double-breasted, three-quarter-length dark blue-grey greatcoat. This unique garment – there was no other comparable coat worn within the Luftwaffe – was worn open at the neck. It had a wide collar, two large side patch pockets both with large squared pocket flaps, and a single external vertical slit pocket with flap on the right side of the coat, slightly above waist level. It had a two-buttoned half-belt at the rear, and on the front a set of six gilt buttons in two rows each of three buttons. Göring's Reichsmarschall collar patches and shoulder-straps were worn on the coat, and he wore his Great War Honour Title on the right forearm (not illustrated here). There were no turn-back cuffs. Göring frequently wore this greatcoat during the period of the Battle of Britain and for a short time afterwards, but it seems to have disappeared from his wardrobe after his failure to destroy the Royal Air Force. Göring also ceased to wear his 'Jagdgeschwader Frhr.v.Richthofen Nr.1, 1917/18' cuff-title once he donned his new-style dove-grey Reichsmarschall uniforms.

441 This was the original 'official' tunic (or, more correctly, blouse) that Göring ordered to be designed, and that he wore after his elevation to the rank of Reichsmarschall der Gross-deutschen Reichs. It was very similar in appearance to the Imperial German 1915 officers' pattern 'Bluse'. It was dove-grey, fly-fronted and single-breasted, the collar normally being closed at the neck. It had two external, slightly curved side pocket openings without flaps. The collar of the tunic was edged with twisted gold cording, and the sleeves had no turn-back cuffs. The Luftwaffe national emblem sewn to the right breast was in fine gold wire hand-embroidered on to a backing of white material. Under the tunic Göring wore a white shirt and, when he left the tunic top button undone, a light grey tie.

Opposite page, top right: Yet another official photograph of Hermann Göring, taken to record his promotion to Reichs-marschall. Göring is wearing the dove-grey uniform with the first pattern of collar patches. He is also wearing three neck orders; his Grand Cross, his Knight's Cross and his Order Pour le Mérite.

Opposite page, lower right: On a visit to a Luftwaffe airfield somewhere in northern France, Göring talks to NCO and officer pilots from an unspecified squadron. The photograph was taken on 12 September 1940, and Göring is wearing the first pattern of Reichsmarschall collar patches.

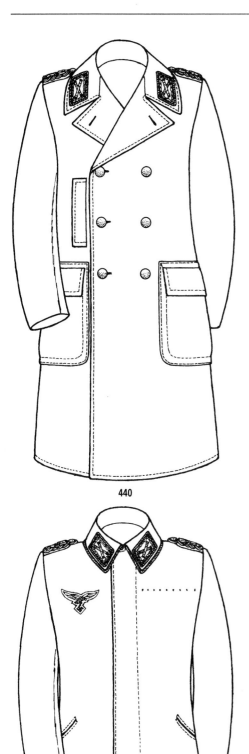

440

441

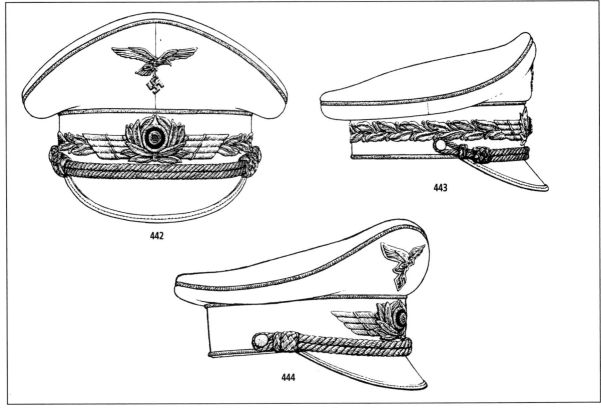

442

443

444

Göring as Reichsmarschall possessed two patterns of uniformed peaked cap, one being somewhat more elaborate than the other.

Left: The less elaborate of the two caps is shown here. Göring confers with General Bruno Loerzer (holding map) and General Hans Jeschonnek, the Luftwaffe Chief-of-Staff (far left), 1 October 1940.

Right: The other, more elaborate, Reichsmarschall cap worn by Göring.

442 and 443 The Uniform Peaked Cap, Full-Dress version.

There were two special peaked caps that Göring wore as part of his Reichsmarschall's uniform. The first could be classed as the full dress version, the cap that formed part of his official uniform, while the second cap, not quite so elaborate, could be said to be his informal or undress Marshal's cap. Both caps exhibited a high standard of workmanship, and details of the design and colouring of the 'full dress' version were published in the German trade magazines *Uniformen-Markt* [1] and *Schwert und Spaten*.[2] The crown and body to the cap was made form 'hellgrau' (light-grey) material of the finest quality, the cap band was of light-grey velvet and the peak was of black patent vulcanised fibre with a narrow stitched rim and a pale green underside (see photos on page 307). The insignia of the cap was also of the highest quality, the gold embroidery work being of 'blankgold'; bullion threads of reflective, glittering gold. The national emblem was embroidered on to a backing of dove-grey material and then sewn to the front of the cap. On later caps this eagle and swastika was worked directly into the cloth of the cap. The size of this emblem was slightly larger than those emblems on normal Luftwaffe officers' caps. The crown to the cap and the top and bottom edge of the cap band were piped with gold cording. The gold-wire hand embroidery worked directly into the front of the velvet cap band took the form of a wreath of laurel leaves made up of twelve individual leaves and four laurel berries surrounding a cockade of concentric rings of black, silver and red.

This cockade was edged with a fine border of silver wire which, in turn, was bordered with a circle of gold, and the whole stood proud from the wreath. On either side of the wreath were stylized 'wings', each of two sets of four lines of feathers. Embroidered around what remained of the cap band was a decorative series of laurel leaves and berries. It is believed that 30 such leaves and berries encircled the cap band. The cap was finished off with a set of gold-coloured cap cords held in place by means of two small pebble-surfaced gilt-coloured cap cord buttons. The original cap was manufactured by the Berlin firm of Robert Lubstein, and the responsibility for the hand embroidery is attributed to two Berliners employed by the firm, Herr Hanselmann and Herr Troltsch. It is evident that Göring had more than one Marshal's cap of both patterns. The full dress cap as illustrated in official photographs of Hermann Göring taken to mark his promotion to Reichsmarschall show that there were only ten laurel leaves and four laurel berries on the wreath, whereas on other, later, caps of this type there are clearly twelve leaves and four berries.

444 The Undress Uniform Peaked Cap.

This was a simpler version of the Full Dress Cap. It was similar in all respects, except that it lacked the golden wreath of laurel leaves embroidered around the grey velvet cap band.

Göring had a variety of Reichsmarschall uniforms. Some were of a distinct cut, while others had slight differences in style or trimmings.

Left: This photograph shows Göring, wearing his uniform as Reichsmarschall des Grossdeutschen Reichs, seated among mourners in the Mosaic Hall of the New Reichs Chancellery listening to an oration in honour of Reichsminister Kerrl. Note the broad white stripes on his breeches.

445 Variant to the Reichsmarschall Tunic. It is self-evident that Göring possessed more than one Reichsmarschall's uniform. The illustration here represents the 'Imperial Bluse'-style tunic (see Fig. 441), but with white piping to the turn-back cuffs.

446 The Special Tunic. On certain occasions Göring wore a tunic that has been described as the 'kleiner Rock für Reichsmarschall'. Apart from its dove-grey colour it was identical to the blue-grey 'Little Coat' worn by Luftwaffe Generals and fully described in Volume 1933–40, pp.228–232. Dove-grey trousers with either broad white stripes or white piping were worn with this coat. As the coat was worn open at the neck, a white shirt and a light grey tie were worn. Brown leather shoes completed the outfit. It is safe to assume that Göring would have worn this uniform as an informal Evening Full Dress and Undress Service Dress.

Left: In the 'The House of Aviation' (Haus der flieger) in Berlin on 11 January 1941, Göring, on the eve of his 48th birthday, presents German Coal Miners with the decoration of the War Merit Cross. Göring is wearing his Reichsmarschall's uniform with trousers that have white piping only.

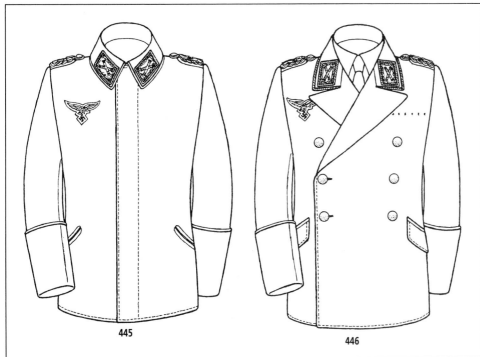

445 446

Below: A variant of the Reichsmarschall's blouse. Note the white piping around the false turn-back cuffs. From left to right, Generalfeld-marschall Ernst Udet, Gener-alleutnant Bodenschatz, Reichsmarschall Hermann Göring and Professor Willy Messerschmitt, during a visit Göring made to the Messer-schmitt works on 20 February 1941.

Above: Among the different styles and variations of uniform garments that Göring wore in his capacity as Reichsmarschall was the so-called 'kliener Rock für Reichsmarschall'. It followed the same cut as the normal officers' 'Little Coat' that Göring wore as a Generalfeldmarschall (see photos on pages 274 and 275), but was produced in dove-grey material with white lapel facings, and cuff-piping and broad white stripes and piping to the matching trousers. Reichsminister Dr Joseph Goebels congratulates Göring on his 48th birthday, 12 January 1941.

Above right: At the start of his state visit to Germany, Field Marshal Slavko Kvaternik, the Deputy Leader of the 'Free and Independent' State of Croatia and Minister for National Defence, is greeted by Hermann Göring at his headquarters. Hrvatski Vojskovodja Kvaternik carries his 'marshal's baton', which took the form of a ceremonial axe. Göring is wearing his 'Little Coat' uniform with trousers that have white piping only.

Opposite page, centre: Göring, wearing a white linen summer tunic, in conversation with Knight's Cross holders Hauptmann Peltz (left) and Hauptmann Baumbach at his headquarters in July 1942.

Opposite page, bottom: Göring in a variant of the white summer tunic illustrated in the preceding photograph. Pocket flaps are visible in that photograph, but this jacket does not have them. Göring is also wearing a white-top summer version of his Reichsmarschall's cap, and it appears that the crown is piped in gold cording. The photograph was taken in the grounds of Karinhall in September 1943, and shows, from left to right, Reichsminister Albert Speer, Hermann Göring, Generaloberst Loerzer (wearing the Luftwaffe officers' white summer tunic) and General Korten, Luftwaffe Chief of Staff.

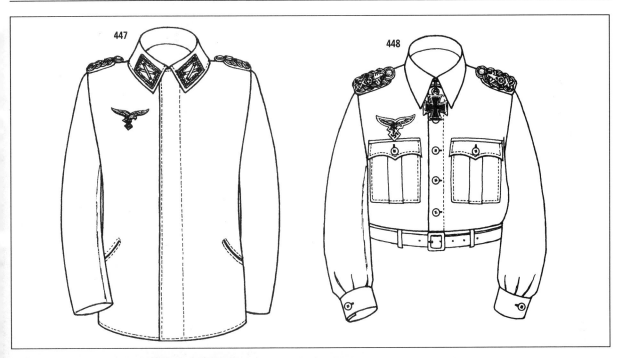

447 Göring wore a white linen summer tunic based on the design of his Reichsmarschall's dove-grey tunic. Fly-fronted, it was normally worn closed at the neck and had two side pockets with curved openings. The photograph left shows the tunic with pocket flaps, and it is possible that these flaps could be tucked into the pocket, giving the tunic the appearance of not having any pocket flaps, as in photo lower left. Göring wore whatever of his decorations and awards he pleased. Under the tunic he wore a white shirt and light grey or black tie. The Reichsmarschall seemed to wear a variety of trousers with this tunic; Luftwaffe blue-grey, dove-grey, and white linen. A white-topped Marshal's summer cap and white buckskin shoes completed this uniform.

448 Summer Shirt. There were times of informality during periods of hot weather, such as a visit the Reichsmarschall made to the Ukraine, when Göring was photographed wearing a summer shirt. This long-sleeved garment, no doubt made for him in fine-quality material, had two box pleated breast pockets, a row of at least six small shirt buttons down the front and, in order to display his Grand Cross, was worn closed at the neck. Göring wore this shirt with a pair of lightweight dove-grey trousers and white buckskin shoes. He displayed his special shoulder-straps, but wore no collar patches. The Luftwaffe breast emblem over the right breast pocket was thought to be in gold embroidery, probably worked on a backing of white material and buckram and pinned to the shirt.

Left and right: From a series of photographs taken in mid-August 1943, recording a visit made by Göring to a Flak battery in the Hamburg area. Also see overleaf.

Left and right: More illustrations from a series of photographs taken in mid-August 1943, recording a visit made by Göring to a Flak battery in the Hamburg area. Also see overleaf.

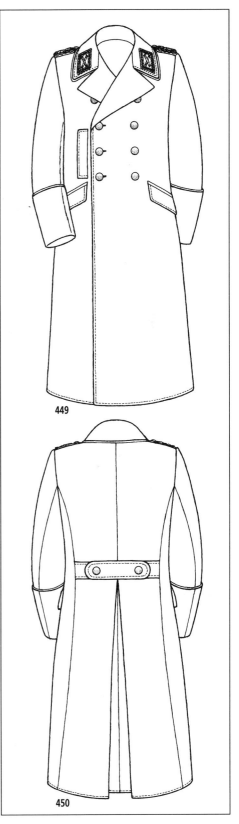

449

450

Left: Final illustrations from a series of photographs taken in mid-August 1943, recording a visit made by Göring to a Flak battery in the Hamburg area.

Above: Wearing his distinctive dove-grey greatcoat, Göring salutes the open grave of Generaloberst Udet.

449 and 450 Göring had a number of dove-grey greatcoats that complemented his Reichsmarschall's uniform. They were all very similar, with only subtle variations in design to distinguish them. All were double-breasted, all had a double row of at least five, possibly six, gilt buttons, and all had white facings to the fold-back lapels. There was white piping to the deep turn-back cuffs, what appeared to be white piping down the front edge of the coat but was in effect the extension of the white lapel facings, and gold twisted cording around the edge of the collar. The Reichsmarschall collar patches were worn and the shoulder-straps were sewn into the shoulder seams. There were two side pockets with squared-off pocket flaps which were also edged in white piping. On at least one variant of this greatcoat there was an extra side pocket, as shown here. On the back of these coats there was a cloth half-belt secured by two gilt buttons, and there was a central vent in the skirt.

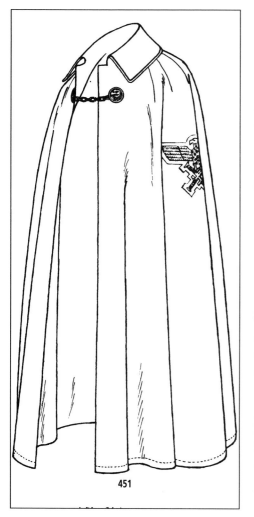

451

452

Above: Part of the complete ensemble of Reichsmarschall uniform items was the dove grey cloak. Apart from its colour, this garment was identical to the blue-grey cloaks worn by Luftwaffe officers before the war as an optional item and described in Volume 1933–40, pp.244–247. In keeping with the previous pattern of officers' cloak, this new garment displayed an elaborate eagle and swastika badge, but now combined with crossed batons and worn as an arm badge on the left shoulder of the Reichsmarschall's cloak.

451 and 452 The Reichsmarschall's Cloak and Eagle emblem. Apart from the colour of the cloak and the special gold, hand-embroidered eagle emblem sewn to the left shoulder, this Reichsmarschall cloak was identical to the style of cloak worn by Luftwaffe general officers (see Volume 1933–40, pp.244–247).

Göring: The Final Days

All this was in sharp contrast to the events that took place five years later, when, in April 1945, Göring was expelled from the Party, stripped of his rank of Reichsmarschall, dismissed from his post as Commander-in-Chief of the Luftwaffe and, on the express order of the Führer, was arrested by the SS on a charge of high treason and came within an ace of being executed by a firing squad. His position as successor to Hitler was withdrawn, and Grossadmiral Karl Dönitz was appointed to succeed the Führer in his place.

Göring was held prisoner at his villa at Obersalzberg from 23 April 1945, and when this was destroyed during an air raid on 29 April he persuaded his captors to allowed him to move to Mauterndorf. He and his family and retinue remained there until 7 May, held prisoners by a detachment of 100 men and their officers from the Leibstandarte-SS 'Adolf Hitler'.

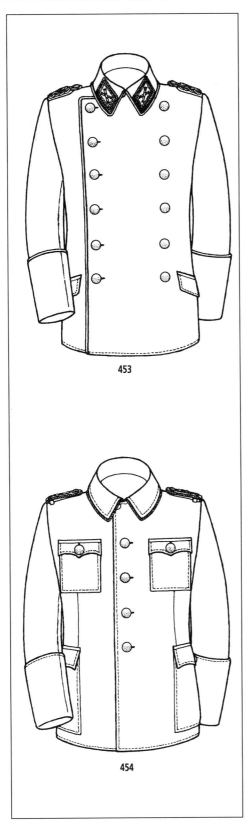

453

453 Reichsmarschall's double-breasted 'Litewka' tunic. This was the tunic, stripped of all insignia and metal items other than the buttons, that Göring wore when he was imprisoned at Nuremberg and arraigned for war crimes. It was another style of tunic that formed part of Göring's Reichsmarschall's wardrobe. Similar in style to the pre-1915 Imperial German 'Litewka', it was a double-breasted garment that could be worn either closed or open at the neck. It had two vertical rows each of six gilt-coloured pebble-surfaced metal buttons. There were two side pockets with pocket flaps, and the sleeves had deep turn-back cuffs. White piping was used around the edge of the collar, the lapels and down the front edge of the tunic. The tops of the turn-back cuffs and the edges of the pocket flaps were also piped in white. The Reichsmarschall's insignia of collar patches and shoulder-straps were worn, as well as his awards and decorations.

454 Special Utility Tunic. In late March 1945, with the defeat of the Third Reich only weeks away, Göring devised and had tailored a form of 'Utility Uniform', complete with special rank insignia, head-dress and greatcoat, that was far less flamboyant and colourful than his Reichsmarschall's uniform. Albert Speer, Minister of Armaments and War Production, mentioned seeing Göring wearing this new uniform for the first time when Göring made his last visit to the Führerbunker on 20 April 1945,[3] ten days before Hitler took his life. The tunic was of a simple cut, single-breasted with four plain patch pockets. It had a single row of five pebble-surfaced matt blue-grey metal buttons to the front, and a single button to each pocket flap. Göring wore this tunic closed at the neck and with his special simplified shoulder-straps trimmed with twisted gold cording. This same cording was used to edge the tunic's collar. Interestingly, there were no collar patches or Luftwaffe breast emblem. The tunic was worn with matching, somewhat baggy, breeches. This was the uniform that Göring wore when he first made contact with the US forces. He wore it again when he presented himself at the interrogation centre and detention camp at Augsburg.

454

Amid the confusion of the closing hours of the war in Europe, and with Hitler having committed suicide in his Berlin bunker on 30 April 1945, the SS had little desire to execute the Reichsmarschall, and a unit of loyal Luftwaffe troops eventually freed him from his SS captors. Göring, accompanied by his family and aides, a small entourage of 30-odd loyal personnel and staff members, set out in a column of staff cars and two lorries loaded with personal luggage to make contact with the advancing Americans. They were taken prisoner by First Lieutenant Jerome N. Shapiro on the refugee-packed road somewhere between Mauterndorf and Fischhorn. The rest of his story, from being taken prisoner to his eventual suicide at Nürnburg, is given in the text describing the photographs reproduced on the remaining pages of this book.

Having escaped the clutches of the SS, Göring and his staff surrendered initially to First Lieutenant Shapiro on the road between Mauterndorf and Fischhorn. Lieutenant Shapiro is on record as noting that, when apprehended, Göring was wearing his 'grey-blue uniform, only three medals and was in need of a haircut'. In all probability the uniform Shapiro refers to was the utility uniform Göring had devised, and which he also wore when he was taken into custody at Augsberg (see photos on page 301). It was also likely that Shapiro noticed only three of the four decorations Göring was wearing; his Grand Cross, his Pilot's Badge and his Iron Cross 1st Class with 1914–18 bar. The Pour le Mérite was probably not visible under the flap of the jacket. From the study of contemporary photographs, some of which are featured here, it is quite obvious that Göring was in need of a haircut.

From Fischhorn, Göring was taken to the divisional headquarters of the US 36th

Above: Immediately after his capture at Fischhorn, Göring was taken to Zell am See where he was met by the Assistant Commander of the 36th US Infrantry, Brigadier-General Robert J. Stack. The Americans accorded him such courtesies as they considered befitted his rank. Göring was invited to take a bath before dinner, after which he was photographed standing in front of the divisional flag.

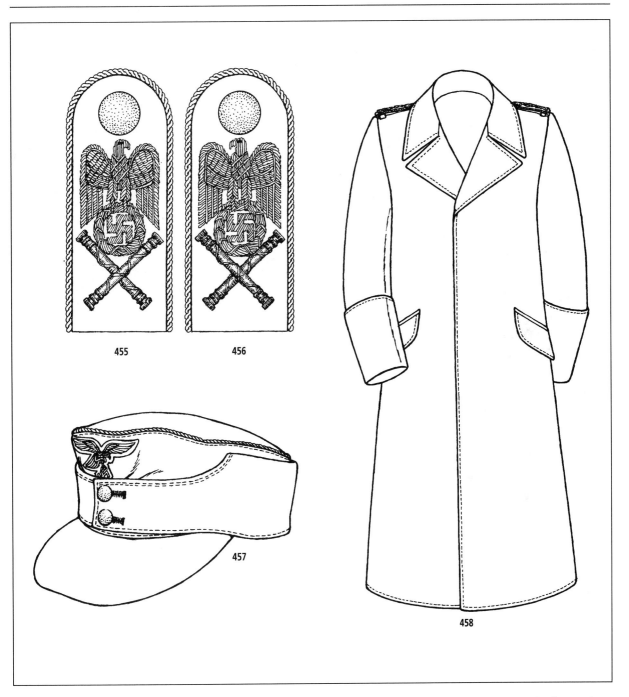

455 **456**

457

458

455 and 456 Special Shoulder-strap Insignia. To match the utilitarian quality of this new uniform, Göring chose to wear shoulder-straps on his tunic, but not collar patches, which were a simplified form of his previous Reichsmarschall insignia. The gold bullion design was worked directly into the blue-grey cloth. The straps were edged in twisted gold cording and the buttons were pebble-surfaced blue-grey painted metal.

457 Part of the utility uniform was a cap, similar in form to the Replacement Flight Cap, although in Göring's case he never wore a flight cap to be replaced. The new cap, made from the same blue-grey material as the uniform, had gold

twisted cording around the crown and a gilt embroidered Luftwaffe national emblem on the front. The curtain was fastened in the front by two small blue-grey buttons.

458 Utility Greatcoat. To complete his new outfit, Göring had a simple greatcoat. It was a single-breasted, fly-fronted coat with two side pockets with flaps and deep turn-back cuffs. The coat was worn open at the neck, and the lapels did not display any facing colour. Shoulder-straps of the same pattern as worn on the utility tunic were worn on the greatcoat.

Infantry Division at Zell am See. He was accompanied, amongst others, by his adjutant, Oberst Berndt von Brauchitsch, the son of the German Field Marshal, and his valet, Robert Krop. His wife Emmy and his daughter were left behind at Fischhorn. They were not to see each other until after the trials in August 1946.

The Reichsmarschall, who still regarded himself as the Führer's rightful successor despite the events of the previous weeks, was convinced that he was eventually to meet with General Eisenhower, the Supreme Commander of Allied Forces in Europe. He wrote that, when they met, he would be able to talk 'man to man, soldier to soldier' with the General.

At Zell am See Göring was met by Brigadier-General Robert J. Stack, Assistant Commander of the 36th US Infantry Division. Here he was extended such courtesies due to his rank. He was invited to take a bath before dinner, after which he was photographed standing in front of the divisional flag. These photographs show that he had changed his blue-grey utility uniform for his Reichsmarschall uniform of the type illustrated as Fig. 441. After lunch

the following day he was driven to the Grand Hotel at Kitzbühel, the headquarters of the US 7th Army, to meet General Spaatz. It was here, on the balcony of the hotel headquarters, that Göring was seen laughing, surrounded by high-ranking US Army officers and with a glass of champagne in his hand, an incident that was to anger General Eisenhower when this fraternisation was reported to him.

This photograph above is captioned as having been taken at the Grand Hotel at Kitzbühel, where Göring is seen in conversation with Brigadier-General Robert J. Stack (on his left), Assistant Commander of the 36th US Infantry Division, and Major-General John Dahlquist (back to camera), Commander of the 36th Division. In all probability the picture was taken just before Göring's departure for the airfield at Kitzbühel, from where he was flown to Augsberg. Once again Göring is wearing his utility uniform, but with the addition of a white arm band around his left upper arm. He still wears his four decorations.

Göring had been driven to Kitzbühl in an American staff car. His own blue-grey supercharged Mercedes 200, driven by his

Above: Göring is seen in conversation with Brigadier-General Robert J. Stack (on his left), Assistant Commander of the 36th US Infantry Division, and Major-General John Dahlquist (back to camera), Commander of the 36th Division

Opposite page: Göring, accompanied by Oberst Brauchitsch, on arrival at the Augsburg detention camp.

personal driver, Willi Schulz, followed. Accompanying the Reichsmarschall to the headquarters were Oberst Brauchitsch, his adjutant, Hauptmann Klass, his personal officer, and Robert Krop, his valet, who accompanied his extensive luggage.

Göring was convinced that he was going to a conference with General Eisenhower. His next move was from the Grand Hotel at Kitzbühl to the nearby airfield. Driven in his own Mercedes and followed by Kropp with a lorry-load of his master's personal baggage, Göring arrived at the airfield to find five large USAAF transport aircraft waiting to fly him, his personnel and his luggage to Augsburg.

Göring landed at Augsburg and, accompanied by his two aides, was immediately and without ceremony taken to a former workers' settlement of small houses on the outskirts of the city. These had been especially adapted as a detention camp for high-ranking officers.

Photos on this page and overleaf show Göring, accompanied by Oberst Brauchitsch, on arrival at the camp, talking with US Colonel William Quinn, G-2 US Seventh Army, and the official inter-

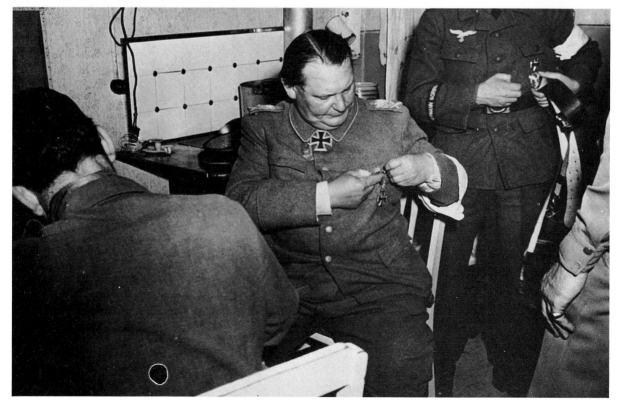

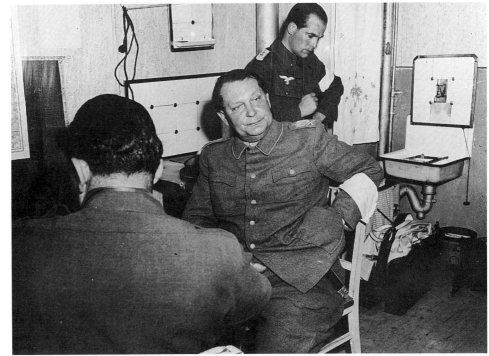

Opposite page, top: Göring, on arrival at the detention camp,

Opposite page, bottom: Both men removing their metal decorations. Göring has already removed his waist-belt and cross-strap, which are held by his aide, and he is in the process of removing his Pilot's Badge.

Right: Göring removes his favourite hunting dagger.

Below: Göring looking thoroughly dejected as his wrist watch is taken from him.

A. See *The Daggers and Edged Weapons of Hitler's Germany* by Major James P. Atwood, published privately by the author, 1965, page 161.

preter, Major Paul Kabala (holding a cane). Other photographs taken at the time show various studies of Göring and provide clear details of his utility uniform and cap, as well as his four decorations. He is carrying his Reichsmarschall's baton wrapped inside a purpose-made cloth cover.

The next series of photographs are of particular interest. They show Göring, still accompanied by his aide, von Brauchitsch, undergoing the initial processing as a prisoner of war.

The photo opposite shows both men removing their metal decorations. Göring has already removed his waist-belt and cross-strap, which are held by his aide, and he is in the process of removing his Pilot's Badge.

The photo above shows Göring about to remove and hand over his hunting dagger, his favourite edged weapon, which he is known to have worn frequently since it was presented to him by the Swedish Count Eric von Rosen, brother-in-law to Göring by his first wife (see page 270). This dagger, together with Göring's baton, was taken by Colonel Quinn, and eventually presented to the Museum of the Military Academy at West Point in the USA, where it remains to this day.[A]

The photo left shows Göring's wrist watch being examined by the US officer in charge of the initial interrogation.

Photos on page 307 show Göring being interviewed by Allied war correspondents in the grounds of the Augsburg detention camp on 11 May 1945. He is wearing his Reichsmarshall's uniform and cap. Interestingly, the captions to some of these pictures claim that: 'He [Göring] has taken off his decorations for the interview'. However, he was no longer in possession of his personal effects, as these had been taken from him on his arrival at the camp. The officer seated next to Göring is Major Paul Kabala, Assistant G-2 (Intelligence) officer for the Seventh US Army. Major Kabala acted as the official interpreter for this and other interviews.

Göring was kept at Augsburg until 20 May 1945, when he was transferred to the Interrogation Centre bearing the US code name 'Ashcan', set up at the Palace Hotel in the spa town of Mondorf-les-Bains in the Grand Duchy of Luxembourg. To forestall any suicide attempts, all prisoners were immediately stripped naked on arrival at the Palace Hotel for a complete physical examination, and their clothing and personal property was minutely examined. Any item that could be used as a weapon or to inflict a wound upon themselves was removed. Amongst these items were all batons, interim staffs, walking sticks, canes, long-pinned medal ribbons, insignia of rank and metal decorations. Military uniforms were stripped of insignia, but col-

Opposite page and above: Perspiring and obviously apprehensive, Göring is shown here at the conclusion of his initial processing session. The photgraph above however, shows that some light relief was possible.

Right: Göring seated in an armchair in a small garden of a private house within the grounds of the Augsburg detention camp. Here the Reichsmarschall was interviewed by members of the Allied press. Seated next to him is Major Paul Kubala, of Elizabeth Town Kentucky, who acted as an interpreter.

The next five photographs show Göring stripped of all his decorations and unnecessary accessories. In the last two photographs it can be seen that he has even removed the white arm band from his left arm.

lar patches, possibly shoulder-straps and the broad stripes on trousers or breeches were left. However, this insignia was missing when the prisoners appeared in the dock at Nuremberg.

On 20 May 1945 Hermann Göring arrived at Mondorf-les-Bains from Augsberg wearing his dove-grey uniform. According to Colonel Brutus C. Andrus, Commandant of 'Ashcan', Göring weighed-in at 264lb and perspired profusely. The former Reichsmarschall brought with him 16 matched and monogrammed suitcases, a red hatbox and his valet, Robert Kropp. In his book *The Infamous of Nürnberg*, Colonel Andrus lists all of the valuables that Göring took with him into captivity, and which were deposited under lock and key in the Gun Room of the Palace Hotel. Among these 49 individual personal objects and 81,268 Reichmarks were the following military items:

One gold Luftwaffe Pilot-Observer badge, one gold Luftwaffe Pilot-Observer Badge with diamonds, one Order Pour le Mérite, one 1914–18 Imperial Iron Cross 1st Class, one Grand Cross of the Knight's Cross and one platinum Iron Cross which, although it was not stated, could well have been Göring's Knight's Cross.

These decorations were removed from Göring during his initial interrogation at Augsburg, as can be seen from the photos reproduced on pages 302 and 303. It seems that they followed him to 'Ashcan', but interestingly no mention is made of his favourite hunting dagger and his Marshal's baton, both of which he had with him when he entered the Augsburg Interrogation Centre and were removed during his first interrogation. (In October 1946 Colonel Andrus was responsible for breaking up Göring's large collection of jewelled items and awards. It was claimed that the military decorations were torn apart, the precious metals melted down and the precious stones gathered together. These, their origin unrecognisable, were handed over to the new German economy. The rest of his inventory of valuables was given to his widow.)

On Sunday 12 August 1945 Göring, together with the other senior Nazis, was flown to the German city of Nuremberg, there to stand trial for war crimes. Colonel Andrus was also appointed Governor of the Nuremberg Jail, in charge of the guard detachment and responsible for all of the high-ranking prisoners held in the prison cells attached to the Nuremberg Palace of Justice, as well as for the overall security of the Tribunal.

On 25 August 1945 it was announced from Nürnberg that Göring, Keitel and Jodl had been deprived of their military ranks. It was explained that, under the Geneva Convention, solitary confinement was forbidden in cases of prisoners of military rank and, as the accused were being held in such confinement as common criminals pending trials, this action had therefore been taken.

The trials opened on 20 November 1945 and ended on 1 October 1946. Article 6 of the International Military Tribunal laid down that the Tribunal had the power to try and to punish persons 'who, acting in the interests of the European Axis countries, whether as individuals or members of organisations' had committed any of the following crimes:

Crimes against peace, namely the planning, preparation, initiation or waging of a war of aggression or a war in violation of international treaties, agreements or assurances or participation in a common plan or conspiracy for the accomplishment of any of the foregoing.

War crimes, namely violations of the laws or customs of war. Such violations included, but were not limited to, murder, ill-treatment or deportation to slave labour or for any other purpose of the civilian population of, or in, occupied territory; the murder or ill-treatment of prisoners-of-war or persons on the seas; the killing of hostages; the plunder of public or private property; and the wanton destruction of cities, towns or villages, or devastation not justified by military necessity.

Crimes against humanity, namely murder, extermination, enslavement, deportation and other inhuman acts committed against any civilian population, before or during the war; or persecutions on political, racial or religious grounds in execution of, or in connection with, any crime within the jurisdiction of the Tribunal, whether or not in violation of the domestic law of the country where perpetrated.

Reading out the judgements on 1 October 1946, Lord Justice Lawrence said of Hermann Göring: '... His guilt is unique in

Right: Göring being interviewed by Allied war correspondents in the grounds of the Augsburg detention camp on 11 May 1945.

its enormity', and that, 'the record discloses no excuses for this man'.

Hermann Wilhelm Göring, 52 years of age, former Commander-in-Chief of the Luftwaffe and Successor-Designate to Adolf Hitler, was found guilty on all four counts:

1. Common plan or conspiracy to wage aggressive war
2. Crimes against peace
3. War crimes
4. Crimes against humanity.

On 2 October 1946 Lord Justice Lawrence passed sentence on Göring with these words: 'Defendant Hermann Wilhelm Göring, on the counts of the indictment of which you have been convicted, the International Military Tribunal sentences you to death by hanging'.

Göring committed suicide at 10.45pm on 15 October 1946, just 2¾ hours before the time appointed for his execution. He was able to escape the hangman by swallowing cyanide from a capsule which he had successfully kept hidden throughout his internment. At his death Göring weighed 192lb and his height was 5ft 10in. At 4am on 17 October 1946, Göring's body and those of the other Nazis who had been

Left: Göring being interviewed by Allied war correspondents in the grounds of the Augsburg detention camp on 11 May 1945.

Right: Göring and Hess in the Nuremberg Courtroom, 17 January 1946.

hanged a few hours earlier were loaded on to two heavily guarded lorries and, it is believed, driven to Dachau. There they were burnt in the ovens at the former concentration camp and their ashes scattered into the River Amper.

Far left: Göring seated next to Alfred Rosenberg in the prisoner's mess situated above the courthouse in Nuremberg, 30 November 1945. Göring, who wears his former Reichsmarschall's uniform devoid of all insignia, refused to eat whilst photographs were being taken of him.

Left: Göring talking with Rudolf Hess, back to camera, during a ten minute recess in the course of the war crimes trials held at the Palace of Justice, Nuremberg, 4 December 1945.

Right: A rare moment of mirth during the war crimes trials. Laughter breaks out amongst the defendants. In the front row, left to right are Göring, Hess, Ribbentrop and Keitel. In the back row are Dönitz, Raeder, Schirach and Saukel. 21 February 1946.

References

The National Emblem of Germany

1. *Luftwaffen-Verordnungsblatt*, Nr. 16, dated 27 May 1935, p.102, Order Nr.225 issued 16 May 1935.

2: The Luftwaffe 1940–1945: Formations and Branches

1. *Luftwaffen-Verordnungsblatt*, dated 18 January 1943, Order Nr. 130 issued 12 January 1943.
2. Order issued by the OKH regarding arm-of-service colours of Jäger Regiments of the Luftwaffe, dated 10 July 1944.
3. *Luftwaffen-Verordnungsblatt*, dated 4 July 1943, p.801, Order Nr. 1498.

3: Badges and Accoutrements

1. *Luftwaffen-Verordnungsblatt*, dated 18 January 1943, p.97, Order Nr.127 issued 4 January 1943.
2. *Luftwaffen-Verordnungsblatt*, for April 1943, p.386, Order Nr.709.
3. *Luftwaffen-Verordnungsblatt*, dated 15 June 1943, p.580, Order Nr.1115 issued 3 June 1943.
4. *Luftwaffen-Verordnungsblatt*, for September 1941, p.797, Order Nr.1361 issued 15 September 1941.
5. *Luftwaffen-Verordnungsblatt* Nr.30, Part C, dated 25 July 1938, pp.217–8, Order Nr.659 issued 7 July 1938.
6. *Luftwaffen-Verordnungsblatt*, dated 15 November 1943, p.1136, Order Nr.2083 issued 5 November 1943.
7. *Luftwaffen-Verordnungsblatt* Nr.52, dated 13 December 1937, p.665, Order Nr.1604 issued 6 December 1937.
8. *Luftwaffen-Verordnungsblatt* Nr.13, dated 30 March 1936, p.146, Order Nr.374 issued 18 March 1936.
9. *Luftwaffen-Verordnungsblatt* Nr.43, Part C, dated 25 September 1939, p.388, Order Nr.846 issued 10 September 1939.
10. *Luftwaffen-Verordnungsblatt* Nr.39, Part C, dated 3 October 1938, p.271, Order Nr.838 issued 22 September 1938.
11. *Luftwaffen-Verordnungsblatt* Nr.30, Part C, dated 25 July 1938, p.218, Order Nr.660 issued 15 July 1938.
12. Instructions introducing the letters 'UVS' to be worn by Officers, NCOs and Men of the NCO Preparatory School (Unteroffiziervorschulen) were published in *Luftwaffen-Verordnungsblatt* for 14 July 1941, p.482, Order Nr.745 issued 30 June 1941. Instructions introducing the letters 'US' which replaced the previous letters 'UVS' when the NCO Preparatory Schools were redesignated as NCO Schools (Unteroffizierschulen) were promulgated in *Luftwaffen-Verordnungsblatt*, dated 8 December 1941, p.1101, Order Nr.1946 issued 22 November 1941.
13. *Luftwaffen-Verordnungsblatt* dated 18 August 1941, p.596, Order issued 6 August 1941.
14. *Luftwaffen-Verordnungsblatt* dated 15 May 1944, Order Nr.607 issued 9 May 1944.
15. The white-aluminium metal Askulapstab shoulder-strap insignia was introduced to be worn by those medical personnel who wore the uniform of an Oberfeldwebel and were described as 'lower grade doctors'. This insignia was worn on the shoulder-strap between the NCOs' two rank stars, and replaced the matt-grey cotton embroidered Serpent and Staff cloth badge worn on the left forearm. Instructions were published in *Luftwaffen-Verordnungsblatt* Nr.18, dated 11 June 1935, p.125, Order Nr.274 issued 5 June 1935.
16. Luftwaffe Medical Officers of the Landwehr were instructed in July 1936 to wear on their shoulder-straps in place of the Roman numerals worn by

Officers of the Landwehr an Askulap-stab of silver oxidised light metal 3.2cm in height. The same instructions also included the shoulder-strap insignia to be worn by Medical Officers of the Luftwaffe Reserve. They were required to wear a gold coloured light metal Askulapstab also 3.2cm in size. These instructions were published in *Luftwaffen-Verordnungsblatt* Nr.28, dated 13 July 1936, pp.340–1, Order Nr.864 issued 6 July 1936.

17. *Luftwaffen-Verordnungsblatt* for January 1943, Order Nr.191, page 124 issued 15 January 1943.

18. According to *Luftwaffe-Verordnungs-blatt* dated May 1942 Order Nr.1423 the wearing of collar patches on the Greatcoat by NCOs and other ranks was to be discontinued from 1 October 1942, and by officers and other personnel who purchased their own uniforms from 1 April 1943. All Luftwaffe units were instructed to observe this ruling with the exception of the Guard Regiment of the Luftwaffe, Berlin and the Führer-Flakabteilung of the Division 'Hermann Göring'.

19. *Luftwaffen-Verordnungsblatt* Nr.11, dated 22 April 1935, p.66, order Nr.137, issued 11 April 1935.

20. These instructions were first published in March 1939 and repeated in April the same year: *Luftwaffen-Verord-nungsblatt* Nr.11 dated 6 March 1939, Part C, p.60, Order Nr.204 issued 22 February 1939, and again in *Luftwaf-fen-Verordnungsblatt* Nr.17, dated 11 April 1939, Part C, p.112, Order Nr.343 issued 1 April 1939.

21. *Luftwaffen-Verordnungsblatt* Nr.10, Part C, dated 7 March 1938, p.78, Order Nr.215 issued 4 March 1938.

22. *Luftwaffen-Verorodnungsblatt* dated 10 February 1941, Order Nr.137 issued 30 January 1941.

23. *Luftwaffen-Verordnungsblatt* dated 8 February 1943, Order Nr.284 issued 28 January 1943.

24. *Luftwaffen-Verordnungsblatt* dated 12 June 1944, Order Nr.781 issued 31 May 1944.

25. *Luftwaffen-Verordnungsblatt* dated 13 July 1942, Order Nr.1744, issued 26 June 1944.

26. *Luftwaffen-Verordnungsblatt*, dated 15 May 1944, Order Nr.615, issued 29 April 1944.

27. *Luftwaffe Verordnungsblatt* Nr.4 dated 27 January 1941, p.37 Order Nr.69 issued 10 January 1941. Designed by the firm of Wilhelm Ernst Peekhaus the drawings for the Luftwaffe Anti-Aircraft Badge were submitted to the Air Ministry on 19 July 1940. Once approved production of the badge was carried out by the Berlin firm of C. E. Juncker.

28. The regulations governing the award of the Luftwaffe Ground Combat Badge were published as Order Nr.1574 dated 3 November 1944 in the *Luftwaffen-Verordnungsblatt* issued on 20 November 1944.

29. Details regarding the introduction of the Luftwaffe Sea Battle Badge, including an illustration of the badge itself, were published in *Luftwaffe-Verdord-nungsblatt* dated 8 January 1945, 2nd Edition, Order Nr.19, page 12, issued 27 November 1944.

30. The Luftwaffe Close Combat Clasp was introduced by authority published in *Luftwaffen-Verordnungsblatt* Nr.49 dated 20 November 1944, Order Nr.1574, p.808 issued 3 November 1944.

31. Information regarding the 21 days privilege leave for those persons awarded the gold, Class III, Luftwaffe Close Combat Clasp was published in *Luft-waffen-Verordnungsblatt*, dated 15 January 1945, Order Nr.61 and issued 8 January 1945.

32. The order introducing the 'Kreta' cuff-title to be worn by certain Luftwaffe and Fallschirmjäger troops was published in *Luftwaffen-Verordnungsblatt* dated 5 October 1942, Order Nr.2519, p.1403 issued 29 September 1942. These instructions were ordered to be promulgated throughout the Luftgaukommandos on 15 November 1942.

33. 27 May 1941 was chosen as this was the date on which the German forces finally began to gain the upper hand over the British, Australian, New Zealand, Maori and Greek troops who were opposing them on the island of Crete.

34. *Luftwaffen-Verordnungsblatt* dated 25 September 1944, Order Nr.1315 issued 15 September 1944.

35. These instructions were published in *Luftwaffen-Verordnungsblatt* dated 16

March 1942, 11th Edition, Order Nr.622, p.333 issued 6 March 1942.

36. In addition to members of the German Army, the Luftwaffe and the Navy, the distinction of wearing the 'Africa' with Palms cuff-title was, on the order of the Reichsführer-SS, extended to members of the SS, provided that they had served honourably and had received the right to wear either the 'Afrika' or 'Kreta' cuff-titles. These instructions were published in *Verordnungsblatt der Waffen-SS*, Order Nr.82 dated 1 March 1943.

37. *Luftwaffen-Verordnungsblatt*, dated 31 January 1944, Order Nr.132 issued 12 January 1944.

38. *Luftwaffen-Verordnungsblatt* dated 31 May 1943, Order Nr.1028 issued 20 May 1943.

39. *Luftwaffen-Verordnungsblatt*, dated 4 September 1944, Order Nr.1180 dated 27 August 1944.

40. *Allgemeine-Heeresmitteilungen*, Order Nr.40, dated 15 January 1941.

41. For photographic illustrations of various types of 'Führer-Hauptquartier' cuff-titles see *Uniforms & Traditions of the German Army, 1939–1945* by John R. Angolia and Adolf Schlicht, Vol.2, pp.102–103.

42. *Luftwaffen-Verordnungsblatt* 1 June 1942, Order Nr.1381 issued 22 May 1942.

43. Luftwaffen-Verordnungsblatt dated 12 January 1942, pp.48–49, Order Nr.59 issued 20 December 1941.

44. *Luftwaffen-Verordnungsblatt* dated 12 January 1942, pp.48–49, Order Nr.59 issued 20 December 1941.

45. *Luftwaffen-Verordnungsblatt* dated October 1941, p.849, Order Nr.1473 issued 9 October 1941.

46. *Allgemeine Heeresmitteilungen* dated 22 January 1945, 2nd Edition, p.16, Order Nr.47 issued by the O.K.L. on 29 December 1944.

47. *Luftwaffen-Verordnungsblatt* dated 17 August 1942, p.1119, Order Nr.2036 issued by the O.K.W. 19 May 1942.

4: Uniforms

1. *Luftwaffen-Verordnungsblatt*, dated January 1943, p.97, Order nr.126 issued 2 January 1943.

2. It was forbidden for any one who had been engaged in the Norwegian Campaign other than for Army Mountain Troops to wear the Edelweiss. These instructions were published in *Luftwaffen-Verordnungsblatt*, Nr.17 dated 21 April 1941, p.270, Order Nr.411, issued 7 April 1941.

3. *Luftwaffen-Verordnungsblatt*, for February 1943 issued 22 January 1943.

4. *Luftwaffen-Verordnungsblatt*, for September 1943, p.1012, Order Nr.1824 issued 27 September 1943.

5. *Luftwaffen-Verordnungsblatt*, dated 14 October 1940, Order Nr.1290 issued 1 October 1940.

6. *Luftwaffen-Verordnungsblatt* for November 1943, p.1136, Order Nr.2084 issued 2 November 1943.

7. *Luftwaffen-Verordnungsblatt*, Nr.57 dated 11 December 1939, p.431 Order Nr.1086 issued 5 December 1939.

8. *Luftwaffen-Verordnungsblatt*, for May 1942, Order Nr.1423 issued May 1942.

9. *Luftwaffen-Verordnungsblatt* Nr.57 dated 11 December 1939, p.431, order Nr.1086 issued 5 December 1939.

10. *Luftgau-Verordnungsblatt XI*, Nr.9, dated 16 June 1944, p.51, Order Nr.201, issued 25 April 1944.

11. *Luftwaffen-Verordnungsblatt*, for August 1944, issued August 1944.

12. *Luftwaffen-Verordunungblatt* Nr.29 dated 20 July 1936, page 348, order Nr.884 issued 8 July 1936.

13. *Luftwaffen-Verordnungsblatt* for September 1943, page 1012, Order Nr.1824 issued 27 September 1943.

14. *Luftwaffen-Verordnungsblatt* Nr.18, dated 11 June 1935, p.116, Order Nr.256 issued 27 May 1935.

15. *Luftwaffen-Verordnungsblatt* Nr.1, dated 6 January 1936, pp.1–2, Order Nr.2 issued 19 December 1935.

16. *Luftwaffen-Verordnungsblatt* Nr.51, dated 6 December 1937, p.652, Order Nr.1571 issued 2 December 1937.

17. The change over of cuff-titles from 'General Göring' to 'Hermann Göring' was announced in *Luftwaffen-Verordnungsblatt* dated 1 June 1942, Order Nr.1381 issued 22 May 1942.

18. *Luftwaffen-Verordnungsblatt* dated 18 January 1943, Order Nr.127, page 97, issued 4 January 1943.

19. *Luftwaffen-Verordnungsblatt* dated April 1943, page 386, Order Nr.709 issued April 1943.

5: Protective and Specialist Clothing

1. *Luftwaffen-Verordnungsblatt*, for May 1941, Order Nr.584, issued 8 May 1941.
2. *Luftwaffen-Verordnungsblatt* Nr.25 dated 24 June 1940, p.318, Order Nr.726 issued 12 June 1940.
3. This listing of Luftwaffe tropical clothing appeared in *Luftwaffen-Verordnungsblatt* Nr.18 dated 5 May 1941, pp.286–287, Order Nr.497 issued 25 April 1941.
4. *Luftwaffen-Verordnungsblatt* May 1943, p.579, Order Nr.1113, issued 4 June 1943.
5. *Luftwaffen-Verordnungsblatt*, dated September 1943, p.1012, Order Nr. 1824 issued 27 September 1943.

6: Luftwaffe Women's services.

1. *Luftwaffen-Verordnungsblatt* dated 1 July 1940, Order Nr.794 issued 11 June 1940.
2. *Luftwaffen-Verordnungsblatt* Nr.33 dated 11 August 1941, Order Nr.896, pages 560–562 issued 27 July 1941. These extensive instructions covered a wide range of introductions, both for items of service clothing as well as the description of different patterns of rank insignia for use by the Luftnachrichten-helferinnen and the Luftschutzwarndienst-Helferinnenschaft.
3. *Luftwaffen-Verordnungsblatt* Nr.33 dated 11 August 1941, Order Nr.896, pages 560–562, issued 28 July 1941.
4. *Luftwaffen-Verordnungsblatt* Nr.29, dated 1 July 1940, Order Nr.794, pages 387–388, issued 11 June 1940.
5. *Luftwaffen-Verordnungsblatt* Nr.33 dated 11 August 1941, Order Nr.896, pages 560 to 562 issued 28 July 1941.
6. *Luftwaffen-Verordnungsblatt* Nr.33 dated 11 August 1941, Order Nr.896, pages 560 to 562 issued 28 July 1941.
7. *Luftwaffen-Verordnungsblatt* Nr.11 dated 10 March 1941, Order Nr.254, pages 162 to 164 issued 26 February 1941.

7: Luftwaffe Heimat Flak Units

1. Instructions regarding the issue and possible surrender of the stick pin insignia presented to members of Heimat Flak units were contained in *Luftwaffen-Verordnungblatt* dated 29 March 1943, Order Nr.602 issued 9 March 1943.

8: Hitler Youth Flak Units

1. The regulations that had been drawn up on 9 November 1942 whereby the Luftwaffe could enlist members of the Hitler Youth into Flakhelfer units was entitled 'Kreigshilfseinsatz der deutschen Jugend bei der Luftwaffe' (Auxiliary War Action of German Youth within the Air Force). These regulations were promulgated on 7 January 1943.

9: Hermann Göring: The Man and his Uniforms.

1. *Uniformen-Markt*, Nr.17, p.131 issued 1 September 1940 plus supplements and announcements published in the August, November and December 1940 issues.
2. *Schwert und Spaten*, Nr.8 issued August 1940, pp.108–109 and further announcement published in July 1940 issue.
3. In his book *Inside the Third Reich* Albert Speer describes seeing Göring wearing this utility uniform:
'Shortly afterwards we were standing, as we had done so often, in the confined space of the bunker, around the situation map. Hitler had taken his seat facing Göring. The latter, who always made such a point of his attire, had changed his uniform quite remarkably in the past few days. To our surprise the silver-grey cloth had been replaced by the olive-drab of the American uniform. Along with this his two-inch wide gold braided epaulets had given way to simple cloth shoulder strips to which his badge of rank, the golden Reich Marshal's eagle, was simply pinned. "Like an American general", one of the participants in the conference whispered to me. But Hitler seemed not to notice even this change.' This is an interesting observation and in essence the description of the uniform is correct, although I would dispute Herr Speer's description of the uniform colour. However, as I have not actually seen the uniform in question, and my observations and conclusions are based on the careful study of contemporary monochrome photographs I stand to be corrected.

Bibliography

Ailsby, Christopher, *Combat Medals of the Third Reich.* Patrick Stephens, Wellingborough, Northamptonshire, 1987.

Andrus, Burton C., Colonel US Army, *The Infamous of Nuremberg.* Leslie Frewin, London, 1969.

Angolia, Lieutenant Colonel John R., *For Führer and Fatherland, Military Awards of the Third Reich.* R. James Bender, San Jose, California, USA, 1976.

Angolia, Lieutenant Colonel John R. (Ret), *Belt Buckles & Brocades of the Third Reich.* R. James Bender, San Jose, California, USA, 1982.

Angolia, John R. and Schlicht, Adolf, *Uniforms and Traditions of the German Army, 1933–1945,* Vol.1. R. James Bender, San Jose, California, USA, 1984.

Angolia, John R. and Schlicht, Adolf, *Uniforms and Traditions of the German Army, 1933–1945,* Vol.2. R. James Bender, San Jose, California, USA, 1986.

Angolia, John R. and Schlicht, Adolf, *Uniforms and Traditions of the German Army, 1933–1945,* Vol.3. R. James Bender, San Jose, California, USA, 1987.

Baer, Ludwig, *The History of the German Steel Helmet, 1916–1945.* R. James Bender, San Jose, California, USA, 1985.

Bender, Roger James, assisted by Taylor, Hugh Page, *Air Organizations of the Third Reich – The Luftwaffe.* R. James Bender, Mountain View, California, USA, 1972.

Bender, Roger James and Law, Richard D., *Uniforms, Organization and History of the Afrikakorps.* R. James Bender, San Jose, California, USA, 1973.

Bender, Roger James and Petersen, George A., *'Hermann Göring' From Regiment to Fallschirmpanzerkorps.* R. James Bender, San Jose, California, USA, 1975.

British Intelligence Objectives Sub-committee (BIOS), *Development in Protective Clothing in Germany.* Final report No.152, Items 22 & 27. 1945.

Davis, Brian L., *German Army Uniforms and Insignia, 1933–1945.* Arms and Armour Press, London, 2nd revised edition with amendments and corrections, 1992.

Davis, Brian L., *Uniforms and Insignia of the Luftwaffe, Volume 1: 1933–1940.* Arms and Armour Press, London, 1991.

Der Reichsminister der Luftfahrt und Oberbefehlshaber der Luftwaffe, *Anzugordnung für die Luftwaffe (LAO)*, Bestimungen über Beschassenheit Sitz und Trageweise der einzelnen Bekleidungs- und Austustungsstücke sowie der Signalinstrumente. vom 27.11.1935. L.Dv.422 Abschnitt A. Neudruck vom 1 April 1938. Verlag 'Offene Worte', Berlin W 35.

Der Reichsminister der Luftfahrt und Oberbefehlshaber der Luftwaffe, *Anzugordnung für die Luftwaffe (L.A.)*, Anhang I, Sonderbekleidung und Sonderausrüstung. L.Dv.422 Abschnitt A. Neudruck von 1 April 1938. Verlag 'Offene Worte', Berlin W 35.

Deeter, Richard E. and Odegard, Warren W., *Gorgets of the Third Reich.* DO Enterprises, Los Angeles, California, USA. 1977.

Deutsche Uniformen-Zeitschrift, combining Schwert und Spaten and Uniformen-Markt. Various issues.

Dodkins, Colonel Clifford M., and Littlejohn, David, *Orders, Decorations, Medals and Badges of the Third Reich (Including the Free City of Danzig).* R. James Bender, Mountain View, California, USA, 1968.

Eichelbaum, Dr Hauptmann (E) im Reichsluftfahrtministerium *Das Buch von der Luftwaffe.* Verlagshaus Bong & Co, Berlin, post-1936.

Erlam, Denys, *Ranks and Uniforms of the German Army, Navy and Air Force.* (Collected from German semi-official sources and largely based upon *Uniformen der Deutschen Wehrmacht* by Eberhard Hettler of the German Air Ministry.) Seeley Service, London, 1939.

Halcomb, Jill and Saris, Wilhelm P.B.R. with Otto Spronk, *Headgear of Hitler's Germany, Vol.1: Heer, Luftwaffe, Kriegsmarine.* R. James Bender, San Jose, California, USA, 1989.

Halcomb-Smith, Jill and Saris, Wilhelm P.B.R. with Otto Spronk, *Headgear of Hitler's Germany, Vol.2: Waffen-SS, Legion Condor, Air, Veterans' and Patriotic Struggle Organizations, Free Corps.* R. James Bender, San Jose, California, USA, 1992.

Handbook for Military Government in Germany Prior to Defeat or Surrender. Supreme Headquarters Allied Expeditionary Force, Office of the Chief of Staff, December 1944.

Hettler, Hauptmann Eberhard, *Uniformen der Deutschen Wehrmacht; Heer, Kriegsmarine, Luftwaffe* mit Zeichnungen von Herbert Knötel, Paul Pietsch, Egon Jantke. (Originally published in 1939, supplement (Nachtrag) issued 1940.) Facsimile reprint by Verlag und Gesamtherstellung Militariarchiv K.D. Patzwall, Hamburg, Germany, 1979.

Irving, David, *The Rise and Fall of the Luftwaffe,* The Life of Luftwaffe Marshal Erhard Milch. Weidenfeld and Nicolson, London, 1973.

Kern, Jean G. CWS HQ ETOUSA, *Special Protective Garments for Aviators (Seenotschutzgerät).* Report prepared by Combined Intelligence Objectives Sub-Committee, CIOS Black List Item 22, 29 May 1945.

Kleitmann, Dr K.G., *Die Deutsche Wehrmacht – Uniform und Ausrüstung, 1934–1945, Vols 1 und 2.* Verlag Die Ordenssammlung, Berlin, 1960 and 1963.

Lange, Eitel, Der Reichsmarschall im Kriege. Curt E. Schwab, Stuttgart, Germany, 1950.

Littlejohn, David, with Hinds, Harry, *The Hitler Youth:* A history of the Hitler Youth both in Germany and abroad and of the non-German youth movements which collaborated with it. Organizations, structure, uniforms, flags, insignia. Agincourt Publishers, USA, 1988.

Luftwaffen-Verordnungsblatt Herausgegeben vom Reichsluftfahrtministerium (Zentralabteilung). All years from 1935 to 1944–45. Printed by Gedruckt in der Reichsdruckerei.

Medem, Hauptmann W.E. Frh.von, *Fliegende Front.* Verlag Die Wehrmacht, Berlin, 1942.

Mollo, Andrew, *Uniforms of the SS,* Volume 6, *Waffen-SS Clothing and Equipment, 1939–1945.* Historical Research Unit, London, 1972. (This is one of seven volumes originally published by Historical Research Unit between 1968 and 1976 and reissued by Windrow & Greene, London, in 1993.)

Nielsen, Generalleutnant Andreas, *The German Air Force General Staff.* United States Air Force Historical Studies No.173. Arno Press, New York, USA, in association with USAF Historical Division, Research Studies Institute, Air University, June 1959.

Obermaier, Ernst, *Die Ritterkreuzträger der Luftwaffe, 1939–1945,* Vol 1, Jagdflieger. Verlag Dieter Hoffmann, Mainz, Germany, 1966.

Obermaier, Ernst, *Die Ritterkreuzträtger der Luftwaffe, 1939–1945,* Vol 2, Stuka- und Schlachtflieger. Verlag Dieter Hoffmann, Mainz, Germany, 1988.

Schwert und Spaten – Älteste deutsche Fachzeitschrift der gesamten Ausrüstungs-Industrie für Heer, Luftwaffe, Kriegsmarine, Reichsarbeitsdienst, Körperschaften, Organisationen und Verbände. Schwert und Spaten, Berlin, various years.

Suchenwerth, Richard, *The Development of the German Air Force, 1919–1939.* United States Air Force Historical Studies No.160. Arno Press, New York, USA, in association with USAF Historical Division, Aerospace Studies Insitute Air University, June 1968.

Surgeon General, US Air Force, German Aviation Medicine, World War II, Vol 1. Department of the Air Force, 1950.

Taylor, Telford, *Sword and Swastika:* Generals and Nazis in the Third Reich. Simon and Schuster, New York, USA, 1952.

Taylor, Telford, *The March of Conquest:* The German Victories in Western Europe, 1940. Simon and Schuster, New York, USA, 1958.

Taylor, Telford, *The Breaking Wave:* The German Defeat in the Summer of 1940. Weidenfeld and Nicolson, London, 1967.

Tschoeltsch, E. (Oberst (1940) and Generalmajor (1943)), *Der Dienstunterricht in der Luftwaffe.* E.S. Mittler & Sohn, Berlin, 1940 and 1943.

Uniformen-Markt. Fachzeitung der gesamten Uniformen-, Austrüstung-, Effekten-, Fahnen-, Paramenten-, Orden-und Abzeichenbranche. Mitteilungsblatt der Fachuntergruppen Uniformen-Industrie, Uniform-

Ausstattungs-Industrie, Mützen-Industrie, Fahnenhersteller und der Fachabtailung Mützen-Zutaten-Industrie. Verlag Otto Dietrich, Berlin, various years.

Voigtlander, W. and Zuerl, H. *Luftwaffen-Fachworterbuch* Teil I, Deutsch/englisch/franzosisch. Hess Verlag, Braunschweig-München, 1940.

Westarp, Oberstleutnant E-J Graf von, *Westarpscher Taschenkalender für die Luftwaffe*, sowie für Luftschutz, Luftverkehr und Luftsport. Unter Mitwirkung des Reichsluftfahrtministerium herausgegeben. Verlag Alfred Waberg, Grimmen in Pommern, 5 Jahrgang, 1 April 1940 to 31 March 1941.

Right and below: German troops taken prisoner by Polish forces during the first week of fighting of the Second World War, September 1939. Of particular interest is the officer with the bandaged head. He wears the Luftwaffe Tuchrock complete with the Luftwaffe national emblem and twisted silver cording to the edge of the tunic collar. However, he is wearing what appear to be shoulder cords for an officer of the Allgemeine-SS. These shoulder cords were worn by officers with ranks from SS-Sturmbannführer to SS-Standartenführer. The collar patches appear to be plain black with twisted silver-aluminium cording. Exactly who this person was and what organization he was from remains a mystery.